GW0083250i

GUIDED MEDITATIONS, HYPNOSIS AND AFFIRMATIONS

2 BOOKS IN 1:

REWIRE YOUR BRAIN FOR RAPID WEIGHT LOSS, POSITIVE THINKING, ANXIETY CURE, DEEP SLEEP AND RELAXATION

Awakening Transformation Academy

Table of Contents

HYPNOSIS AND GUIDED MEDITATIONS FOR RAPID WEIGHT LOSS, DEEP SLEEP AND RELAXATION..11

An introduction to meditation 12

    The power of meditation 13

    The Benefits of meditation 14

Chapter 1.   Why Meditation Is Important? 17

    How Can I establish a Good Meditation Practice?.....18

    Benefits of Establishing a Meditation Practice.........18

    When Is a Good Time to Meditate?.......................21

    Making Use of Meditation Anchors 22

Chapter 2.   Benefits Of Guided Meditation 24

    What is a guided meditation? 24

    Mental Health Benefits.....................................25

    Performance Benefits 27

    Physical Benefits 29

    Relationship Benefits 31

PART 1: HYPNOSIS AND GUIDED MEDITATIONS FOR RAPID WEIGHT LOSS...............................33

Introduction 34

Chapter 3.   What Is Hypnosis For Weight Loss?........35

    Why Is It Hard To Lose Weight 38

    The Importance Of Genetics 40

    Weight Stigma..42

Chapter 4.   Guided Meditation For Weight Loss........47

Meditation exercise 1: Release of bad habits.......... 47

Meditation exercise 2: Forgiving yourself.............. 49

Chapter 5.   Meditation For A Mindfulness Diet 52

Mindful Eating Meditation 52

Chapter 6.   Meditation To Burn Fat 57

Fat Burn Meditation 57

Chapter 7.   Heal Your Relation With Food 62

Mindful Eating Meditation 62

Changing Your Mindset 70

Chapter 8.   Meditation For Weight Loss 73

The 5 best Meditation Weight Loss Techniques....... 73

Chapter 9.   Portion Control Hypnosis (Go In-Depth And Very Accurate) 82

Natural Weight Loss Hypnosis............................ 82

Chapter 10. Stop Emotional Eating Hypnosis............87

Emotional Hunger 87

The 3 Causes of Emotional Eating 90

Using Awareness or Mindfulness to Beat Emotional Eating... 94

Chapter 11. Weight Loss Hypnosis.........................97

Hypnosis for Natural Weight Loss 97

Chapter 12. Eat Healthy With Subliminal Hypnosis...103

Chapter 13. Loss Weight Fast And Naturally With Hypnosis 110

Hypnosis As A Means Of Losing Weight 110

What Hypnosis Feels Like 112

How Hypnosis Aids In Weight Loss 113

Understanding The Hypnotic Gastric Band And How It Works 114

What Is A Gastric Band? 115

Chapter 14. 100 Positive Affirmations For Weight Loss. 116

Chapter 15. Daily Habits For Weight Loss 124

Understanding Mindful Eating 124

Mindful Eating Benefits 125

A Guide To Mindful Eating 126

General Principles Of Mindful Eating 127

The Most Effective Method to Start Eating More Intentionally 129

Tips in Mindful Eating that Transform how you Relate to Food. 132

Chapter 16. Learning To Avoid Temptations And Triggers 135

Keep your emotions in check 135

Practice detachment 136

Accept what is beyond your control 137

Always be prepared 137

Take the time to embrace success 138

Be happy with what you have 139

Be happy with who you are 140

PART 2: HYPNOSIS AND GUIDED MEDITATIONS FOR DEEP SLEEP AND RELAXATION 141

Introduction 142

Chapter 17. The Importance Of A Good Sleep 143
  What Keeps People Up at Night? 145

Chapter 18. Guided Meditations For Deep Sleep 148
  Guide Meditation to Improve Insomnia 148
  Guide Meditation for Super Motivation 150
  Guide Meditation for Boost Positivity.................. 152

Chapter 19. Meditations For Better And Deeper Sleep.. 158
  Basic Sleep Meditation Script............................. 158
  Guided Meditation to Get Back to Sleep Script 161
  Nap Time Meditation Script................................ 163

Chapter 20. Meditation Scripts 166
  Relaxing into Sleep Meditation 166
  Sleep Body Scan Meditation............................... 168
  Sleep Countdown Meditation.............................. 171

Chapter 21. Sleep Scripts 175

Chapter 22. Sleep Talkdown Script 179
  Sleep Talkdown (30mns).................................... 179
  Sleep Talkdown (2) (20mns) 185

Chapter 23. Hypnosis For Sleeping Better............... 189
  Better Sleep Guided Hypnosis............................. 189

Chapter 24. Deep Sleep Hypnosis - Sleepy Ocean Visualization 194

Chapter 25. Principles For Self-Hypnosis For Sleep..... 201

Chapter 26. Induction Techniques To Get Self-Hypnosis
.... 207

Chapter 27. Deep Sleep Hypnosis Script 213

Chapter 28. Relaxation And Stress Scripts.............. 220

Chapter 29. Positive Affirmations For Better Sleep... 230
    Affirmations For Falling And Staying Asleep 230
        Healthy Sleep Dedication 232
        Relaxing.. 234

Conclusion 239

POSITIVE THINKING AFFIRMATIONS AND GUIDED MEDITATIONS FOR ANXIETY 243

PART 1: POSITIVE THINKING AFFIRMATIONS... 245

Positive thinking affirmations: introduction 246

Chapter 1.   Positive Thinking and the Law of Attraction
.... 248

Chapter 2.   14 Powerful Positive Thinking Practices .. 259

Chapter 3.   The Spiritual Value of Positive Thinking 269
    Self-love 269
    Meditation.. 271
    Finding meaning in life.................................... 271
    Like attracts like 272

Chapter 4.   Being Positive In Bad Situations 275

Chapter 5.   Bring On Positivity 279

Chapter 6.   Assess Your Way of Thinking 283

Be responsible with your attitude 283

Keep a journal or diary to reflect on your thoughts 284

Chapter 7.   Strategies to be Happy 286

Setting up your goal...................................287

Chapter 8.   5 Ways to Overcome Negative Thoughts .292

Chapter 9.   Affirmations 296

What is an Affirmation?...................................296

How Affirmations Work 297

Activating Your RAS..297

Creating Dynamic Tension in Your System.........298

Chapter 10. Affirmations Decoded 300

Creating a Positivity Base...................................302

Chapter 11. Happiness Affirmations 304

Chapter 12. Health Affirmations 309

Chapter 13. Success Affirmations 313

Chapter 14. Affirmations and Prayer 317

Chapter 15. How to Use Affirmation Effectively 321

Chapter 16. Using Affirmations to Speak to Your Finances 324

Chapter 17. 10 Tips to Avoid Wrong Affirmations.....330

Chapter 18. 6 Steps to Create Powerful and Workable Positive Affirmations 334

Chapter 19. Meditation for positive thinking...........338

Meditation Script...339

Chapter 20. Negativity Has No Place Here 345

The Effects of Negativity and How to Counteract Them
....346

Understanding Relationships and How to Make the Most
of Them...347

Characteristics of a Healthy Relationship.................349

How to Focus on the Good Parts of Life and
Relationships..351

Chapter 21. Living The Life................................356

PART 2: GUIDED MEDITATIONS FOR ANXIETY.. 365

Guided meditations for anxiety: introduction 366

Chapter 22. Anxiety..370

Chapter 23. What Is Meditation? 379

Why We Meditate..380

The Conscious 381

The Subconscious..381

The Superconscious......................................382

Other Reasons Why We Meditate 383

Meditation Eliminates Stress..........................383

It Increases Your Level of Happiness 384

Meditation Relaxes You 384

It Helps Boost Cerebral Activity......................384

Chapter 24. Getting Started....................................385

Chapter 25. How To Calm The Body......................391

Chapter 26. Breathing Exercises Throughout the Day .398

Chapter 27. Meditation for Anxiety 407

Chapter 28. Guided Meditation for Anxiety.............416

Chapter 29. Guided Body Scan Meditation for Anxiety .421

Chapter 30. Benefits of meditation 428

Chapter 31. Mindfulness Meditation 438
Meditation for Self-Healing Mindfulness...............438

Chapter 32. How to Meditate 444
Practical Advice on meditation 446
Knocks along the Road 448

Chapter 33. How to Practice Mindfulness Meditation .450

Chapter 34. Dealing with Stress 460

Chapter 35. Stress and Workplace Awareness Meditation
....472

Chapter 36. Meditative Guide For Positive Consciousness
....477

Chapter 37. Daily Meditation Affirmation Routines ...481

Chapter 38. Affirmations For Over Coming Anxiety ..492

Conclusion 498

HYPNOSIS
AND GUIDED MEDITATIONS
FOR RAPID WEIGHT LOSS,
DEEP SLEEP AND RELAXATION

REWIRE YOUR BRAIN
TO STOP EMOTIONAL EATING,
LOSE WEIGHT, FALL ASLEEP FAST,
RELIEVE STRESS AND ANXIETY

Awakening Transformation Academy

An introduction to meditation

Meditation comes from the word "medicina", which is a Latin word and originally means natural medicine. Meditation signifies that we do not identify our thoughts with the voice and emotions in our heads, but go beyond them and notice them objectively without negative or positive judgments. This technique can be practiced even while cleaning, and we don't need specific circumstances to meditate. If we do something from the heart, we can say that we are meditating. Meditation is the art of entirely redirecting focus to only one thing.

Meditation is a changed state of awareness that cannot be produced by will or forced. In this regard, it is similar to sleep, because the more we want to sleep, the more alert we will be. Meditation usually refers to a state of mind whereby the body is consciously carefree and relaxed, and our spirit is let go of peace and concentration within ourselves. Meditation does not merely imply sitting or lying down for five to ten minutes in silence. Meditation indeed demands mindful work. The mind must be relaxed and balanced. At the same time, the brain must be alert so that it does not allow any disturbing thoughts or desires to penetrate. We begin meditation with our effort. Still, when we delve intensely into ourselves, we see that it is not our individual self that allows us to enter the state of meditation. The Supreme or Creator meditates within and through us, with our deliberate attention and permission.

The aim is to seek peace and freedom from disturbing thoughts. In such cases, the meditator achieves an escape from the environment so that from a psychological point of view, the experience could even be called a changed state of consciousness. When we can make our minds calm and still, we will touch a new existence awakened within us. If our mind is discharged and tranquil, and our entire being becomes an empty vessel, then our internal presence can call upon eternal peace, light, and mercy to flow into and fill this vessel. This happens during meditation.

The power of meditation

Meditation has impressive power because we associate emotions coming from the depths of the soul with conscious thought. In meditation, the individual is brought into the same frequency as the origin of the Inner Self, that is, the Universe itself, and thus is directly connected to the consciousness sphere of the Universe. In this state, there is no time limit, so the visualized fulfillment can immediately expand to the physical level. As a result of regular meditation, we obtain numerous benefits in a physical and mental sense. We will be healthier because when we focus on our breathing, our blood pressure drops, our heart rate slows down; consequently, we become calmer. It helps us have a clearer mind, sort out our thoughts and emotions, making our communication more productive both at work and in social life. We can focus more easily and accordingly feel less stressed. We become more aware of our emotions; hence, we can manage them more effectively. We find a solution sooner in areas of our lives where we feel stuck. It promotes the processing of mental problems. It helps to find peace and balance. We get closer to understanding ourselves, the people around us, our lives, and our mission. When we accept ourselves as we are, we become positive, joyful, and attractive. This will make our existing relationship more intimate or, if we are alone, the desired partner will come into our lives.

The Benefits of meditation

Meditation has been used in many cultures for thousands of years because of its numerous benefits: it reduces anxiety, and makes people feel happy. In the short term, meditation has mainly psychological advantages, but in the long run, it has physical outcomes. Those who try meditation can enjoy its benefits in the short term such as balance, greater peace and vitality, and a decreased need for sleep. Physical effects can be experienced in just a few months: among other things, blood pressure may return to normal, or digestion may improve. So you can imagine how beneficial it can be in the long run.

The University of California's Neuroscience Laboratory has been researching the impacts of meditation on the brain's structure for years. Their most recent research has studied long-term effects in the minds of habitual meditators compared to non-meditators. According to their results, the cerebral cortex of long-term meditators is more marked than that of non-meditators, indicating increased cognitive performance. The Frontiers in Human Neuroscience published research which became a milestone in science because it has long been believed that the brain mass reaches its peak in the early twenties, and then begins to narrow slowly (Bae, Hur, Hwang, Jung, Kang, Kim, Kwak, Kwon, Lee, Lim, Cho, & Park, 2019). Previously it was a widespread opinion that there was no way to interrupt this process. However, it is now known that the brain retains its plasticity to some extent, and it can physically change as a result of meditation. Earlier studies have shown that for long-time meditators, both gray matter and white matter in the brain have increased in weight. (The former contains the cells of the brain nerve cells; the latter contains the neuronal cell-forming projections). The number of neurons in the cortex changes only very rarely in adulthood. One group of the current research involved 28 men and 22 women, their average age was 51, and they had all been meditating for an average of 20 years. The oldest participant was 71, and the most experienced meditator had been practicing daily for 46 years. The researchers performed MRI scans of participants' brains and compared them to 50 non-meditating members of the control group.

Regular practice can increase the advantages of meditation. According to research, the more practitioners repeated deep breathing techniques and other meditation methods, the more they relieved the symptoms of arthritis, reduced their pain, increased their immune systems, manifested healthier hormone levels, and lowered blood pressure. According to the researchers, this explains that a person's mental state can change his physical condition and gives an added motivation to why traditional Tibetan, Indian, and Ayurvedic medicine view meditation and the repetition of mantras as therapeutic.

Hundreds of scientific documents confirm the positive healing and health benefits of meditation. Here are some of them.

During the first twenty minutes of meditation, metabolism is reduced by sixteen percent. The body deeply calms down during transcendental meditation, which is the result of decreased cellular oxygen utilization due to reduced metabolism. It also decreases heart rate and stabilizes blood circulation (Dillbeck, & Orne-Johnson, 1987). Besides, the blood pressure decreases, and muscular tension and anxiety consequently disappear. Meditation has proven to be effective in overcoming chronic anxiety and in increasing self-esteem

(Eppley, Abrams, & Shear, 1989). Meditation is also an effective way to create relaxation and reduce physiological stimulation. The essence of the phenomenon is a decrease in respiratory rate, oxygen consumption and carbon dioxide exhalation. Breathing is not only rarer but more profound, vital capacity increases from resting 450-550 ml to 800-1300 ml (up to 2000 ml for some master meditators) and remains consistent throughout. However, a lower respiratory rate is not offset by deeper breathing, resulting in a 20% reduction in respiratory volume under rest.

Several sports psychologists think that meditation may be appropriate for improving athletic performance (Syer, & Conolly, 1984). Meditation can help lessen the stress of competition, but with some practice, an athlete can also learn how to relax different muscle groups individually and detect complex differences in muscle tension.

Throughout meditation, the athlete can anticipate the next event (such as skiing downhill) in such detail that the visualization of the action can be almost perfectly synchronized with the action itself. The skier anticipates how he will start from the starting position, gliding down and accelerating, avoiding the gates, and doing the entire race in his head. By framing images of successful performance, an athlete may attempt to program their muscles and body for the best results.

Chapter 1. Why Meditation Is Important?

Such as simple thing meditation is yet it is extremely powerful. You never think that something so simple can have an immense effect on your until you try it and you feel the benefits of meditation. You might be wondering what has this got to do with mindfulness and really, what is the difference between meditation and mindfulness?

You can meditate for 5 minutes, 10 minutes, or longer as long as you do it right. That is, you want to have a purpose when you began your meditation. The best part is there are many ways to meditate, and anyone can learn how to do it effectively with the right tools, teachings, and techniques.

For beginners learning to meditate, the hardest aspect would be to quiet the mind and achieve focus. But with practice, you'd find that it becomes easier and easier.

When it comes to mindful meditation, it also means to be in a mindful and calm state. But what do all of these terms mean? Don't worry about the terms; we will explore them.

Mastering the art of meditation, like everything else, takes patience, time, and practice. You are putting far too much pressure on yourself if you expect to get it right from the moment you sit cross-legged on your mat and shut your eyes, hoping to achieve deep meditation right from the get-go. No, it takes time and practice, and you need to be patient with yourself. In this book, you will find a plan that will help you achieve deep meditation, and the key to succeeding in this is to remember that you need to be patient. Practice makes perfect, which is why your goal of achieving deep meditation is more of a journey than a destination. There is no expiry date; neither is there a master level you need to achieve.

How Can I establish a Good Meditation Practice?

One effective way to consistently practice meditation is to create and plan out a practice that you can follow, according to your needs, your daily schedule, routines, and timing.

The thing about meditation is that you need to be mindful of everything that you experience in your session. With mindful meditation, there is a goal and a purpose. It is to help you be conscious and mindful of everything you do.

Benefits of Establishing a Meditation Practice

A foundation of your meditation session is important because, in many ways, when you set the stones to your practice, your brain will start moving toward making this practice happen. For example, if you decide to buy a new meditation mat, your mind will be reminded (or you will remember) that you purchased the mat, and you want to know the feeling of sitting on the mat and practicing.

1. Without a firm foundation, you will not be consistent.

It won't be long before whatever you're doing eventually crumbles and falls because there's nothing supporting it. That's just one way of describing how important it is to develop a sound meditation practice right from the very beginning of the process.

2. It helps you create a habit.

But although meditation is something that is beneficial for everyone, not everyone is currently putting it into practice. Some people are not practicing meditation at all. Why? Because it isn't a habit. A lot of us lead very busy lives, so sometimes our plates seem too full to take on anything else. There will always be a reason not to start something, which is why it is entirely up to you to make time for it.

The purpose of establishing a meditation practice is because you want to make meditation a habit, a part of your daily life, and something that you are willing to do every day without even thinking twice or resisting it because you are pressed for time.

3. It makes your practice ingrained, almost second-nature activity in your life

Meditating will become much like how brushing your teeth or showering, preparing something to eat, and even going on a daily commute to work. Those habits are so deeply ingrained in you that you do them without any effort or a lot of thought put into it.

That is what establishing a meditation practice aims to do for you right now, and it is something you need to establish as a foundation to make your practice consistent.

Here is how you can start establishing a meditation practice for yourself.

Start small. Start small at first by meditating for short periods of time, maybe 5-10 minutes a day, especially if you're new at it. You can do anything for 5-10 minutes a day with no resistance, and the time will pass before you even know it. When you see how easy that was, it keeps you motivated to keep adding onto that. By creating small, achievable goals, you begin building the habit of making meditation a part of your daily life.

Use tools to help you. There is an app for just about everything these days, even meditation, so why not make the most of the tools you have to help you establish a successful daily practice? There are several apps, such as Headspace and Calm, which can help you enhance your meditation sessions, with everything from timers to ambient sounds to help set the mood. If it helps make your daily practice more enjoyable, why not? You are more likely to stick to something if you like what you're doing.

Use YouTube. Guided meditations that you like on YouTube can be a great tool, especially for beginners on this journey. It helps you stay on track and on the right path. Some meditations are given on a daily basis, whereas some are based on your goals, such as Meditation for Focus and Meditation for Sleep. Guided meditations make it much easier for beginners, especially to start getting into the flow of things and helps you progress in the right direction with your meditation sessions, especially when you're doing it alone as a solo practice. It would be good to know that you are heading in the right direction.

Make space. This is extremely important. Making space in your home or anywhere you feel comfortable is a vital part of your practice. A space that is dedicated solely for your meditation sessions should be a place that is safe and comfortable for you, and preferably quiet. Fill that space with anything you need to make you feel comfortable or something that makes you feel like you want to be there for a while. You can fill it with pillows, cushions, pictures that inspire you, incense or scented candles if it helps, and anything that helps soothe your soul and brings you a sense of calm. That will go a long way toward helping you make meditation a consistency in your life if you have a space that you look forward to spending some time in each day because of the comfort and calm that it envelopes you in.

Make it a schedule. Okay, so not many people like routine and schedule, but if you are starting in meditation practices, this is essential. Make it a point to pencil it into your calendar or make a note of it on your calendar app on your phone. It can be easy for other things going on during the day to take precedence over your meditation session, which is why you need to purposely make that time just to stop and meditate before the day comes to an end, and you realize you didn't get to spend any time meditating at all.

When Is a Good Time to Meditate?

The short answer to this is preferably at a quiet time and as long as this time works for you. You can choose to meditate in the morning, afternoon, evening, or even before you go to bed. That's the beauty of this practice; it is entirely up to what works best for you. Every individual is different, and no two people are going to be doing things the exact same way with the same experience. Some people prefer to meditate in the morning because it sets the tone for the rest of the day, while some prefer to do it at night because it helps them unwind, calm down, and relax after a long and hectic day.

The best time of the day for you to meditate would be any time that you can consistently and realistically commit to it. It can be in the morning, in the afternoon, in the evening, or at night; it doesn't matter. As long as you are getting it done, that is the only thing that matters, even if it is for just 10 minutes a day. A short meditation session is better than nothing at all.

When I'm meditating, is there a specific posture I need to follow?

No, there isn't because again, everyone is different, and some people may prefer one posture, while someone else may prefer another. That is okay. The posture you decide to go with should be the one that feels most comfortable and what you are happy with. If sitting in a chair works better for you, go ahead and do that. If you prefer to sit cross-legged on a mat, that's alright. If you prefer to lie down, that's alright too. It is important to do what is right for your body and what you feel most connected with, which will allow you to relax yet stay alert during your session at the same time.

Making Use of Meditation Anchors

Even the most advanced meditation practitioners could use an anchor every now and then. Our minds are such a versatile thing that sometimes it can get easily distracted and wander before we become aware and bring it back to focus again. This is why meditation anchors are helpful, especially if you are new to this practice. It will help you find the focus and concentration that you need during your meditation session. Even if you're an advanced practitioner, having an anchor is still going to be helpful to you on the days when your mind may be struggling to grasp the concentration that it needs.

A meditation anchor will allow you to steady your mind and maintain focus on what you are doing. An anchor gives you a point to bring your mind back to whenever it deigns to wander of. An anchor gives you something to connect your mind as you strengthen and build on mindfulness, a practice that will eventually come with time.

A meditation anchor can be anything that you find useful and which helps you to maintain your focus. Some suggestions of what could be used as an anchor when you meditate include the following:

- Focusing on your breath as it moves in and out of your body
- What your body feels like with each deep breath you take
- Your chest as it rises and falls slowly and rhythmically with each breath that moves in and out
- If you're using music or any ambient tones to help set the mood, you can focus on that and the way it makes you feel as you listen to the rhythm
- Physical sensations that slowly emerge as you progress throughout the meditation, for example, the way your hands feel or the way the muscles in your body feel

Are you starting to get the idea? Your anchor can be anything that you want it to be. It doesn't have to be specific to the list. It just has to be something that you can connect on, something that your mind can focus on while you meditate. It helps you give you a purpose, especially when you're just starting out. Otherwise, you could find yourself aimlessly sitting on the mat, wondering if you're doing it right or not being able to meditate at all.

This would be a good time to find an anchor that works best for you and helps you with your meditation practice. Being able to bring your thoughts back to your anchor when needed will be a great help in your four-week plan to achieve a deeper state of meditation.

Having a regular anchor that is consistent would be helpful, but if you ever feel that you want to choose or use something else as your anchor, go ahead and do it. If it helps you stay focused, and it works for you, your anchor can be anything you want it to be. Remember, it is all about finding what works best for you because meditation is such a personal experience, one that is entirely yours.

Chapter 2. Benefits Of Guided Meditation

You are most likely here right now because you have heard amazing, life-changing aspects meditation can bring to your life. Whether you are looking to improve your mental health, performance, physical health, or better your relationship with yourself or others; meditation could be the perfect practice for you. We'll be going over just some of the benefits meditation can bring into your life.

What is a guided meditation?

Unlike the traditional type, guided meditation is aimed at a specific purpose, and for beginners, it is one of the best ways to approach this practice. It is also called guided visualization. In this type of meditation, you form mental images of places or situations where you can feel relaxed. Most of the time, this is practiced with a teacher's help or a leader who is not necessarily present in the room where the meditation occurs. It's enough to include listening to a recording and meditating on it.

Guided meditations are not all the same: it depends on the purpose you want to achieve through this practice. Do you just want to relax? Fight insomnia? Become more resilient? Accept a major change? Lose weight?

In most guided meditations, it's essential to try to use as many senses as you can: the smells, the lights, the sounds, the textures. Usually guided meditations have a musical background that invites the mind and body to relax: sounds of nature such as rain, rainforest, sea waves or the sound of a waterfall; or more traditional music like that of the Native American characterized by the sound of flutes, tubes and rattles. Choose the musical background you prefer, what is important is to create the best condition to relax. To start, you can do a very quick guided meditation for beginners. The basic principle is to pay attention to what you do, always keep it in mind from the beginning to the end of the practice. Close your eyes and start taking three deep breaths, inhaling through your nose and exhaling from your mouth. When you breathe in you are full of positive energy and when you exhale all kinds of negative energies, such as stress, tension and worries, abandon you. Find your breath and feel your body. Simply observe it (Headspace, n. d.).

Mental Health Benefits

Unfortunately, there are many individuals who suffer from mental health issues. Whether you are dealing with anxiety, depression, or something along those lines; meditation can help place you in a better mindset when practiced on a regular basis.

Meditation decreases Depression

In a study done in Belgium, four-hundred students were placed in an in-class mindfulness program to see if it could reduce their stress, anxiety, and depression. It was found that six months later, the students who practiced were less likely to develop depression-like symptoms. It was found that mindfulness meditation could potentially be just as effective as an antidepressant drug!

In another study, women who were going through a high-risk pregnancy were asked to participate in a mindfulness yoga exercise for ten weeks. After the time passed, it was found there was a significant reduction in the symptoms often caused by depression. On top of the benefit of less depression, the mothers also showed signs of having a more intense bond with their child while it was still in the womb.

25

Meditation reduces Anxiety and Depression

In general, meditation may be best known for the mental health benefits of reducing the symptoms associated with anxiety and depression. It was found that through meditation, individuals who practiced meditation such as Vipassana or "Open Monitoring Meditation," were able to reduce the grey-matter density in their brains. This grey-matter is related to stress and anxiety. When individuals practice meditation, it helps create an environment where they can live moment to moment rather than getting stuck in one situation.

While practicing meditation, the positive mindset may be able to help regulate anxiety and mood disorders that are associated with panic disorders. There was one article published in the American Journal of Psychiatry based around twenty-two different patients who had panic or anxiety disorders. After three months of relaxation and meditation, twenty of the twenty-two were able to reduce the effects of their panic and anxiety.

Meditation Quiets the Mind

When you no longer overthink things, or you do not have to worry or have the feeling of constant fear, or when you stop worrying endlessly about what the future holds, you get to experience a silence that is intoxicating. Meditation allows your mind to explore this side of your natural state, the stillness that is true and pure.

When you meditate constantly, you eventually start to silence your mind and stop thinking about the ticking clock, the chores you have to do, and the work you need to get done. You silence your mind to spend a few minutes in bliss, and these few minutes can benefit you in longer and more pronounced aspects of your life.

Performance Benefits

When you are able to relax, you would be amazed at how much better your brain will be able to function. By letting go of stress, you leave room for positive thoughts in your head and will be able to make better decisions for yourself. It's a win-win situation when you can improve your mood and your performance simply from meditation.

Better Decision Making

A study done at UCLA found that for individuals who practiced meditation for a long time, had a larger amount of gyrification in the brain. This is the "folding" along the cortex, which is directly related to processing information faster. Compared to individuals who do not practice meditation, it was found that meditators were able to form memories easier, make quicker decisions, and could process information at a higher rate overall.

Improve Focus and Attention

Consistent meditation disables the distractions we face by filtering it before it starts to bottleneck. Think of this like a river dam that ensures the right amount of water to be released to households, industries, and agriculture. Meditation, in the same way, filters the less important data that we are exposed to and sends only the necessary and important info into our brain. In other words, it helps us determine what information should we focus on and what we do not need to focus on that may cause chronic anxiety.

A study performed at the University of California suggested that through meditation, subjects are able to increase their focus on tasks, especially ones that are boring and repetitive. It was found that even after only twenty minutes of meditation practice, individuals are

27

able to increase their cognitive skills ten times better compared to those who do not practice mindfulness.

Along the same lines, it's believed that meditation may be able to help manage those who have ADHD, or attention deficit hyperactivity disorder. There was a study performed on fifty adults who had ADHD. The group was placed through mindfulness-based cognitive therapy to see how it would affect their ADHD. In the end, it was found that these individuals were able to act with awareness while reducing both their impulsivity and hyperactivity. Overall, they were able to improve their inattention.

Relieve Pain

It has been said that it's possible that meditation could potentially relieve pain better when compared to morphine. This may be possible due to the fact that pain is subjective. There was a study done on thirteen Zen masters compared to thirteen non-practitioners. These individuals were exposed to painful heat whilst having their brain activity watched. The Zen masters reported less pain, and the neurological output reported less pain as well. This goes to show that pain truly is a mental aspect.

Along the same lines, mindfulness training could also help patients who have been diagnosed with Fibromyalgia. In one study, there were eleven patients who went through eight weeks of training for mindfulness. At the end of the study, the overall health of these individuals improved and reported more good days than bad.

Avoid Multitasking Too Often

While multitasking can seem like a good skill to have at some points, it's also an excellent way to become overwhelmed and stressed out. Unfortunately, multitasking can be very dangerous to your productivity.

When you ask your brain to switch gears between activities, this often can produce distractions from your work being done. A study was performed on students at the University of Arizona and the University of Washington. These people were placed through eight weeks of mindfulness meditation. During this time, the students had to perform a stressful test demonstrating multitasking before and after the training. It was shown that those who practiced meditation were able to increase their memory and lower their stress while multitasking.

Physical Benefits

While mental improvements are fantastic benefits of meditation, physical benefits can help motivate individuals to begin meditation as well. Unfortunately, the standard of health is to turn to medication. If you are an individual who hates popping pills for every issue you have; meditation may be just what you need to help improve your health.

Meditation reduces cortisol

Researches from Rutgers University and the University of California also conducted research relating to mindfulness meditation and the effects on cortisol. The study shows that consistent meditation reduced cortisol dramatically, with some results showing at least a 50% drop.

Daily meditation for even 3 minutes is effective for the brain. You do not need to be a yogi with years of training to do this. Meditation is like the firefighters you call to extinguish this hormone that brings in so many diseases that can protect your health and happiness. When you do mindfulness exercises, you create an environment that is 100% inharmonious with anxiety. This mental environment prevents anxiety from manifesting in your mind and brain.

Meditation reduces Risk of Stroke and Heart Disease

It has been found that heart disease is one of the top killers in the world compared to other illnesses. Through meditation, it's possible you could lower your risk of both heart disease and stroke. There was a study done in 2012 for a group of two hundred high-risk people. These individuals were asked to take a class on health, exercise, or take a class on meditation. Over the next five years, it was found that the individuals who chose meditation were able to reduce their risk of death, stroke, and heart attacks by almost half!

Meditation reduces High Blood Pressure

In a clinical study based around meditation, it was also found that certain Zen meditations such as Zazen, has the ability to lower both stress and high blood pressures. It's believed that relaxation response techniques could lower blood pressure levels after three short months of practicing. Through meditation, individuals had less need for medication for their blood pressure! This could potentially be due to the fact that when we relax, it helps open your blood vessels through the formation of nitric oxide.

Meditation for a Longer Life

When you get rid of stress in your life, you may be amazed at how much more energetic and healthier you feel. While the research hasn't been drawn to a conclusion yet, there are some studies that suggest meditation could have an effect on the telomere length in our cells. Telomeres are in charge of how our cells age. When there is less cognitive stress, it helps maintain telomere and other hormonal factors.

Relationship Benefits

There are some people who are looking for a little bit more peace in your life. In the world we live in today, times can be very trying. There are constant deadlines, bills to pay, people to deal with; but now is the time to look at stressors in your life under a different life. Through meditation, you can become a more caring and empathetic individual to create a more peaceful life for yourself.

Improve Positive Relationships and Empathy

When we undergo stressful situations with obnoxious people, it can be very trying to remain empathetic. There is a Buddhist tradition of practicing loving-kindness meditation that may be able to help foster a sense of care toward all living things. Through meditation, you'll be able to boost the way you read facial expressions and gain the ability to empathize with others. When you have a loving attitude toward yourself and others, this helps develop a positive relationship with them and a sense of self-acceptance.

Decrease Feelings of Loneliness

There are many people who are not okay with being alone. Often times, we try to fill our time with activities so that we are never alone with ourselves. The truth is, it can be healthy to spend some time with yourself so that you can self-reflect on your life choices. In a study published in Brain, Behavior, and Immunity, it was proven that after thirty minutes of meditation per day, it was able to reduce individuals' sense of loneliness while reducing the risks of premature death, depression, and perhaps even Alzheimer's.

Along with feeling less lonely, meditation also opens up new doors to feeling a positive connection to yourself. When you love yourself, and you are happy with your own company, you may spend a lot less time on negative thoughts and feelings of self-doubt; both of which can lead to self-caused stress.

PART 1: HYPNOSIS AND GUIDED MEDITATIONS FOR RAPID WEIGHT LOSS

Introduction

One of the hardest parts about losing weight is having to wait so long to see the results. While there isn't a way to lose 20 pounds overnight, you can reshape your mentality so that you can grow your patience for the process. When you fully recognize time and how that plays into weight loss, you won't be looking at the scale every hour, begging for results. Instead, you will be happy with your journey and able to recognize the incredible way that your body is changing.

This is a visualization exercise that is going to help you get in the right mindset to lose weight fast.

This meditation is going to be a visualization. You are going to want to make sure that you are in a comfortable place where you can drift off and go to sleep if you want to. We are going to take you through the scene that will await you at the end of your natural weight loss journey. We often have many ideas of what we want to get from our weight loss process, but we don't always visualize what the actual setting could be. In this meditation, we are going to help you understand the realistic scenario that you could find yourself in after you've managed to lose the weight. Close your eyes and keep your body as relaxed as possible. Start to focus on your breathing. Breathe in through your nose and out through your mouth. Concentrate the air as it travels through your body so that you will be able to shut out any negative or toxic thoughts more easily than you have in this moment.

Chapter 3.   What Is Hypnosis For Weight Loss?

This hypnosis program is for people who want to lose weight, feel confident about their bodies, get toned and be healthy. If you're reading this right now, one thing is for certain and that is that you want to make some serious changes to your body. As a woman, your self-confidence and self-esteem is highly influenced by how you feel about the current state of your body. Make no mistake about it, when you wake up and don't like the appearance staring back at you in the mirror, it sets the whole tone for the rest of the day – negative, for the most part.

You know very well that when you feel great in your own skin, your day just moves along better. You've put your heart into trying to achieve a body that you can feel good about, but alas, not much has come from your efforts. All of this is about to change.

This hypnosis program will help you to:
- Stay committed into trying to achieve a body that you have been searching for all this time.

- Naturally burn up more calories on a day to day basis doing nothing.

- Set up a proper plan that is going to work with your body and help you release fat storage from all the trouble spots on your body.

The program includes:

Hypnosis for naturally losing weight: The hypnosis will help you to change your negative mental views and turn them into positive ones, practice gratitude for weight loss, visualize, accept and appreciate your fabulous healthy body. It will emphasize on how to set and focus on your goals to keep that negativity at bay since losing weight needs consistent reminders and focus on proper mental preparations. Always keep yourself motivated and train yourself to think positive all the time.

Meditation for relaxation: A meditation to reduce muscle tension, lower blood pressure, calm the mind, eliminate stress and achieve mental and physical condition. You can practice it into your everyday life to help you deal with stress, relax and have peace of mind. Deep rest and relaxation achieved through meditation is therefore great for rejuvenating the body to leave you well and mentally serene.

Positive affirmations for weight loss: You will find a sequence of powerful affirmations for weight loss which are intended to magnify your focus on the positive reality you desire and the possibility thereof. They will help you take control of your motivation and release doubt, giving you the power to pave the steps in front of you, as you stride confidently toward your manifesting goals. You are now striding confidently toward manifesting your weight loss goals!

Well, you had better accept it if you want to see optimal results. But as a woman, you need to be on top of your game. To get the most out of the program you need to choose one of the aforementioned hypnosis and focus on it. Once you have finished this program, you should then feel ready and confident to put your best foot forward and see the optimal results that you are looking for.

Dieting plans using to these restrictions can definitely work, but only in the short run. In spite of avoiding regaining those lost pounds, there is a better way to choose.

With the right approach, you get to satisfy your sugar cravings, you get to enjoy some of your favorite foods and you still get to reach your optimal weight.

It should be noted that there are many weight gain triggers other than food. For instance, living in a stressful environment or not getting enough sleep can affect your waistline.

Accordingly, in spite of losing weight and keeping it that way, you need to work on your weight gain triggers just as you need to work on your meal plans.

Moreover, you need to work on changing your weight loss mindset, you need to rewire your thoughts about fitness and healthy living in the in order to stay on the right track in the long run.

Making the decision to lose weight was easy because everyone wants to look good. However, to enjoy success in the long run, you need dedication and commitment to truly follow through on your decision.

This is when things become more difficult as following your decisions over some time can be daunting. This is the main reason why people tend to quit.

For the sake of avoiding this happening to you, in addition to working on slightly changing your dieting pattern, you also need to embrace simple, easy-to-follow, yet effective weight loss tips which will keep you focused and motivated.

Moreover, losing weight is not only about looking good, but way beyond this. Losing weight can benefit you in numerous ways and your dieting choices can definitely make a difference both in the present and in the future.

The best way to go is to follow a dieting plan you can make work in the long run. Once there, with simple weight loss tips you get to stay on the right track, you get to keep your motivation and you get to work on your fitness and weight loss mindset.

These, when combined, lead you towards a healthy lifestyle you have always wanted to embrace, but you have lacked motivation, inspiration or knowledge.

In the direction of starting the journey on the right foot, it is important you understand why you gain or lose weight, what different weight gain factors are and other scientific facts revolving around shedding and gaining pounds.

Why Is It Hard To Lose Weight

You can say goodbye to obsessing over your daily calorie intake, over obsessing over how many carbs you ingested today.

You can say goodbye to extremely restrictive bans on foods as well as on other forced behaviors in pursuance of focusing on getting back into shape in a healthy, natural way by following your body's biology.

You have probably blamed yourself, or your lack of self-discipline in the past. You probably have blamed calories and your dieting formulas which most certainly did not bring anything good your way.

The truth is that there is no one and nothing to blame here. Every step you have taken in the past can teach you something which will help you to succeed in the future.

Another truth is that losing weight can be an extremely difficult thing to do and there are several different reasons behind this.

If you are focused on the weight loss industry, you have probably been told many times before how easy it is to shed those additional pounds.

The industry generally suggests you take this pill, drink that beverage or buy this equipment and simply enjoy your additional pounds melting on their own.

The truth is that the industry generates billions of dollars every year thanks to individuals who spend their money on different weight loss tools and products which can only be effective in the short-run.

Accordingly, many people struggling with weight are still overweight despite hundreds of dollars spent in the industry.

Now, you probably wonder why it is so hard and challenging to lose those additional pounds. It should be noted that there is no magical pill, magical tool or magical equipment that can make the process runs smoothly.

Dieting plans which suggest you completely change your dieting pattern, quit eating your favorite foods and similar restrictions do not work.

There is also scientific evidence as clear as it can get that suggests that cutting your daily calorie intake will not by any means lead to health gains or long-term weight loss.

It would be logical that most dieters have realized they have wrong dieting patterns, but still, individuals set those same weight goals every year.

The truth is that dieting failures are the norm. There is also a massive stigma surrounding heavier people and, on many occasions, we can witness the massive blame game which is directed towards dieters who are not able to shed those additional pounds.

On the other hand, looking from a scientific point of view, it is clear that dieting most certainly sets up a truly unfair fight.

Many people are confused to learn that dieting plans suggesting extreme dieting changes, but that this only comes as a result of the statements does not square with their previous observations.

There are some thin people who consume junk food and still stay thin without their food choices affecting their weight.

These people most usually think that they stay in shape due to their dieting habits, but the truth is that genetics plays a massive role in helping them stay fit.

These people are praised over their dieting choices as others can only see what they consume, but they cannot examine what is inside their genes.

The Importance Of Genetics

Due to the role of genetics, many individuals struggling with excess pounds will not be as thin as other people even if they embrace the same dieting choices as them and consume them in the exact same quantities.

The bodies of those heavier people can run on fewer calories than thin people require which may sound like a promising thing.

On the other hand, this means that they have more calories left, stored as fat in the body after eating the same food in the same quantities as thinner people.

This means that they need to consume fewer foods than thin people in order to shed pounds. Once they have followed some dieting plan for some time, their overall metabolic state changes which means that they need to consume even fewer calories in pursuance of losing further weight.

It isn't only genetics which makes thin people stay thin, but it is also their mindset revolving around dieting and fitness.

For thin people, as they are non-dieters, it is very easy to ignore those sugary treats and desserts which for heavier people seem like a massive challenge and obstacle on their weight loss journey.

For heavier people, these treats and sugary candies seem as if they are almost jumping around cheerfully making them approach and eat them.

This being said, dieting of any kind causes specific neurological changes which make people more likely to be focused on foods and notice foods everywhere.

Once they notice foods, those neurological changes happening in the brain are what makes it almost impossible to not think about food.

Thin people more often than not forget about those sweet treats on the desk, but dieters tend to keep obsessing over them.

As a matter of fact, dieters seem to crave these foods even more due to those neurological changes.

Moreover, these neurological changes make food taste better due to the fact they cause a greater rush of dopamine or the reward hormone.

This is the exact same hormone releases when drug addicts or substance abusers use their drug. Individuals who are non-dieters do not suffer from these kinds of rushes, so they can peacefully leave a piece of cake untouched.

Dieters also tend to struggle with another issue revolving around neurological changes which affect their hormonal balance.

They face another uphill battle when their leptin hormone or satiety hormone levels go down. Due to this hormonal change, dieters require even more foods to consume in pursuance of feeling full.

This means that they felt hungry following their dieting plans and over some time they feel even hungrier once again due to hormonal changes.

Weight Stigma

Individuals usually see thin people and are impressed by their self-discipline, self-determination or their willpower and self-control.

Yet, should it be considered great self-control or great willpower to avoid consuming foods, when you are actually not hungry.

It really is a true willpower or true self-control when you are able to avoid eating foods you do not notice at all and you do not get any reward rush out of it.

The plain truth is that anyone would be able to resist sugary sweets or any food under these specific circumstances, as there is no need for any willpower or great self-control to avoid foods when you are not actually hungry and when you have no rushes to worry about.

Even though thin people do not need any extra self-control or willpower in these cases, if they do need it, their self-control and willpower would function optimally due to the fact that they are non-dieters.

On top of these extreme circumstances, dieters who need to struggle with dieting of any kind also disrupt their cognition which is especially effective over their executive function.

The executive function is a process which promotes and helps with self-control. Hence, people following strict dieting plans have less self-control and willpower in those situations when they need more willpower.

On the other hand, in the same situations during which dieters struggle, non-dieters have plenty of self-control and willpower even though they do not need it.

And there is also another fact, if thin people were to eat delicious cakes, treats, and other tempting foods, their metabolism burns more calories by far when compared with the dieter's metabolism state.

All of this means that thin people are mistakenly given some credit for staying fit and in shape at this job that comes easier to them than for those individuals following some dieting plan.

These facts lead to the very cruel irony which makes it very hard to keep losing weight for individuals who have been following some dieting plan.

Yes, it is physically possible to lose weight in the long-run, but just a small minority of dieters actually manages to keep losing weight for months or years.

Following the trend, this battle does not come without demoralization, stigma, and damages to their mindset which dieting does to their physiology both in the short-run and in the long-run.

It is very easy to see why the majority of dieters regain the weight they have lost.

No matter the obstacles and challenges, we have to work on changing the stigma surrounding weight, especially weight gain.

You struggling with additional pounds does not make you weak in any way. The factors affecting weight gain and weight regain and they have nothing do to with your dieting choices.

Hence, be impressed by every single step you take, be grateful for every small goal you reach and remind yourself that you are not weak, but you are a victim of a very unfair battle.

This battle is won by only a few who are more focused on staying healthy than losing weight, who are determined to improve their weight not by any artificial means, but only in a natural way.

The Impact of Weight Stigma

The main question here is whether anti-obesity and anti-overweight attitudes are the ones contributing to these outcomes in obese and overweight individuals.

First, we need to clarify this term of weight stigma. It is stereotyping or discrimination towards individuals based on their weight. Weight stigma is also known as weight-based discrimination or weight bias.

One of the major health risks of weight stigma lies in the fact that it can lead to extremely increased body dissatisfaction which is one of the leading factors contributing to the development of various kinds of eating disorders.

When it comes to the best-known factor leading to the development of an eating disorder, it is definitely the very common and highly present idealization of being thin as seen in media as well as other social-cultural environments.

However, it is never acceptable by any means to discriminate against someone based on any physical features and weight is one of them.

On the other hand, weight stigma which includes blaming, shaming and concern trolling individuals who struggle with their weight happens more commonly than we want to admit.

The fact is it happens everywhere, at home, at school, at work and in some cases even in the doctor's office.

This tells us that weight discrimination is more prevalent then we think and according to the latest studies on the topic, it even occurs more often than age or gender discrimination.

Another truth is that weight stigma is very dangerous increasing the risk for different behavioral and psychological issues such as binge eating, poor body image, and depression.

In fact, weight stigma has been documented as one of the risks for low self-esteem, depression and extreme body dissatisfaction.

Moreover, those individuals who struggle with weight stigma also tend to engage more often in binge eating.

They are also at a significantly increased risk for developing some type of eating disorder and they are more likely to be diagnosed for BED or binge eating disorder.

Those individuals struggling with weight stigma also generally report that their family members, friends, and their physicians are the most common sources of their weight stigma struggles.

When it comes to family members and friends, diet talk and weight-based teasing are more often than not related to extreme weight control patterns, unhealthy behaviors, and weight gain as well as binge eating.

This being said, weight stigma in health care is yet another very important concern showing the magnitude of this problem.

The topic which show health care professionals and providers, when talking to overweight and obese patients tend to provide them with not valuable health information, tend to spend not enough time with them and tend to see them as annoying, and undisciplined as well as uncompliant with their weight loss treatment.

There is also a massive issue regarding popular obesity and overweight prevention campaigns. Attention given to weight control and obesity definitely has skyrocketed in the past several years.

By doing so, the industry has ingrained words such as diet, obesity epidemic and BMI into our regular vocabulary.

Chapter 4. Guided Meditation For Weight Loss

Meditation exercise 1: Release of bad habits

Sit comfortably. Relax your muscles, close your eyes. Breathe in and breathe out. Do not cross your feet because this will lock you away from the desired experience. Hold your hands together to connect your logical brain hemisphere with your instinct.

Concentrate on your back now and notice how you feel in the bed or chair you are sitting in. Take a deep breath and let your stress leave your body. Now focus on your neck. Observe how your neck is joined to your shoulders. Lift your shoulders slowly. Breathe in slowly and release it. Feel how your shoulders loosen. Lift your shoulders again a little bit then let them relax. Observe how your neck muscles are tensing and how much pressure it has. Breathe in and breathe out slowly. Release the pressure in your neck and notice how the stress is leaving your body. Repeat the whole exercise from the beginning. Observe your back. Notice all the stress and let it go with a profound breath. Focus on your shoulders and neck again. Lift up your shoulders and hold it for some moments, then release your shoulders again and let all the stress go away. Sense how the stress is going away. Now, focus your attention to your back. Feel how comfortable it is. Focus on your whole body. While breathing in, let relaxation come, and while you are breathing out, let frustration leave your body. Notice how much you are relaxed.

Concentrate on your inner self. Breathe slowly in and release it. Calm your mind.

Observe your thoughts. Don't go with them because your aim is to observe them and not to be involved. It's time to let go of your overweight self that you are not feeling good about. It's like your body is wearing a bigger, heavier top at this point in your life. Imagine stepping out of it and laying it on an imaginary chair facing you. Now tell yourself to let go of these old, established eating and behavioral patterns. Imagine that all your old, fixed patterns and all the obstacles that prevent you from achieving your desired weight are exiting your body, soul, and spirit with each breath. Know that your soul is perfect as it is, and all you want is for everything that pulls away to leave. With every breath, let your old beliefs go, as you are creating more and more space for something new. After spending a few minutes with this, imagine that every time you breathe in, you are inhaling prana, the life energy of the universe, shining in gold. In this life force you will find everything you need and desire: a healthy, muscular body, a self that loves itself in all circumstances, a hand that puts enough nutritious food on the table, a strong voice to say no to sabotaging your diet, a head that can say no to those who are trying to distract you from your ideas and goals. With each breath, you absorb these positive images and emotions.

See in front of you exactly what your life would be like if you got everything you wanted. Release your old self and start becoming your new self.

Gradually restore your breathing to regular breathing. Feel the solid ground beneath you, open your eyes, and return to your everyday state of consciousness.

Meditation exercise 2: Forgiving yourself

Sit comfortably. Do not cross your feet because this will lock you away from the desired experience. Hold your hands together to connect your logical brain hemisphere with your instinct. Relax your muscles, close your eyes.

Imagine a staircase in front of you! Descend it, counting down from ten to one.

You reached and found a door at the bottom of the stairs. Open the door. There is a meadow in front of us. Let's see if it has grass, if so, if it has flowers, what color, whether there is a bush or tree, and describe what you see in the distance.

Find the path covered with white stones and start walking on it.

Feel the power of the Earth flowing through your soles, the breeze stroking your skin, the warmth of the sun radiating toward you. Feel the harmony of the elements and your state of well-being.

From the left side, you hear the rattle of the stream. Walk down to the shore. This water of life comes from the throne of God. Take it with your palms and drink three sips and notice how it tastes. If you want, you can wash yourself in it.

Keep walking. Feel the power of the Earth flowing through your soles, the breeze stroking your skin, the warmth of the sun radiating toward you. Feel the harmony of the elements and your state of well-being. In the distance, you see an ancient tree with many branches. This is the Tree of Life. Take a leaf from it, chew it, and note its taste. You continue walking along the white gravel path. Feel the power of the Earth flowing through your soles, the breeze stroking your skin, the warmth of the sun radiating toward you. Feel the harmony of the elements and your state of well-being.

You have arrived at the Lake of Conscience, no one in this lake sinks. Rest on the water and think that all the emotions and thoughts you no longer need (anger, fear, horror, hopelessness, pain, sorrow, anxiety, annoyance, self-blame, superiority, self-pity, and guilt) pass through your skin and you purify them by the magical power of water. And you see that the water around you is full of gray and black globules that are slowly recovering the turquoise-green color of the water. You think once again of all the emotions and thoughts you no longer need (anger, fear, horror, hopelessness, pain, sorrow, anxiety, annoyance, self-blame, superiority, self-pity, guilt) and they pass through your skin and you purify them by the magical power of water. You see that the water around you is full of gray and black globules that are slowly obscuring the turquoise-green color of the water. And once again, think of all the emotions and thoughts you no longer need (anger, fear, horror, hopelessness, pain, sorrow, anxiety, annoyance, self-blame, superiority, self-pity, guilt) as they pass through your skin, you purify them by the magical power of water. And you once again see that the water around you is full of gray and black globules that are slowly obscuring the turquoise-green color of the water.

You feel the power of the water, the power of the Earth, the breeze of your skin, the radiance of the sun warming you, the harmony of the elements, the feeling of well-being.

You ask your magical horse to come for you. You love your horse, you pamper it, and let it caress you too. You bounce on its back and head to God's Grad. In the air, you fly together, become one being. You have arrived. Ask your horse to wait.

You grow wings, and you fly toward the Trinity. You bow your head and apologize for all the sins you have committed against your body. You apologize for all the sins you have committed against your soul. You apologize for all the sins you committed against your spirit. You wait for the angels to give you the gifts that help you. If you can't see yourself receive one, it means you don't need one yet. If you did, open it and look inside. Give thanks that you could be here. Get back on your horse and fly back to the meadow. Find the white gravel path and head back down to the door to your stairs. Look at the grass in the meadow. Notice if there are any flowers. If so, describe the colors, any bush or tree, and whatever you see in the distance. Feel the power of the Earth flowing through your soles, the breeze stroking your skin, the warmth of the sun radiating toward you. Feel the harmony of the elements and your state of wellbeing. You arrive at the door, open it, and head up the stairs. Count from one to ten. You are back, move your fingers slowly, open your eyes.

Chapter 5. Meditation For A Mindfulness Diet

One of the best ways to transition into a diet that's centered around weight loss is to do so using mindful eating. All too often, we eat well beyond what is needed, and this may lead to unwanted weight gain down the line.

Mindful eating is important because it will help you appreciate food more. Rather than eating large portions just to feel full, you will work on savoring every bite.

This will be helpful for those people who want to fast but need to do something to increase their willpower when they are elongating the periods in between their mealtimes. It will also be very helpful for the individuals who struggle with binge eating.

Portion control alone can be enough for some people to see the physical results of their weight-loss plan. Do your best to incorporate mindful eating practices in your daily life so that you can control how much you are eating.

This meditation is going to be specific for eating an apple. You can practice mindful eating without meditation by sharing meals with others or sitting alone with nothing but a nice view out the window. This meditation will still guide you so that you understand the kinds of thoughts that will be helpful while staying mindful during your meals.

Mindful Eating Meditation

You are now sitting down, completely relaxed. Find a comfortable spot where you can keep your feet on the ground and put as little strain throughout your body as possible. You are focused on breathing in as deeply as you can.

Close your eyes as we take you through this meditation. If you want to actually eat an apple as we go through this, that is great. Alternatively, it can simply be an exercise that you can use to envision yourself eating an apple.

Let's start with a breathing exercise. Take your hand and make a fist. Point out your thumb and your pink. Now, place your right pinky on your left nostril. Breathe in through your right nostril.

Now, take your thumb and place it on your right nostril. Release your pink and breathe out through your nostrils. This is a great breathing exercise that will help to keep you focused.

While you continue to do this, breathe in for one, two, three, four, and five. Breathe out for six, seven, eight, nine, and 10. Breathe in for one, two, three, four, and five. Breathe out for six, seven, eight, nine, and 10.

You can place your hand back down but ensure that you are keeping up with this breathing pattern to regulate the air inside your body. It will allow you to remain focused and centered now.

Close your eyes and let yourself to become more relaxed. Breathe in and then out.

In front of you, there is an apple and a glass of water. The apple has been perfectly sliced already because you want to be able to eat the fruit with ease. You do not need to cut it every time, but it is nice to change up the form and texture of the apple before eating it.

Breathe in for one, two, three, four, and five. Breathe out for six, seven, eight, nine, and 10.

Now, you reach for the water and take a sip. You do not chug the water as it makes it hard for your body to process the liquid easily. You are sipping the water, taking in everything about it. You are made up of water, so you need to constantly replenish yourself with nature's nectar.

You are still focused on breathing and becoming more relaxed. Then, you reach for a slice of apple and slowly place it in your mouth. You let it sit there for a moment and then you take a bite.

It crunches between your teeth, the texture satisfying your craving. It is amazing that this apple came from nature. It always surprises you how delicious and sweet something that comes straight from the earth can be.

You chew the apple slowly, breaking it down as much as you can. You know how important it is for your food to be broken down as much as possible so that you can digest it. This will help your body absorb as many vitamins and minerals as possible.

This bit is making you feel healthy. Each time you take another bite, it fills you more and more with the good things that your body needs. Each time you take a bite, you are making a decision in favor of your health. Each time you swallow a piece of the apple, you are becoming more centered on feeling and looking even better.

You are taking a break from eating now. You do not need to eat this apple fast. You know that it is more important to take your time.

Look down at the apple now. It has an attractive skin on the outside. You wouldn't think by looking at it about what this sweet fruit might look like inside. Its skin was built to protect it. Its skin keeps everything good inside.

The inside is white, fresh, and very juicy. Think of all this apple could have been used for. Sauce, juice, and pie. There are so many options when it comes to what this apple may have become. Instead, it is going directly into your body. It is going to provide you with the delicious fruit that can give you nourishment.

You reach for your glass of water and take a long drink. It is still okay to take big drinks. However, you are focused now on going back to small sips. You take a drink and allow the water to move through your mouth. You use this water not just to fill your body but to clean it. Water washes over you, and you can use it in your mouth to wash things out as well.

You swallow your water and feel it as it begins to travel through your body. You place the water down now and reach for another apple slice.

You take a bite, feeling the apple crunch between your teeth once again. You feel this apple slice travel from your mouth throughout the rest of your body. Your body is going to work to break down every part of the apple and use it for nourishment. Your body knows how to take the good things that you are feeding it and use that for something good. Your body is smart. Your body is strong. Your body understands what needs to be done to become as healthy as possible.

You are eating until you are full. You do not need to eat any more than what is necessary to keep your body healthy. You are only eating things that are good for it.

You continue to drink water. You feel how it awakens you. You are like a plant that starts to sag once you don't have enough water. You are energized, hydrated, and filled with everything needed to live a happy and healthy life.

You are still focused on your breathing. We will now end the meditation, and you can move onto either finishing the apple or doing something relaxing.

You are centered on your health. You are keeping track of your breathing. You feel the air come into your body. You also feel it as it leaves. When we reach zero, you will be out of the meditation.

Twenty, 19, 18, 17, 16, 15, 14, 13, 12, 11, 10, nine, eight, seven, six, five, four, three, two, one.

Chapter 6.   Meditation To Burn Fat

Our bodies were designed to burn fat. It is the way that they provide the body with energy when we haven't given it enough through the foods we eat. We require more energy when we workout, so our bodies will burn more fat during these processes.

Though it can sound so simple on paper, it will be rather challenging to always include these things in our lives. This meditation is going to help guide you through the journey of getting the body you want, with a visualization exercise to help you see your goals laid out clearly. Listen to this first when you are in a relaxed position in case you become calm to the point of sleep.

After you know how you react, you might include this when you are doing yoga or another form of light exercise to help keep you grounded and relaxed.

Fat Burn Meditation

Narrator: This is a visualization meditation. I am going to take you on a mindfulness journey through your body. To start, ensure that you are somewhere that you can be fully relaxed. You don't want to have any distractions around, and the only thing that you are going to focus on now is the air that is coming in and out of your body.

(Narrator pauses for 3 seconds)

Narrator: Let your mind go blank. As thoughts begin to creep in, gently push them out with each exhale. Focus on nothing else other than the air that enters your body, and how it exits.

(Narrator pauses for 3 seconds, breathing in and out)

Narrator: When we count down from ten, you are going to imagine that you are in the middle of the woods. There is a light trail and you are walking down it.

Breathe in for one, two, three...

And out for three, two, one...

You will be in the woods in ten, nine, eight, seven, six, five, four, three, two, and one.

(Narrator pauses for 3 seconds)

Narrator: You are walking through the woods, noticing everything that surrounds you. There are trees, birds, and even a little stream that you can hear the water running from.

You are feeling incredibly good in this moment, healthy and focused. You haven't eaten in a little bit, but you aren't very hungry just yet. You felt your stomach grumble, but it was just a small signal that you need to eat. Nothing is causing you pain or discomfort. You are focused on right now only, and nothing else.

You are walking up a hill now, a slight incline. You feel the burn start to occur in your legs. As you continue to walk, you begin to realize that your body is starting to burn fat.

You don't have to tell your body to do this. You don't have to take a pill to do this. Your body knows how to do it on its own.

You supply it with healthy food that doesn't add as many calories as you need for energy to your body, meaning that you are burning fat faster.

You put it through workouts in order to burn fat. The combination of both of these are helping you to lose weight.

(Narrator pauses for 3 seconds)

Narrator: You won't notice in the mirror immediately after burning the fat, but you are feeling it immediately

58

in the way your body functions. Each time your stomach growls, you feel it. Every time you take a step, you feel it. As your body is continuing to get stronger and stronger, and push you closer and closer to the goals that you want, you feel lighter and lighter.

Your body is burning more and more fat. You are becoming more and more relaxed, focusing only on your breathing and the good feeling circulating through your entire body. The only thing that you concern yourself with is shedding the pounds.

(Narrator pauses for 3 seconds)

Narrator: You are only burning fat. You aren't doing anything to add fat, which means that your body's only option is to use what is already there as an energy source.

You consistently make choices to burn the fat from your body. You are always looking for ways to become lighter and lighter. You feel as your waist is getting slimmer and slimmer.

It feels good to drop the weight. It feels amazing to finally let go of all that has been holding you back.

The more weight that you are burning, the easier it is to lose even more. There is nothing that is going to keep you from getting the things that you want in this life. You are working with your body to get the things that you have been hoping for.

(Narrator pauses for 3 seconds)

Narrator: You continue to walk through the woods with the realization that you are a part of nature just like all that surrounds you. Your body was made in order to keep you as healthy as possible. Now, it is time to train your brain so that it is optimized for health as well.

Your brain will try to do what it thinks is right for your health. It wants you to eat ice cream, so you feel better right now. It wants you to sit on the couch instead of workout so that you can save your energy. Your body is only thinking of the "now."

You are training your brain to think about the future. You are accepting all that surrounds you, and that you are a part of this nature just as the rest. You are connected to the earth and feel the natural processes flow through your body. You are highly aware of all of the things that you need to do in order to keep your body as healthy as possible.

(Narrator pauses for 3 seconds)

Narrator: Your body feels better and better the further that you walk. Sometimes you feel a slight strain in your legs, but nothing that is painful. It is simply your body doing its best to burn as much fat as possible. It is your body working hard. It is a good pain, one that makes you feel healthier, stronger.

You have water with you that you take a drink of. This is the fuel that helps to keep your body going. You provide it with everything necessary in order to continually work hard.

Your body will always burn fat. It is designed to use what you already have stored within you. Each time you make a healthy choice, it makes you feel healthier.

Every time you do something good for your body, you are burning fat. You continue to burn fat, always feeling lighter and lighter.

(Narrator pauses for 3 seconds)

Narrator: You are more relaxed now. Your mind understands what it needs to do to be healthy. You are starting to feel lighter every day.

The forest around you is fading.

As we come to the end of the meditation, remember to focus on your breathing. You will either be able to drift off to sleep or move onto other meditations needed for weight loss mindset.

As we reach ten, come out of the forest and back into reality where you will be focused only on burning fat and losing weight.

(Narrator counts to ten)

Chapter 7. Heal Your Relation With Food

All too often, we eat well beyond what is needed, and this may lead to unwanted weight gain down the line.

Mindful eating is important because it will help you appreciate food more. Rather than eating large portions just to feel full, you will work on savoring every bite.

This will be helpful for those people who want to fast but need to do something to increase their willpower when they are elongating the periods in between their mealtimes. It will also be very helpful for the individuals who struggle with binge eating.

Portion control alone can be enough for some people to see the physical results of their weight-loss plan. Do your best to incorporate mindful eating practices in your daily life so that you can control how much you are eating.

This meditation is going to be specific for eating an apple. You can practice mindful eating without meditation by sharing meals with others or sitting alone with nothing but a nice view out the window. This meditation will still guide you so that you understand the kinds of thoughts that will be helpful while staying mindful during your meals.

Mindful Eating Meditation

You are now sitting down, completely relaxed. Find a comfortable spot where you can keep your feet on the ground and put as little strain throughout your body as possible. You are focused on breathing in as deeply as you can.

Close your eyes as we take you through this meditation. If you want to actually eat an apple as we go through this, that is great. Alternatively it can simply be an exercise that you can use to envision yourself eating an apple.

Let's start with a breathing exercise. Take your hand and make a fist. Point out your thumb and your pink. Now, place your right pinky on your left nostril. Breathe in through your right nostril.

Now, take your thumb and place it on your right nostril. Release your pink and breathe out through your nostrils. This is a great breathing exercise that will help to keep you focused.

While you continue to do this, breathe in for one, two, three, four, and five. Breathe out for six, seven, eight, nine, and 10. Breathe in for one, two, three, four, and five. Breathe out for six, seven, eight, nine, and 10.
You can place your hand back down but ensure that you are keeping up with this breathing pattern to regulate the air inside your body. It will allow you to remain focused and centered now.

Close your eyes and let yourself to become more relaxed. Breathe in and then out.

In front of you, there is an apple and a glass of water. The apple has been perfectly sliced already because you want to be able to eat the fruit with ease. You do not need to cut it every time, but it is nice to change up the form and texture of the apple before eating it.

Breathe in for one, two, three, four, and five. Breathe out for six, seven, eight, nine, and 10.

Now, you reach for the water and take a sip. You do not chug the water as it makes it hard for your body to process the liquid easily. You are sipping the water, taking in everything about it. You are made up of water, so you need to constantly replenish yourself with nature's nectar.

You are still focused on breathing and becoming more relaxed. Then, you reach for a slice of apple and slowly place it in your mouth. You let it sit there for a moment and then you take a bite.

It crunches between your teeth, the texture satisfying your craving. It is amazing that this apple came from nature. It always surprises you how delicious and sweet something that comes straight from the earth can be.

You chew the apple slowly, breaking it down as much as you can. You know how important it is for your food to be broken down as much as possible so that you can digest it. This will help your body absorb as many vitamins and minerals as possible.

This bit is making you feel healthy. Each time you take another bite, it fills you more and more with the good things that your body needs. Each time you take a bite, you are making a decision in favor of your health. Each time you swallow a piece of the apple, you are becoming more centered on feeling and looking even better.

You are taking a break from eating now. You do not need to eat this apple fast. You know that it is more important to take your time.

Look down at the apple now. It has an attractive skin on the outside. You wouldn't think by looking at it about what this sweet fruit might look like inside. Its skin was built to protect it. Its skin keeps everything good inside.

The inside is white, fresh, and very juicy. Think of all this apple could have been used for. Sauce, juice, and pie. Instead, it is going directly into your body. It is going to provide you with the delicious fruit that can give you nourishment.

You reach for your glass of water and take a long drink. It is still okay to take big drinks. However, you are focused now on going back to small sips. You take a drink and allow the water to move through your mouth. You use this water not just to fill your body but to clean it. Water washes over you, and you can use it in your mouth to wash things out as well.

You swallow your water and feel it as it begins to travel through your body. You place the water down now and reach for another apple slice.

You take a bite, feeling the apple crunch between your teeth once again. You feel this apple slice travel from your mouth throughout the rest of your body. Your body is going to work to break down every part of the apple and use it for nourishment. Your body knows how to take the good things that you are feeding it and use that for something good. Your body is smart. Your body is strong. Your body understands what needs to be done to become as healthy as possible.

You are eating until you are full. You do not need to eat any more than what is necessary to keep your body healthy. You are only eating things that are good for it.

You continue to drink water. You feel how it awakens you. You are like a plant that starts to sag once you don't have enough water. You are energized, hydrated, and filled with everything needed to live a happy and healthy life.

You are still focused on your breathing. We will now end the meditation, and you can move onto either finishing the apple or doing something relaxing.

You are centered on your health. You are keeping track of your breathing. You feel the air come into your body. You also feel it as it leaves. When we reach zero, you will be out of the meditation.

Twenty, 19, 18, 17, 16, 15, 14, 13, 12, 11, 10, nine, eight, seven, six, five, four, three, two, one.

As mentioned previously, you should work and invest time and effort into reaching your desired body weight, not because of some thin body ideal circling around and not because of other people around you, but because weight gain in addition to helping you be more satisfied with your body image also brings numerous health benefits which are crucial on top of all other weight loss effects on your life.

The truth is that you do not have to lose some excess amount of weight to experience weight loss health benefits as losing only several pounds can make a huge difference.

For instance, losing ten pounds for a person weighing two hundred pounds improves her overall health state, make her feel better, more energized and much more.

Losing only ten pounds can rapidly ease up on your joints, remove some pressure off your knees as well as remove pressure off your other lower body joints which can wear out easily when you have to carry around those additional pounds.

Additional fat accumulated in the body can also cause various types of chronic inflammatory disorders as chemicals contained in the body, which tend to do tissue damage while damaging your joints as well.

Therefore, losing weight can prevent this from happening as well as reduce your risk for developing arthritis at some point later in life due to your weight.
Losing those extra pounds also can decrease your chances of developing some types of cancers. In fact, there is one study showing that a female who lost at least five percent of her body weight lowered her chances for developing breast cancer by twelve percent.

There is no clear proof that losing weight can protect you from other types of cancer, but even the slightest weight loss progress decreases the chances of developing breast cancer.

For instance, overweight females who lose extra pounds also tend to lower their hormone levels which are linked to the development of cancer cells including androgens, insulin, and estrogens.

If you are more likely to develop type 2 diabetes, weight loss is absolutely your way to go to delay or even prevent it from occurring.

Moreover, in addition to losing weight in these cases, moderate exercise for at least thirty minutes per day is also highly recommended.

On the other hand, if you have already been diagnosed with diabetes, losing those additional pounds can help you in many different ways such as keeping your blood sugar levels in control, lowering your odds of the condition causing some other health issues and lowering your need for taking all of those medications.

By losing additional pounds, you can also lower your levels of bad LDL cholesterol just by embracing healthy dieting options.

Unlike balancing those LDL cholesterol levels, balancing those levels of good HDL cholesterol is harder, but not impossible by losing body fat and by exercising regularly.

Just as you can balance your cholesterol levels, by losing those additional pounds, you can also bring down your triglyceride levels which are responsible for transporting energy and fat storage throughout the body.

High triglyceride levels mean you are more likely to have a stroke or heart attack, so moving closer to those healthy triglyceride levels is crucial for maintaining an optimal health state.

Those who are overweight and struggle with high blood pressure can absolutely make a huge change by losing those additional pounds.

As you know, having excess body weight puts the body under more stress so the blood starts pushing harder against the artery walls.

In these cases, the heart needs to work harder as well. In order to avoid suffering complications related to high blood pressure, trimming only five percent of your total body mass can make a massive change.

Another dieting tip for lowering high blood pressure includes eating plenty of low-fat dairy products, plenty of foods and veggies and cutting down on salty foods.

Individuals who struggle with excessive weight are at much greater risk for developing sleep apnea due to the excess fat situated in their throat tissue.

When the body relaxes when sleeping, that throat tissue can slightly drop down blocking the airway which can make people stop breathing periodically over the night.

Fortunately, shedding only several pounds of your overall body mass is in some cases enough to prevent sleep apnea and avoid the health issues which it brings.

Body fat accumulated on the abdomen or belly area tends to give off damaging chemicals which interfere with insulin effects which balance blood sugar levels.

Despite the fact that the pancreas works harder in order to produce more insulin, blood sugar levels can still go up. Fortunately, losing excess weight even only several pounds can prevent or reverse this from occurring.

There are numerous studies conducted on the topic which suggest that losing weight brings good night sleep which is less possible when you are overweight or obese.

Losing excess weight also leads to better mood as it may surely chase away your blues.

Moreover, weight loss will also make you feel better and more satisfied with yourself bringing a better body image and improved sleeping pattern due to weight loss may be one of the reasons.

There is also one study conducted on the topic showing that depressed individuals who are also overweight felt much better after losing an average of eight percent of their body weight.

The same study also suggests that they will feel even better if they keep losing weight in the future.

Shedding additional pounds also brings down various types of inflammation. Fat cells which are located on the abdominal area, in some cases, release damaging chemicals which inflame and irritate tissues throughout the body.

This is connected to various health issues such as heart attack, arthritis, stroke, and heart disease.

Fortunately, moving towards your optimal weight can easily lower the amount of those damaging chemicals in the body reducing the chances of developing these illnesses.

There are also some lifestyle benefits which weight loss brings such as greater self-esteem, improved energy and focus, decreased stress, improved mood, and improved vitality as well as greatly improved body image.

Weight loss also brings several social benefits as well such as greater motivation to stick to your exercise program or to your dieting program.

There are some individuals reporting that weight loss improved their mood and decreased stress also improved their personal relationships with family members and friends.

Changing Your Mindset

The very first step you need to take on your weight loss journey requires you to change your weight loss mindset. This is the first as well as the most important step for sustainable weight loss.

As you work on changing your weight loss mindset, you, in fact, rewire what you actually think about weight loss, so your overall weight loss journey can serve you better.

In other words, you need to cultivate your own weight loss state of mind. This psychological change you need to embrace can be even more challenging than adding a few additional greens to your plate.

This is something which needs to be done. First of all, keep in mind that there are three words you should ban from your mind as you embark on this journey.

These words are "I do not", "will not" and "cannot." These are three short words you need to ban in order to succeed as they just come from your mind and have nothing to do with your inner strength or with what you can achieve.

If you use them often, they can have a massive indirect impact on your weight-loss journey as well as on your fitness level.

Therefore, you need to flip the entire script and leave that negative talk behind. Individuals who are trying to lose weight commonly say do not simply due to their negative past experiences.

For instance, someone saying I do not like veggies simply reminds herself of those old experiences which do not have anything to do with her current behavior.

For this reason, your old experiences should not dictate your present behavior. If there are some I cannot or I do not terms in your vocabulary, you need to flip the script and turn them into I do and I can.

This will motivate and encourage you to move further and after several days you will be able to pick your new pace with ease.

If your current fitness level is low, your "I cannot" words may be blocking your success. Instead of saying I cannot do ten push-ups, say I will try and I will succeed. You need to try as it is better to try and fail than fail to try.

You can start with two push-ups and every new day you add one more push-up, so you move further until you reach your fitness goal.

Your weight loss journey must start with you changing your mindset and rewiring what you think about weight loss.

There are numerous physical ways for overcoming your weight loss plateau such as changing your dieting habits and embracing physical activity.

Nonetheless, without changing your mindset, these tricks will only work in the short-run providing no sustainable weight loss journey as there is always some underlying thought keeping you from sustainable weight loss.

Unless you go out there and address it, you will keep struggling on the road. For instance, many females tend to lose pounds as soon as they start making healthier dieting choices, but their weight loss progress tends to stop before they are completely satisfied with what they see in the mirror.

The truth is that losing weight in a sustainable way is much more than shedding those additional pounds which seem to be melting away at the very beginning of the journey.

The trick is to keep losing weight after that initial period. Many females fail in this step as after periods of losing weight, their progress simply freezes.

The main reason for this happening is that very common weight loss plateau present keeping you from losing weight in the long run.

In order to overcome this issue, there is no any magic trick you can do except changing your weight loss mindset.

Chapter 8.   Meditation For Weight Loss

There are various meditation techniques to lose weight because there are various ways to meditate. In this practice, breathing is fundamental as it is for our life. In some techniques it only consists of controlling well the way of breathing.

There are meditation exercises to lose weight, which greatly reduce anxiety since in many cases it is one of the main causes of a person having a hard time losing weight.

There are many meditation techniques that will help you lose weight because there are various ways of meditating and in this case breathing is essential.

The 5 best Meditation Weight Loss Techniques

1. Pratyahara

Pratyahara is a technique in which the negative information entering the mind is reduced and the positive information is increased.

When you spend too much time around a negative person, for example, who pressures you and makes you eat emotionally, you can isolate yourself from this adult, which helps to reduce emotional eating.

Alternatively, if you find yourself inspired by some of your friends and you want to lose weight, you can start hanging around more with those friends, which will increase your weight loss motivation.

Pratyahara is a mechanism where negativity is minimized and positivity is enhanced. Look at the above connection.

Applied to get in shape, that simply means you take in more positive information and experiences to help support your weight loss journey and take in less information that keeps you from getting in shape.

2. Mindfulness

Mindfulness is about understanding what's happening in your mind.

Most people are not aware of their thinking, which is why they are so greatly affected by their feelings.

They think, for example, "I need to eat chocolate," and go and get chocolate automatically.
A careful approach would be to say, "Alright, that's just a chocolate feeling, just an idea, it's not real, I don't really need candy in my head." Distancing yourself from your cravings in this way gives you power over them. It helps you avoid the cravings.

- Instructions

You'll need 1 piece of comfort food / junk food you'll still consume for this workout. Your pick.

Go in a quiet and peaceful place.

Place the junk food in front of you a few feet on the table / board.

Using good posture to sit comfortably.

Relax for two minutes Train your attention on the fact that your breath will come and go through the gap between your nose and mouth.

74

Take 25 attentive breaths.

Mind your dream junk food (the one before you).

Focus your mind on this food's effect in your head (don't look at the food itself, center on the food's mental impression).

You will find that certain feelings emerge when you concentrate your attention on the meal. You're going to have specific food ideas. The detrimental interaction with food is created by these emotions. We need these feelings to get rid of.

Each time you feel Each thought, SEE the thinking to get rid of the feelings (imagine that you are staring at yourself as if you were spectating yourself). First, tell yourself, "It's just an idea. At last, imagine blowing the idea away from you until it disappears completely.

Take the food.

You will experience different emotions again while holding the food in your mouth.

Take a minute to see the kinds of thoughts you're going through.

Tell yourself again that they're just thoughts. They're not facts in your head, they're just fantasies.

Now, I'm going to use the analogy of a chocolate bar to continue this workout, but you can start with whatever food you have.

Remove the bar of chocolate. Thought about it. Focus your mind on the flavor, colors, scent, sound, and any other part of the food 100 percent.

Notice again the kinds of thoughts that you are experiencing. Speak to yourself, "It's just feelings. They're not reality. "Imagine the thoughts floating in the distance.

Slowly eat the food. Bite into it, catch it and quit in your mouth. Don't go drinking. Think of the taste.

Stay mindful of your emotions with the food in your mouth. Speak to yourself, "It's just feelings. They're not true. "Imagine the thoughts in the distance floating away.

Swallow. Swallow.

Start until there's no food left.

You're shifting your thoughts and feelings about food with the weight loss meditation technique above.

This helps eliminate the negative thoughts about food that you have.

This method helps the subconscious to get rid of your food-related negative and illogical thoughts and feelings. In other words, you tell the mind that food is not pleasure, enjoyable, comfort, or anything else. Nutrition is nourishment.

You may have been a little shocked when you did the exercise above when I instructed you to delete ALL ideas, even good thoughts, during the exercise. At one point you might have thought (for example) "Food is nutrition. I will sleep right. "That's a good idea, isn't it? And why do you get rid of it?

The explanation to get rid of all emotions and not just the bad ones is that thoughts live as a matrix of our head. Thoughts are like a string fragment that is really poorly twisted. It doesn't necessarily lead to another good thought to consider one good thought. If you say "I'm going to eat well," your next idea is just as likely to be "No

I'm probably not going to eat because I have a bad diet" as it is "Yeah, I'm going to eat healthy and exercise."

This is a simple exercise that will change the way you feel about your favorite food completely. It will change your mindset to junk food absolutely. And it will greatly reduce your cravings and make your diet better.

3. Visualization Meditations For Weight Loss

Visualizations are methods of therapy including visualization and visual imagery. You construct a mental picture of who you really want to be when you do a visualization meditation. Then you meditate on this image, which makes you feel that you can achieve your goal. It greatly increases the fitness drive and weight loss.

Try this method. "Sit quietly and concentrate on your breath for a few minutes. That's going to help you relax.

Now imagine the whole body as you would like it to be. What are you going to look like? What are you going to feel like? What's special about you? Imagine the specifics of these things now tell yourself how you're going to get there. Which moves do you take to get in shape?

Now see the steps above until you reach the ideal type of body.

4. Mind Body Meditation For Weight Loss

This method increases the connection between your mind and body, improving your self-control. It's a technique for changed body scanning.

- Lie down with a good posture or sit down.

77

- Close your eyes and focus on breathing. Fill your nose with 10 deep breaths.

- We're going to guide the body's consciousness. This will increase the connection between mind and body. Start at your bottom. Just be aware of your feet. Concentrate on them. Observe and sound in or out of your feet. Explore the emotions there. Touch your feet (mentally).

- Now move your body up systematically. Shift from your knees to your calves to your lower legs to your upper legs to your pelvis to your chest to your arms, wrists, back to your shoulders, to your body, chin, and finally head.

- Sometimes you will feel discomfort in your body parts. Imagine breathing warm air in that area asking your body to relax if this is the case. This is going to ease the stress.

- Now be mindful of the whole body and the emotions that run through you. This will increase your sensitivity. You will be more conscious of the sensation that precipitates the hunger the next time you experience a desire for food. That knowledge is going to give you more self-control.

5. *Meditation for Weight Loss Visualization (Dhyana Meditation Technique)*

This is a very powerful meditation technique for weight loss. It's going to help you lose weight and keep your diet alive.

You must create a very convincing mental image of a better you in this diagram.

You'll see yourself as all you want to be. You must prepare your mind to know what you really want.

This will turbo-charge the loss of weight.

- Use good posture to sit comfortably. Make sure that your body is aligned correctly.

- Close your eyes and concentrate a few minutes on breathing. Breathe, breathe.

- That's the fun bit. You will create a mental picture of yourself regularly as the person you really want to be. And you don't want to part from me. I want you to be absolutely amazing to see yourself. I want the same thing you want to be your own. It's all right. You're ready?

- Start with the nose. What would look like your face? See that. See that. See your lovely skin. Notice how the wrinkles are zero. You look pretty. Consider that in DETAIL.

- The upper portion of your body. You might want a six pack if you're a male. You may want a lean and sleek look if you're a kid. Dream that your upper body is perfect.

- Tone of the legs? Smooth? How are you going to want them? Picture that in depth.

- Everything else: fill in your ideal body with any other info.

- Imagine that this perfect thing you're doing with weight loss is incredible. You are doing something that you can only do once you have been able to lose weight. Maybe you've just run a marathon. Maybe you're on a stage with people watching you. Whatever it is that you like, imagine it in depth.

- Bring it all together so you can picture something spectacular accomplishing your best self.

- Affirmation: after accomplishing this amazing thing, what would your ideal self say? Choose an affirmation and imagine in your mind saying it LOUD.

- Imagining the ideal self in depth is important. You really need to see that perfect body and really imagine getting that amazing thing done and really hear the positive affirmation in your head.

Using Meditation For Weight Loss When Depressed Most people who overeat do so because they have a negative food relationship. Maybe the best example of this is eating comforting people.

Nutrition is not just protein for comfort eaters, it is a method of protection that they use when they feel depressed or anxious. They feel stressed, they want something beautiful, they eat some delicious food, they feel better. But then, for eating too much, they feel bad. It makes them mindful of their diet. We felt stressed and depressed afterwards. So they're eating something good again and the vicious cycle begins anew.

A relaxed eating person correlates diet with sadness, pain, and relaxing. Food is what they are going to do when they feel depressed. This provides healing for them. It's all a habit in thought.

The same applies to people who, for other reasons, overeat.

Many people associate a luxurious lifestyle with good food. They want the luxury lifestyle to eat lots of food.

Others associate food with socialization.

None of these are safe connections.

Meat is nourishment, nothing.

The key to have a healthy food partnership is to remove the illogical food thoughts and beliefs and see that food is just protein. Live, not for any other reason, to nourish the body.

The perfect body and mind you're after can be accomplished. The meditation techniques for weight loss that we have looked at will help.

Enlightened people like you and I know the loss of weight occurs in the head.

The power of the subconscious to resist cravings, to inspire us to lose weight, and to help us through stressful times... these talents are worth much more than anything you can get at the gym.

The best way of thinking produces the right body.

Chapter 9. Portion Control Hypnosis (Go In-Depth And Very Accurate)

It can be tempting to give into the promises we see from celebrities and other big brand ads about losing weight. They make it seem so effortless and fun, but when we start the journey ourselves, we soon discover that it is not so simple. This hypnosis is a process that will aide in your weight loss journey and provide for you a natural way to shed the pounds.

You will be guided through the process of feeling better, mindful eating, goal-oriented thoughts, and dedication to the body. This hypnosis is a little different than others and will involve "I" statements. Allow these thoughts to come into your brain as if they were your own.

Natural Weight Loss Hypnosis

Narrator: First you will need to find a calm and quiet place with little distraction. Lay down flat on the ground or bed, or sit with your legs crossed and back comfortably straight, your palms face up and resting on your knees. Once you are in this position begin taking long deep breaths from the stomach, in through the nose, and out the mouth.

(Narrator breathes with listener for 5 seconds)

Narrator: Good. As you breathe focus in on each of your muscles, letting them constrict and then retract. Move on to the next one. Constrict, retract. Once all of your muscles are relaxed and your mind has focused on your inner and outer breaths, you'll want to clear your mind of all distractions. Imagine as you exhale, all the worries in your life leave with that one outward breath. Continue this until your mind is completely clear and your breath naturally falls into a rhythm.

(Narrator pauses for 3-5 seconds)

Narrator: As you continue to focus on these breaths, listen to the words carefully, repeat them in your head if you need to. These are affirmations that will change the way your mind thinks about weight loss and a healthier you. I do not need to participate in any diet plan. I do not need to sign up for one specific workout. I am able to go through with the weight loss all on my own. I am capable and ready to lose the weight naturally, using my own body to do this.

(Narrator pauses for 3 seconds)

Narrator: My body was designed to keep me as healthy as possible. The first step is deciding that I want to lose weight. This is a step that I have already agreed to. I have continually wanted to lose weight and have this be a part of my lifestyle.

(Narrator pauses for 3 seconds)

Narrator: I am devoted to making the best decision possible for my health. I am learning self-control and focusing on knowing what the best thing for my body is going to be. I understand when I should say "no," and when I need to push myself through something that might be a bit more challenging. I have recognized what bad habits I have done in the past, and I have created new habits that I can start to add to my future.

(Narrator pauses for 3 seconds)

Narrator: I understand why I need to lose the weight. I am no longer doing this just for looking good. I am doing this because I need to be healthier. I want to feel good

83

all the time. I want to be able to have confidence and love myself easier.

(Narrator pauses for 3 seconds)

Narrator: I recognize that I need to love myself in this present moment. I cannot do this journey if I do not believe in myself. I am my own trainer. I am the person that is going to be encouraging me more than anyone else. I am the one who is going to be holding all of the power over my life for the rest of my time on this Earth. I am the one who needs to remember the things that are most important for achieving my dreams.

(Narrator pauses for 3 seconds)

Narrator: I love myself more than I ever have, which is why I am making this journey. If I do not learn to accept myself the way I am right now, then I will never fully be able to love the person that I am, even after I have made the transformation.

I am my own best friend. I have the ability to lose all of the weight that I want because it is part of who I am. It is natural for me to lose the weight the way that my body designed me to do so.

(Narrator pauses for 3 seconds)

Narrator: I am going to eat less calories than what I am used to eating right now. I am going to exercise more than what I am used to doing right now. I am going to do this so I can burn more calories and lose even more weight. I am dedicated to this lifestyle because I deserve it. I am focused on shedding the pounds because of all the various health benefits that come along with being more in shape.

(Narrator pauses for 3 seconds)

Narrator: I am going to eat foods that are healthy for me. I will not deprive myself of any nutrition. I will eat in moderation, but I will never starve myself. I will make sure to not overeat, but I will never completely keep food from my body.

I will exercise as often as I can. I will push myself on days that I feel like staying home instead, but I will never push myself to a point that I physically hurt myself. I will know when I need to try a little harder, and I will know when it is OK to lighten up.

(Narrator pauses for 3 seconds)

Narrator: I will learn all of these things through trusting my body. Not only do I have the natural processes to lose weight already inside of me, but I have what is needed to trust myself through my own intuition. I understand the importance of listening to my gut. I recognize how I can read what I need to do, and know what isn't necessary.

(Narrator pauses for 3 seconds)

Narrator: I have made mistakes in the past, and there were moments where I didn't judge the situation properly. I will always know how to best listen to my voice as I continue to move forward in this life. I will only grow stronger that voice in the back of my head which tells me what to do. I will listen to my conscious and my subconscious and know how to read both in order to get the truth. I will always be prepared to have to face myself and look deep within my character to get to the root of my issues.

(Narrator pauses for 3 seconds)

Narrator: I will continue to do this because it is going to help me to lose weight. I will always look for ways to improve the natural methods that I can use to shed the pounds. I am confident in my own abilities to say "no" when it is needed. I won't act on impulse and I will always do my best to control my emotions. The better I can have a handle on my emotions, the easier it will be to know what I need to do to reach my goals and achieve my dreams.

(Narrator pauses for 3 seconds)

Narrator: I am focused on myself. I am doing this for myself. I am taking care of myself.

(Narrator pauses for 3 seconds)

Narrator: Each promise that I make to myself is one that brings me closer to my goals. I can feel the air coming in and out of my body. I am focused on relaxing, because reducing my stress will be important in achieving my goals. I am making a dedication to my body.

(Narrator pauses for 3 seconds)

Narrator: I am going to provide my body with all of the healthy food, water, air, and sun that it can get. I am like a gorgeous plant that needs the attention it deserves to have a vibrant and healthy blossom. I am devoted to myself. I love myself. I love my body. I am going to take care of my body. I am ready for the future. I am not afraid. I am accepting of the bad. I am excited for what is to come.

(Narrator pauses for 3 seconds)

Narrator: Take in several deeper breaths, just focusing on your body, your promises, and your goals. As you begin to bring yourself into the conscious, slowly open your eyes, press your palms together at your chest, and smile.

Chapter 10. Stop Emotional Eating Hypnosis

Emotional Hunger

Emotional hunger and physical hunger are two very different things. Many individuals may claim that they're just trying to fill their empty stomach whenever they're taking a ton of food out of the fridge. However, they may just be trying to fill their empty heart or at least, to take their mind of something.

It's easy for many to not see the differences, especially when they're really depressed, stressed out, and troubled. If you're still stuck in a cycle of emotional hunger, frustration, and negativity, you're encouraged to take note of the things explained below.

Mindless Eating Usually Follows After Emotional Hunger

Mindless eating is characterized by a lack of awareness of what's going into your body or the amount of food you're stuffing yourself with. After several hours, you may have already consumed a whole bag of chips or a whole pint of ice cream without paying much attention and without fully enjoying the meal. You're emotional, not necessarily hungry.

Even after you've eaten a huge amount of food, you can still go at it because your mind's not registering what has been happening for the past few hours. When you're physically hungry, though, you're usually more mindful of what you're doing. You're just responding to the hunger, not the emotional instability.

Emotional Hunger is Sudden

Emotional hunger does not follow a specific schedule. It will hit you instantly, filling you with a sense of urgency that's simultaneously overwhelming and very tempting. Since emotions are also quite difficult to manage and predict, emotional hunger can surprise you in many instances. On the other hand, physical hunger is gradual.

Unless you haven't eaten in a very long time, you wouldn't want to eat as soon as possible. The hunger builds up because since your last meal this morning, you haven't had anything to eat. There's still an hour away before lunch break and your stomach's already rumbling a bit.

For example, you broke up with a long-time boyfriend or girlfriend. The immense sadness can lead you to consume a ton of potato chips and gallons of ice cream in the next few days.

You're not necessarily hungry, but your emotions have immediately kicked into gear, pushing you to eat despite the relative fullness. You may have seen a number of people who have put on a few pounds just a few days after their "personal tragedy." They quickly turned to food for comfort, hence the term "Comfort Food."

Being Full Won't Satisfy Emotional Hunger

Physical hunger can be satisfied when you've had your fill. After a healthy amount of food, you can continue being productive or doing various activities. On the other hand, emotional hunger continues to demand more and more. You're led to eat more because the bad or negative feelings haven't been addressed yet.

You're so focused on drowning your sorrows and disappointments with different types of "Comfort Food" that you forget about what your body actually needs. You're already full if you'll consider your physical needs, but your heart and mind aren't done yet. For so many reasons, they won't be done until you gain much weight; until you see what you've become because of emotional hunger.

Once you're full, but you're body's still searching for more food, consider the possibility of being emotionally hungry. Some people fall into a dangerous cycle of binge eating because they don't want to admit that they're emotionally troubled. They turn to food because they think they're just hungrier than usual. This isn't the case most of the time, though.

The fact that food can give you a good feeling makes it a formidable adversary in some cases, especially if you're prohibited to consume certain types of food due to health risks. There are other ways to satisfy your emotional needs and it's not through food.

Specific Comfort Foods are sought during Emotional Hunger

Physical hunger can be satisfied by virtually any type of food. Those who are simply hungry can get by with a vegetable salad with steamed tuna. Basically, healthy food are also considered—most likely even preferred more than unhealthy choices. You just want to respond to the hunger and get to such a goal in a healthy manner. Emotional hunger craves for specific and usually unhealthy snacks.

Your goal isn't to deal with the hunger, but to escape or cover up the pain you're feeling. For some, it's not necessarily pain, but a sense of helplessness or a couple of frustrations. It's essentially the negativity that you're trying to defeat with positive feeling you're getting from the delicious cheese pizza or vanilla mint ice cream you're eating.

Guilt, Regret, or Shame Usually Follow After Emotional Hunger

People know what's bad and good for them. When they make healthy choices with regard to food, they are filled with satisfaction and genuine joy because they know they're taking good care of themselves. They eat only when they are hungry and they don't let their emotions dictate their food choices.

Sadly, for those who are emotionally hungry, guilt, regret, and shame can become frequent companions. After you finish that large bag of chips or that extra-large coke, you're filled with so much regret because you know it's not right. You're guilty because once again, you've allowed yourself to get caught up in the moment. You're also ashamed because you weren't strong enough to make the right decision.

There's one thing you have to know: everyone is prone to emotional hunger. Some are actually doing it unconsciously. No matter how old or young you are and what your circumstances may be, binge eating is a constant option.

Now that you have a better idea of what the differences are between physical or typical hunger and an emotional one, you can better explore the concept. You can now identify what is binge eating and what is not. The next step is to know the different causes of such an unhealthy activity.

The 3 Causes of Emotional Eating

Childhood Habits

Look back at your experiences with food as a child. How did your parents associate food or eating to various circumstances in your life? If you were rewarded with food whenever you did something good or amazing, then you must have unconsciously considered food as a reward for good behavior.

Another way of looking at it is if your parents gave you sweets or a tasty meal whenever you were feeling down. In the early years, one's perspective regarding the role of food in his life is primarily influenced by his parents or guardians. Essentially, the overall view of the family towards food also creates a foundation for the young one's view of food when he grows older.

Emotionally-based childhood eating behaviors, which later on develop into habits, usually extend to adulthood. It's also actually possible for someone to eat based on nostalgic feelings. Eating because you remember how your dad grilled a couple of patties for you when you were younger definitely feels good.

At one point in your childhood, you may have baked a cake with your sweet mother. This may be why you're also eating a lot of pastries right now. You're very troubled and it's these types of food that help you feel secure. Many people want to feel like a child again, particularly during difficult moments.

Influence of Social Activities

One good way of relieving stress is to meet with your close friends or loved ones. Their presence and their tolerance of your food choices give a great feeling. You feel at home with them and because they may also be eating due to emotional hunger, you may end up doing the same.

There's a high tendency that overeating may occur because you're in the company of overeaters. You just decide to do what they're doing because all of you are going through tough challenges as well. You may want to empathize with them.

91

Another reason why overeating or binge eating may occur during social gatherings is nervousness. Things can get even worse if you're encouraged by your loved ones to eat a lot. They don't mind your current body mass because they love you too much to see you not eat and just sit at a corner.

When people go home to their families after being away for a very long time, the immense feeling of joy and relief can also cause them to consume a ton of food. They're not necessarily sad, but the occasion itself causes them to be so emotional, which can lead them to overeat.

Food turns into a medicine, which isn't really as effective as it's viewed to be. People just want to bury their negative emotions under huge pile of food. When they break up with someone, they turn to food. When they lose one of their loved ones, they think of the best possible way to stuff themselves up. When things don't go according to plan, a local binge eater shows his immense faith in the local supermarket and his great adoration for his refrigerator.

When you're stuffed with food, you feel like all the negativity just disappears, but they don't. When you stuff yourself to the point where you gain weight—when you apparently don't want to—you're just filled with a whole new batch of negative emotions.

As the binge eating continues, a very sturdy habit is formed. This means the person will just get used to filling himself up when he has a problem. According to psychologists, a habit can be formed in just 21 days or 3 weeks. So if you've just started your binge eating journey, there's much time for positive transformation.

A Feeling of Emptiness or Extreme Boredom

Some people eat a ton of food just because they're bored. When they have nothing to do, they most likely don't even try to look for some activity to keep themselves busy. Boredom is sometimes a sign of laziness.

Basically, since an individual doesn't want to do what he's supposed to do, he ends up feeling empty. Instead of using this time to be productive or to help himself, he turns to food. This behavior can also turn into a habit if not detected, admitted, and addressed promptly.

If one delves into the matter more deeply, he'll see that boredom can also be considered as "free time," which can be utilized in a way that can help him and other people. Instead of opening the refrigerator whenever you have nothing to do or you're not in the mood yet to work on something, look for a better alternative. An empty space can be effectively filled by making the right or rational decisions, not emotional ones.

Have you ever noticed that stress can also make you hungry? It's actually not just in your head. Having chronic stress in this past-faced and chaotic world often leads to increased levels of cortisol, the stress hormone. Cortisol will trigger cravings for salty, sweet, and high-fat foods. These types of food will give you a burst of energy and pleasure, which is why they're so tempting to consume. The more stressed out you are, the more likely it is for you to turn to unhealthy food.

Unfortunately, so many things can act as stressors, so it's also a challenge for several people to handle themselves. At the workplace, school, and even at home, certain things stress people out. Avoiding stress would be another issue altogether, but making wise decisions on how to manage yourself during tense situations can make a difference.

You may not be able to control the circumstances you face at all times, but you can choose peace over turmoil and healthy living to unhealthy food choices. Know now that stress can turn most people into binge eaters. With this knowledge at hand, you can start being aware of yourself when you're in a pinch.

Using Awareness or Mindfulness to Beat Emotional Eating

You either eat with your emotions or with your mind. You can't really work with both. This is why mindful eating is considered to be the exact opposite of emotional eating. Awareness is a powerful tool in defeating binge eating. Once you become less emotional and more rational with regard to problem-solving or self-management, you'll be able to overcome this seemingly unbeatable foe.

You simply have to start with the identification of the triggers of emotional hunger. After that, you should look for better alternatives. As you work on these, you're also encouraged to savor the eating experience. Lastly, remember to live in the present.

Identify Triggers of Emotional Hunger

Many things can trigger emotional eating. Basically, whatever triggers your emotional outbursts or whatever fills you with negativity are the same factors that influence your diet. It may be a bit challenging to accomplish this step, but you can seek assistance from your loved ones.

You can do it, though. You just have to believe in your ability to not be biased when assessing yourself. Be more observant of your day-to-day activities and regard your problems through positive lenses.

Push pessimism away because this will hinder you from seeing the picture clearly. Instead of thinking that you'll just end up counting your problems, see it as an effective method of analyzing your enemies so that you can take them down. Great soldiers or warriors are aware of what they're feeling during various circumstances. They know what they should do because they look at each and every detail.

They're familiar with their weaknesses and it's this knowledge that enables them to turn such frailties into specialties or strengths. Whether it's stress, depression, a lack of validation or approval from your peers, or tension inside the household, the triggers of emotional hunger must be identified.

Find Alternatives to Address Negative Emotions

Emotional eating isn't the only path towards relief. Actually, it's not even a good path to begin with. Instead of eating to your heart's content whenever you're feeling down, look for other ways to lift yourself up. The greatest solutions to emotional hunger are of love.

This essentially means that if you do things that you're passionate about, you can feel more fulfilled and satisfied. The list of things that can make you happy certainly isn't only filled with different types of food. You will find other things to do in your free time and during those very difficult moments.

The alternatives need not be expensive. They don't even have to cost you a dime. Simply meditating a few times a week, talking to a good friend, or taking a walk at the park every day can take the blues away.

It's also advisable that you don't spend too much time in the kitchen whenever you're down. As you seek to be liberated from the clutches of emotional hunger, you

95

must willingly distance yourself from temptation. The farther you are from your refrigerator, the better.

Savor the Eating Experience

Some say that obesity isn't a huge concern in France because they know how to enjoy their food. They're able to avoid a wider waistline by having a wider grin whenever they're eating. Generally, the French enjoy eating as much as they have fun cooking a variety of healthy and hearty meals.

You may not be a professional cook or chef, but you can choose to savor the eating experience whenever you're at home or when you're eating out. You can have fun eating, exploring the different flavors and textures of the meal before you.

Binge eaters "enjoy" food in a different way. They use it to conceal serious emotional struggles. Instead of eating to be healthy and to do away with their hunger, they use food to break out of their gloomy state. Unfortunately, they're not really free. If you seek freedom, one effective way of achieving it is to savor every bite and to not rush to the refrigerator during a crisis. Enjoy your salad, steak, or whatever it is in front of you. Don't eat more than you're supposed to because your sadness and disappointments won't vacate your heart just because your stomach's filled with so much food.

Chapter 11. Weight Loss Hypnosis

This hypnosis is going to be a way that will validate your weight loss goals. You will be able to recognize how relaxing and being peaceful throughout the weight loss process makes it easier to keep the pounds off. Keep an open mind with this, and remember to let thoughts flow naturally into your brain as if they were your own.

Hypnosis for Natural Weight Loss

You know how to relax your body. You are an expert at making sure that your limbs can hang freely without tension. We need to let our minds relax now.

Don't just let your body feel like jelly floating through water. Let your mind be as malleable in this process too. With hypnosis, you have to let others into your head for just a moment. So allow your thoughts to flow freely and don't put any pressure on yourself to think a certain thing. Focus now on your breath.

Breathe in for five and out for five. Breathe in through your nose and out through your mouth. This is a way that's going to help make sure that you are focused on healthy living. Breathe in for one, two, three, four, and five, and out for five, four, three, two, and one.

Now we're going to do something a little different. Breathe in for five and then out for one long second. This time, we're only going to breathe in and out through your nose. Breathe in through your nose for one, two, three, four, and five, and out for one and a long and forceful breath.

You are slowly breathing in new air, and then you forcefully push it out as fast as you can. Breathe in for one, two, three, four, and five, and out for one with a quick snap. This way, you focus your breathing and make it easier for the air to flow in and out of your body.

You are going to want to snap your attention on nothing. You can look ahead of you now, but make sure that you get all of your sights out. On the count of three, you're going to snap your eyes closed and also breathe out at the same time.

So look around you and breathe in for one, two, three, four, and five. Now quickly shut your eyes and breathe out in one long breath.

You can go back to regular breathing now but continue to focus on breathing in through your nose and out through your mouth. Try to do it in a pattern of five, but don't get too hung up on the strict structure. Instead, you'll want to focus on letting your thoughts come into your brain as if they were your own.

Keep your mind focused and breathe in. In front of you, in your mind, only with your eyes closed, see the emergence of a spinning wheel. This wheel has nothing special about it. It is simply silver with rubber tires, and it is spinning fast. It is not attached to anything. It is simply a spinning wheel. It spins faster and faster and faster. Stare directly at the silver center. Notice how it continues to cycle through quickly.

Now that tire is turning into a circle of water. The water is flowing around as if it were a washing machine with water being spun in a circle.

The water is spinning and spinning. It is splashing against itself, but it is all still contained within this one simple silver circle. Continue to look at the center. There is nothing else around; everything is black. Notice this silver spinning water. It goes over and over and over in a simple cycle in a simple loop. Focus on the center again as we count for your breathing. Breathe in for one, two, three, four, and five, and out for five, four, three, two, and one.

Suddenly, on the count of three, this spinning cycle is going to snap into every corner of your mind. You are going to be engulfed in this spinning water.

One, two, and three.

You are now in the water. You see around you that you are on a calm beach. The water is not spinning anymore and is completely serene and clear. You walk towards the edge of the beach. You see it now that the water is slapping against the shore. This is the way that it was spinning around in circles in your mind.

No longer is it spinning now, and it is simply a normal ocean slapping against the beach. You can feel the water dripping off your skin, but the sun above you is already drying out. The sun is a vibrant yellow, and it casts a warm glow over your body. The sun kisses you at the top of your head and spreads down all the way to the tip of your toes. You look down at your feet and see that they're submerged in the sand. There is still water gently coming over and washing against your feet. You move your toes upwards, and they break through some of the sand, only for it to quickly form over them again. As the water smooths it out, you look ahead of you and breathe in again. You breathe in for one, two, three, four, and five, and out for five, four, three, two, and one, and notice all of these smells that come in with that. You breathe again for one, two, three, four, and five, and out for five, four, three, two, and one. You feel refreshed, energized, and free.

You are natural, pure, clean, and clear. You are part of this beach now with your feet stuck in the sand. You are like a tree with roots deep under the surface.

You decide now to sit down. You let your bum sink into the sand a little bit more as well. Water continues to emerge around you now like a warm blanket, all the way up to your hips. It keeps you feeling completely centered and pure on the now.

You look around you, to your right and left, and see that there are plenty of rocks. These, of course, don't hurt you. They just simply are part of the sand. You dig your fingers into the sand, a little bit feeling the cold packed down underneath the initial warm on the top of the surface. You dig out a rock and see that it is flat and smooth. You clear a little bit of this rock off using water as it passes over. You throw the rock quickly and sharply against the top of the water and watch as it jumps. It was a nice skipping rock that effortlessly glided across the top.

You do this a few more times with other smooth and flat rocks that surround you. It is a reminder of how you can manipulate nature.

The water is getting higher and higher now, and you are chest-deep in the water. It is perfectly warm and calm, bringing plenty of waves back to the surface. You want to feel the sun on your skin again now, so you decide to stand up.

You walk across the sand, now in the dry area. Sand begins to stick to your legs, but still, it is nice and warm. You walk across, feeling your feet sink deep in. Each new step you take, the bottom of your foot is hot from the surface of the sand. It adjusts quickly as it sinks down, and you feel a sensation over and over again as you continue to walk. You see ahead of you that there is what looks to be a sandcastle. As you get closer and closer, you see that there is no castle at all. It is simply a wall that somebody has built with the sand. You decide to walk all the way through this wall now.

No longer is there something that is going to block off part of the beach. It was simply made by sand, so it was easy for you to destroy with your feet and legs only. You recognize that this is a representation of the walls that you have built around yourself. No longer are you going to let yourself be afraid of the things that you want. You can't just be comfortable with the situation you're in anymore. Being comfortable does not always mean being happy. You want to be able to feel completely fresh and pure. You're not attached to the things that you used to be or the person that used to keep your mind stuck in the same situations over and over again.

You sit in the middle of the now-destroyed wall and look out on the beach again. The sun continues to send warm feelings all across your skin.

You breathe in deeply, feeling this ocean air fill your body once again. These oceans are responsible for so much. They are the life force that keeps everybody moving. We take fish from the ocean, and it helps us travel and carry things across waters. You breathe. All of this is a reminder of the incredible world that you're a part of.

While your problems and issues are valid, this is also a reminder of how small some things that seem like such big deals to us really are in the grand scheme of things. There is a great and powerful force that exists just within the world alone.

You are an important part of this, and it is a reminder of the incredible and powerful person that you are.

The sun is setting, so you decide to go for one last and final dip before you don't have the chance anymore. You don't want to swim in the dark, so you decide to wade in a little bit and get your last dose of ocean water right now. You walk in, and the water is all the way up to your hip. You can look down and see the ocean floor because the water is so clear.

You don't really see any fish, but you can see the old shells left over by different crabs or other ocean critters.

You walk a little bit further, and now the water is up to your chest. The waves are so gentle you barely feel them. It's almost as if you were in a deep and warm bath because the water is so relaxing.

You decide to lift your legs up now. Floating on top of the water, you simply move around, letting the waves take you where you need to go. If you go out too far from the shore or off to the side too much, you can gently guide yourself back to where you want to be with a simple arm or leg movement.

You are simply free in the water, almost as if you're flying through the sky. There is no gravity in this moment. You breathe in and out, in and out. The water is surrounding you now. A few droplets will get on your face here and there as the water continues to splash around you, but nothing too extreme.

You close your eyes for just a moment, letting water wash over your face. You are clean, pure, natural, and energized in this moment. Breathe in for five and out for five. Breathe in for five and out for five. Everything around you is turning black. Darkness begins to consume you once again, and you realize you are now back in your bed on the couch, ready to start a new life.

You are pure, energized, and prepared. As we count on from 20, you will be out of this hypnosis. You can then either drift asleep or move on to another mental exercise.

Chapter 12. Eat Healthy With Subliminal Hypnosis

Make yourself comfortable.

Find the perfect sleep position.

Inhale through your nose and exhale through your mouth.

Again inhale through your nose and this time as you exhale close your eyes.

Repeat this one more time and relax.

Sharpen your breathing focus.

Find stillness in every breath you take, relieve yourself from any tension and relax.

Let your body relax, soften your heart, quiet your anxious mind and open to whatever you experience without fighting.

Simply allow your thoughts and experiences to come and go without grasping at them.

Reduce any stress, anxiety, or negative emotions you might have, cool down become deeply and comfortably relaxed.

That's fine.

And as you continue to relax then you can begin the process of reprogramming your mind for your weight loss success because with the right mindset, then you can think positively about what you want to achieve. It begins with changing your mindset and attitude, because the key to losing weight all starts in the mind. One of the very first things you must throw out the window (figuratively) before you start your journey to weight loss is negativity. Negative thinking will just lead you nowhere. It will only pull your moods down which might trigger emotional eating. Thus, you'll eat more, adding up to that unwanted weight instead of losing it. Remember that you must need to break your old bad habits and one of them is negative self-talk. You need to change your negative mental views and turn them into positive ones. For example, instead of telling yourself after a few days of workout that nothing is happening or changing, tell yourself that you have done a set of physical activities you have never imagine you can or will do. Make it a point to pat yourself on the back for every little progress you make every day, may it be five additional crunches from what you did yesterday. Understand and accept that this process is a complete transformation, a metamorphosis if you will. This understanding is going to make the process smoother, and less painful.

Aside from being positive, you should also be realistic. Don't expect an immediate change in your body. Keep in mind that losing weight is not an overnight thing. It is a long term process and gradual progress. Set and focus on your goals to keep that negativity at bay. Losing weight needs consistent reminders and focus on proper mental preparations. Always keep yourself motivated. Train yourself to think positive all the time.

Don't compare yourself to others, because it will not help you attain your goals in losing weight. First and foremost, keep in mind that each one of us has different body types and compositions. There is a certain diet that may work on you, but not so much for the others. Possibly, some people might need more carbohydrates in their diet, while you might need to drop that and add more protein in your meals. Each one of us is unique. Therefore, your diet plan will surely differ from the person next to you.

Comparing yourself to other people's progress is just a negative thought and will just be unhelpful to you. Remember, always keep a positive outlook and commit to it before you start your diet. For the sake of your long-term success, leave the comparison trap. You're not exactly like the people you idolize and they're not exactly like you and that's perfectly fine. Accept that, embrace that and move on with your personal goals.

Be realistic in setting your goals. Think about small and easy to achieve goals that will guide you towards a long term of healthy lifestyle changes. Your goals should be healthy for your body. If you want to truly lose weight and keep it off, it will be a slow uphill battle, with occasional dips and times you'll want to quit. If you expect progress too fast, you will eventually not be able to reach your goals and become discouraged. Don't add extra obstacles for yourself, plan your goals carefully.

If possible, try to find someone who has similar goals as you and work on them together. Two is always better than one, and having someone who understands what you are undergoing can be such a relief! An added benefit of having a partner-in-crime (or several) is that you can always hold each other accountable. Accountability is one thing that is easy to start being lax after the first few weeks of a new weight loss program, especially if results aren't quite where you want them to be.

Write down a realistic timetable that you can follow. Start a journal about your daily exercises and meal plan. You can cross out things that you have done already or add new ones along the way. Plot your physical activities. Make time and mark your calendar with daily physical activities. Try to incorporate at least a 15-minute workout on your busy days.

When you become aware of a thought or belief that pins the blame for your extra weight on something outside yourself, if you can find examples of people who've overcome that same cause, realize that it's decision time for you. Choose for yourself whether this is a thought you want to embrace and accept. Does this thought support you living your best life? Does it move you toward your goals, or does it give you an excuse not to go after them?

If you determine your thought no longer serves you, you get to choose another thought instead. Instead of pointing to some external, all-powerful cause for you being overweight, you can choose something different. Track your progress by writing down your step count or workouts daily to keep track of your progress.

Celebrate and embrace your results. Since the path to a healthy lifestyle is mostly hard work and discipline, try to reward yourself for every progress even if it is small. Treat yourself for a day of pampering, travel to a place you have been wanting to visit, go hiking, have a movie date with friends or get a new pair of shoes. These kinds of rewards provide you gratification and accomplishments that will make you keep going. Little things do count and little things also deserve recognition. But keep in mind that your rewards should not compromise your diet plan.

You can also do something like joining an athletic event, a fun run, where you can meet new people that share the same ideals of a healthy lifestyle. You get to learn more about weight loss from others and also share your knowledge. You need to find a source of motivation and keep that source of motivation fresh in your mind so you don't forget why you embarked on this journey to begin with.

As you focus on your journey of weight loss, keep your stress at bay because too much stress is harmful for the body in many ways, but it also can cause people to gain weight. When the body is under stress, the body will automatically release many hormones and among one of them is cortisol. When the body is under duress and stress, cortisol is released, is can ignite the metabolism, for a period of time. However, if the body remains in stressful conditions, the hormone cortisol will continue to be released, and actually slow down the metabolism resulting in weight gain.

Everyone experiences stress; there is just no getting around that fact. However, minimizing stressors, as well as learning how to manage the stress in your life will not only help you with you with losing weight, but it will also make a more attractive you! High stress in anyone's life often brings out the worst in people. When you are trying to get a man, you want them to see the best of you, not the stressed out you. While you are decreasing your stress level, you will want to increase the amount of sleep you get each night. Lack of sleep is a link to weight gain and because of this, ensuring adequate and appropriate sleep is crucial when trying to lose weight. Sleep is vital for the well being of the body, and the ability for the mind to function, but it is also related to maintaining weight. If you are tired, make sure you sleep, rest or relax, so you are not prone to gaining weight. When a person gets more sleep, the hormone leptin will rise and when this happens the appetite decreases which will also decrease body weight.

Gratitude is important in this journey because it teaches you how to make peace with your body, no matter what shape, size or weight it has at the moment. It makes you look at your body with full acceptance and love, saying: "I'm grateful for my body the way it is." It stops you from beating yourself up for being overweight, unhealthy or out of shape. Be grateful for this learning experience, accept yourself the way you are, and take massive action to get your balance back.

When you express gratitude, you vibrate on a higher energy level, you are positive and happy, and you are simply in the state of satisfaction.

The more things you can find to be grateful for during your weight loss journey, the easier it will be to maintain a positive attitude and keep your motivation up.

It will also get you past those tough moments when you are feeling demotivated to take action and stick to the exercising or eating plan.

This means that you start expressing gratitude for the aspects of your body you would like to have, as if you already have them now. Be grateful for your sexy legs and slim waist. Be grateful for your increased energy levels and strength. Be grateful for the ability to wear smaller clothes. You get the drill. Feel the positive energy of gratitude flowing through your body as you imagine these things are true. By going through this exercise you'll notice the positive change in your thought patterns.

With the level of personal growth, you will achieve and the habits you will change on this session of hypnosis, you will feel like a completely different person. You will have more power, self–confidence and love yourself more than you ever thought possible before. That's change from the inside out. That's what lasts. And, at the end of the day, that's what truly matters.

Take a deep breath and allow your breath to return its natural rate as you return to your normal consciousness.

As you continue to breath, note that, right now, in this moment, you have no worries. You are just a relaxed body. Any distractions that arise while you tell yourself this can wait.

Repeat the following phrases:

I am relaxed

I am balanced

I can deal with any worries later

I am relaxed

I am balanced

The whole earth supports you in your relaxation and balance. Feel yourself supported and held.

Feel that everything you have done in your life has brought you to this moment without errors or mistakes.

This moment is perfect.

When you feel doubt, say hello to it and let it know it can't distract you from your purpose.

You are relaxed

You are balanced

You can deal with all doubts and worries.

Know that you can achieve this at any time because you are supported and held in balance.

Thank yourself for taking this time to connect with your body and balance.

Open your eyes and gently move your hands and feet.

Three eyes open and completely awake.

Chapter 13. Loss Weight Fast And Naturally With Hypnosis

Hypnosis As A Means Of Losing Weight

Hypnosis might be best known as the gathering stunt used to make people move the chicken in front of an audience. However, an ever-increasing number of people go to the psychological control system to help them make more beneficial choices and get in shape. A valid example: The consuming fewer calories master changed to spellbinding when Georgia, 28, chose she required to shed the 30 pounds she put on after foot medical procedure in 2009. The technique for mind-control had helped her in the past to conquer a dread of flying, and she trusted that it would likewise enable her to make good dieting practices.

Georgia subsequently decided to engage in hypnotherapy to help her lose weight. In short, each session was focused on planting positive thoughts in her mind such as knowing when to stop eating and finding the best way to help her stop overeating based on emotional reactions. The treatment proved to be progressively effective as she was able to curb her appetite and manage her eating habits more effectively. She was able to drop the weight that she wanted based on improving her overall eating habits, curbing her cravings and limiting the instances of binge eating.

Mesmerizing is for anybody searching for a mellow way to get thinner and make smart dieting a propensity. Is it safe to say that it isn't for one person? Any individual who needs a quick fix. It expects time to reframe issue thoughts regarding sustenance Georgia reveals to her trance inducer eight times each year, and it took a month before she started to see a genuine change. "The weight fell gradually and definitely, without tremendous adjustments in my way of life. I was all the while eating out many times each week, yet regularly sending plates back with sustenance on them! I truly tasted my sustenance unexpectedly, investing energy in flavors and surfaces. It was as though I had begun my illicit affection relationship with nourishment, no one, but I could get thinner," she said.

Spellbinding isn't planned to be a "diet," but instead an apparatus to help you prevail with regards to eating and practicing nutritious sustenance, states Traci Stein, Ph.D., MPH, an ASCH-ensured clinical entrancing wellbeing clinician and previous Director of Integrative Medicine at Columbia University's Department of Surgery. "Spellbinding enables people to encounter what they feel when they are ground-breaking, fit, and indirection in a multi-tactile way and conquer their psychological hindrances to accomplish those goals," she guarantees. "In particular, trance can help people unravel the hidden mental issues that reason them to abhor work out, experience extreme longings, gorge during the evening, or eat heedlessly. It empowers them to recognize the triggers and incapacitate them.

"As a general rule, it is valuable not to consider mesmerizing an eating regimen by any stretch of the imagination, says Joshua E. Syna, MA, LCDC, an authorized trance specialist at the Houston Hypnosis Center." It works since it changes their perspective about sustenance and eating and empowers them to figure out how to be increasingly quiet and agreeable in their life. So as opposed to being a passionate answer for sustenance and eating, it turns into a reasonable answer for craving, and new personal conduct standards are being made that enable the person to adapt to sentiments and life, "he depicts." Hypnosis works for weight reduction since it enables the person to isolate nourishment and eat from their enthusiastic lives.

Dr. Stein proposes that utilizing at-home independently directed sound projects produced by a gifted subliminal specialist (search for an ASCH affirmation) is alright for people with no other emotional wellness issues. Be that as it may, be careful with all the new online market applications, one investigation found that most applications are untested and regularly make affected cases about their viability that can't be substantiated.

What Hypnosis Feels Like

Forget what you found in movies and front of an audience is more like a treatment session than a carnival stunt. "Trance is a community-oriented encounter and at all times ought to be very much educated and agreeable," says Dr. Stein.

What's more, she adds to individuals stressed over being fooled into accomplishing something odd or hurtful, even under entrancing on the off chance that you would prefer truly not to accomplish something, you won't. "Consideration is simply focused," she portrays. "Normally everybody goes into light daze articulations a few times each day-accept about when you daydream while a companion shares everything about their vacation and trance just figures out how to think that internal consideration in a supportive way." Dispelling the legend that entrancing feels weird or terrifying from the patient's side, Georgia claims she generally felt exceptionally clear and leveled out.

There were even entertaining occasions such as envisioning steps on the scale and seeing the heaviness of her target. "My excessively inventive personality needed to envision initially taking off all garments, all of the gems, my watch, and barrette before hopping on naked. Any other individual does that, or is it just me?" (No, it's not simply you, Georgia!)

It's not intrusive, it functions admirably with other weight reduction medications, and it doesn't include any pills, powders, or different enhancements. Nothing occurs even from a pessimistic standpoint, placing it in the camp "may help, can't hurt." But Dr. Stein concedes that one drawback is there: cost. Expenses every hour contrast dependent on your place, yet for helpful spellbinding systems, it differs from $100-$250 an hour and when you see the specialist for a month or two once per week or more that can include rapidly. What's more, trance isn't secured by most insurance agencies. Be that as it may, Dr. Stein proposes it very well may be secured whenever utilized as a major aspect of a greater arrangement for psychological wellness treatment, so check with your provider.

A surprising perk of weight loss hypnosis isn't only a psychological thing, it's likewise a medicinal component, says Peter LePort, MD, a bariatric specialist, and Memorial Care Center for Obesity's therapeutic chief in California. "You should initially adapt to any hidden metabolic or natural weight increase causes yet utilizing spellbinding can kick start sound propensities while that is no joke," he proposes. Furthermore, there is another great advantage of utilizing spellbinding: "The component of reflection can diminish pressure and lift mindfulness, which can likewise help with weight reduction," he added.

How Hypnosis Aids In Weight Loss

There is an amazing measure of logical research that takes a gander at the viability of weight reduction mesmerizing, and a lot of it is sure. One of the underlying

113

1986 research found that overweight females utilizing a mesmerizing project shed 17 pounds contrasted with 0.5 pounds for females just advised to watch what they ate. A mesmerizing weight reduction study meta-investigation during the 1990s found that members who utilized trance lost more than twice as much weight as the individuals who didn't. Also, an examination in 2014 found that females who utilized entrancing were improving their weight, BMI, eating conduct, and even certain parts of self-perception.

In any case, it's not all uplifting news: A Stanford study in 2012 found that about a fourth of individuals just can't be mesmerized, and it has nothing to do with their characters, as opposed to basic conviction. Or maybe, the minds of certain individuals simply don't appear to work that way. "In case you're not inclined to staring off into space, you regularly think that it's difficult to stall out in a book or endure a motion picture, and don't believe you're innovative, you may be one of the individuals for whom trance isn't functioning admirably," says Dr. Stein.

Georgia is one of the examples of overcoming adversity. She guarantees it helped her lose the extra pounds as well as helped her keep them off also. After six years, she kept her weight reduction joyfully, now and then returning in with her trance specialist when she requires a boost.

Understanding The Hypnotic Gastric Band And How It Works

Gastric band hypnotherapy is a technique used to propose that you have a gastric band connected around your stomach to the intuitive to enable you to get more fit.

Gastric band medical procedure, thought about a final retreat, incorporates fitting a band around the upper segment of the stomach. This confines the amount of sustenance that you can expend physically, advancing weight reduction. It is an activity and, in this manner, involves future dangers and confusion.

Hypnotherapy of the gastric band or fitting a' virtual gastric band' doesn't include the medical procedure. Trance inducers utilize this technique to get the subliminal to think a gastric band has been fitted. The objective is to believe that you have had the physical activity on an oblivious level and that your stomach has diminished in size.

There is no medical procedure or medicine associated with the procedure, and it is thoroughly secure. In this segment, we will explore what is engaged with gastric band hypnotherapy, how it works, and on the off chance that it can work for you or not.

What Is A Gastric Band?

A stomach band is a silicone flexible apparatus utilized in weight reduction medical procedure. To create a modest pack over the gadget, the band is put around the upper part of the belly. This restrains the amount of sustenance that can be put away in the stomach area, making eating enormous amounts hard.

A gastric band will likely constrain the amount of sustenance that an individual can expend physically, making them feel full in the wake of eating next to no to advance weight reduction. It is a final hotel for most people who have this medical procedure after endeavoring for other weight reduction systems. Like any medical procedure, there are perils in fitting a gastric band.

Chapter 14. 100 Positive Affirmations For Weight Loss

According to dietitians, the success of dieting is greatly influenced by how people talk about lifestyle changes for others and for themselves.

The use of "I should" or "I must" is to be avoided whenever possible. Anyone who says, "I shouldn't eat French fries" or "I have to get a bite of chocolate" will feel that they have no control over the events. Instead, if you say "I prefer" to leave the food, you will feel more power and less guilt. The term "dieting" should be avoided. Good nutrition should be seen as a permanent lifestyle change. For example, the correct wording is, "I've changed my eating habits" or "I'm eating healthier".

Diets are fattening. Why?

The body needs fat. Our body wants to live, so it stores fat. Removing this amount of fat from the body is not an easy task as the body protects against weight loss. During starvation, our bodies switch to a 'saving flame', burning fewer calories to avoid starving. Those who are starting to lose weight are usually optimistic, as, during the first week, they may experience 1-3 kg (2-7 lbs.) of weight loss, which validates their efforts and suffering. Their body, however, has deceived them very well because it actually does not want to break down fat. Instead, it begins to break down muscle tissue. At the beginning of dieting, our bodies burn sugar and protein, not fat. Burned sugar removes a lot of water out of the body; that's why we experience amazing results on the scale. It should take about seven days for our body to switch to fat burning. Then our body's alarm bell rings.

Most diets have a sad end: reducing your metabolic rate to a lower level. This means that if you only eat a little more afterward, you regain all the weight you have lost previously. After dieting, the body will make special efforts to store fat for the next impending famine. What to do to prevent such a situation?

We must understand what our soul needs. Those who really desire to have success must first and foremost change their spiritual foundation. It is important to pamper our souls during a period of weight loss. All overweight people tend to rag on themselves for eating forbidden food, "I ate too much again. My willpower is so weak!" If you have ever tried to lose weight, you know these thoughts very well.

Imagine a person very close to you who has gone through a difficult time while making mistakes from time to time. Are we going to scold or try to help and motivate them? If we really love them, we would instead comfort them and try to convince them to continue. No one tells their best friend that they are weak, ugly, or bad, just because they are struggling with their weight. If you wouldn't say it to your friend, don't do so to yourself either! Let us be aware of this: during weight loss, our soul needs peace and support. All bad opinions, even if they are only expressed in thought, are detrimental and divert us from our purpose. You must support yourself with positive reinforcement. There is no place for the all or nothing principle. A single piece of cake will not ruin your entire diet. Realistic thinking is more useful than disaster theory. A cookie is not the end of the world. Eating should not be a reward. Cakes should not make up for a bad day. If you are generally a healthy consumer, eat some goodies sometimes because of its delicious taste and to pamper your soul.

I'll give you a list of a hundred positive affirmations you can use to reinforce your weight loss. I'll divide them into main categories based on the most typical situations for which you would need confirmation. You can repeat all of them whenever you need to, but you can also choose the ones that are more suitable for your circumstances. If you prefer to listen to them during meditation, you can record them with a piece of nice relaxing music in the background.

General affirmations to reinforce your wellbeing:

1. I'm grateful that I woke up today. Thank you for making me happy today.

2. Today is a very good day. I meet nice and helpful people, whom I treat kindly.

3. Every new day is for me. I live to make myself feel good. Today I just pick good thoughts for myself.

4. Something wonderful is happening to me today.

5. I feel good.

6. I am calm, energetic and cheerful.

7. My organs are healthy.

8. I am satisfied and balanced.

9. I live in peace and understanding with everyone.

10. I listen to others with patience.

11. In every situation, I find the good.

12. I accept and respect myself and my fellow human beings.

13. I trust myself, I trust my inner wisdom.

Do you often scold yourself? Then repeat the following affirmations frequently:

14. I forgive myself.

15. I'm good to myself.

16. I motivate myself over and over again.

17. I'm doing my job well.

18. I care about myself.

19. I am doing my best.

20. I am proud of myself for my achievements.

21. I am aware that sometimes I have to pamper my soul.

22. I remember that I did a great job this week.

23. I deserved this small piece of candy.

24. I let go of the feeling of guilt.

25. I release the blame.

26. Everyone is imperfect. I accept that I am too.

If you feel pain when you choose to avoid delicious food, then you need to motivate yourself with affirmations such as:

27. I am motivated and persistent.

28. I control my life and my weight.

29. I'm ready to change my life.

30. Changes make me feel better.

31. I follow my diet with joy and cheerfulness.

32. I am aware of my amazing capacities.

33. I am grateful for my opportunities.

34. Today I'm excited to start a new diet.

35. I always keep in mind my goals.

36. I imagine myself slim and beautiful.

37. Today I am happy to have the opportunity to do what I have long been postponing.

38. I possess the energy and will to go through my diet.

39. I prefer to lose weight instead of wasting time on momentary pleasures.

Here you can find affirmations that help you to change harmful convictions and blockages:

40. I see my progress every day.

41. I listen to my body's messages.

42. I'm taking care of my health.

43. I eat healthy food.

44. I love who I am.

45. I love how life supports me.

46. A good parking space, coffee, conversation. It's all for me today.

47. It feels good to be awake because I can live in peace, health, love.

48. I'm grateful that I woke up. I take a deep breath of peace and tranquility.

49. I love my body. I love being served by me.

50. I eat by tasting every flavor of the food.

51. I am aware of the benefits of healthy food.

52. I enjoy eating healthy food and being fitter every day.

53. I feel energetic because I eat well.

Many people are struggling with being overweight because they don't move enough. The very root of this issue can be a refusal to do exercises due to negative biases in our minds.

We can overcome these beliefs by repeating the following affirmations:

54. I like moving because it helps my body burn fat.

55. Each time I exercise, I am getting closer to having a beautiful, tight shapely body.

56. It's a very uplifting feeling of being able to climb up to 100 steps without stopping.

57. It's easier to have an excellent quality of life if I move.

58. I like the feeling of returning to my home tired but happy after a long winter walk.

59. Physical exercises help me have a longer life.

60. I am proud to have better fitness and agility.

61. I feel happier thanks to the happiness hormone produced by exercise.

62. I feel full thanks to the enzymes that produce a sense of fullness during physical exercises.

63. I am aware even after exercise, my muscles continue to burn fat, and so I lose weight while resting.

64. I feel more energetic after exercises.

65. My goal is to lose weight, therefore I exercise.

66. I am motivated to exercise every day.

67. I lose weight while I exercise.

Now, I am going to give you a list of generic affirmations that you can build in your own program:

68. I'm glad I'm who I am.

69. Today, I read articles and watch movies that make me feel positive about my diet progress.

70. I love when I'm happy.

71. I take a deep breath and exhale my fears.

72. Today I do not want to prove my truth, but I want to be happy.

73. I am strong and healthy. I'm fine and I'm getting better.

74. I am happy today because whatever I do, I find joy in it.

75. I pay attention to what I can become.

76. I love myself and am helpful to others.

77. I accept what I cannot change.

78. I am happy that I can eat healthy food.

79. I am happy that I have been changing my life with my new healthy lifestyle.

80. Today I do not compare myself to others.

81. I accept and support who I am and turn to myself with love.

82. Today I can do anything for my improvement.

83. I'm fine. I'm happy for life. I love who I am. I'm strong and confident.

84. I am calm and satisfied.

85. Today is perfect for me to exercise and being healthy.

86. I have decided to lose weight and I am strong enough to follow my will.

87. I love myself, so I want to lose weight.

88. I am proud of myself because I follow my diet program.

89. I see how much stronger I am.

90. I know that I can do it.

91. It is not my past but my present that defines me.

92. I am grateful for my life.

93. I am grateful for my body because it collaborates well with me.

94. Eating healthy foods supports me to get the best nutrients I need, to be in the best shape.

95. I eat only healthy foods, and I avoid processed foods.

96. I can achieve my weight loss goals.

97. All cells in my body are fit and healthy, and so am I.

98. I enjoy staying healthy and sustaining my ideal weight.

99. I feel that my body is losing weight right now.

100. I care about my body by exercising every day.

Chapter 15. Daily Habits For Weight Loss

Understanding Mindful Eating

There are various scopes of cautious eating techniques, some of them established in Zen and different kinds of Buddhism, others connected to yoga.

Here, we are taking a simple technique, and that is the primary concern.

My careful eating procedure is figuring out how to be cautious. Rather than eating carelessly, putting nourishment unknowingly in your mouth, not so much tasting the sustenance you eat, you see your thoughts, and feelings.

- Learn to be cautious: why you want to eat, and what emotions or requirements can trigger eating.

- What you eat, and whether it's solid.

- Look, smell, taste, feel the nourishment that you eat.

- How do you feel like when you taste it, how would you digest it, and go about your day?

- How complete you are previously, during, and in the wake of eating.

- During and in the wake of eating, your sentiments.

- Where the nourishment originated from, who could have developed it, the amount it could have suffered before it was killed, regardless of whether it was naturally developed, the amount it was handled, the amount it was broiled or overcooked, and so on.

This is an ability that you don't simply increase medium-term, a type of reflection. It takes practice, and there will be times when you neglect to eat mindfully, beginning, and halting. However, you can get generally excellent at this with exercise and consideration.

Mindful Eating Benefits

The upsides of eating mindfully are unimaginable and realizing these points of interest is fundamental as you think about the activity.

- When you're anxious, you figure out how to eat and stop when you're plunking down.

- You figure out how to taste nourishment and acknowledge great sustenance tastes.

- You start to see gradually that unfortunate nourishment isn't as scrumptious as you accepted, nor does it make you feel extremely pleasant.

- Because of the over three points, if you are overweight, you will regularly get more fit.

- You start arranging your nourishment and eating through the passionate issues you have. It requires somewhat more, yet it's basic.

- Social overeating can turn out to be less of an issue—you can eat mindfully while mingling, rehearsing, and not over-alimenting.

- You begin to appreciate the experience of eating more, and as an outcome, you will acknowledge life more when you are progressively present.

- It can transform into a custom of mindfulness that you anticipate.

- You learn for the day how nourishment impacts your disposition and vitality.

- You realize what fuel your training best with nourishment, and you work and play.

A Guide To Mindful Eating

Keeping up a contemporary, quick-paced way of life can leave a brief period to oblige your necessities. You are moving always starting with one thing then onto the next, not focusing on what your psyche or body truly needs. Rehearsing mindfulness can help you to comprehend those necessities.

When eating mindfulness is connected, it can help you recognize your examples and practices while simultaneously standing out to appetite and completion related to body signs.

Originating from the act of pressure decrease dependent on mindfulness, rehearsing mindfulness while eating can help you focus on the present minute instead of proceeding with ongoing and unacceptable propensities.

Careful eating is an approach to begin an internal looking course to help you become increasingly aware of your nourishment association and utilize that information to eat with joy.

The body conveys a great deal of information and information, so you can start settling on cognizant choices as opposed to falling into programmed — and regularly feeling driven — practices when you apply attention to the eating knowledge. You are better prepared to change your conduct once you become aware of these propensities.

Individuals that need to be cautious about sustenance and nourishment are asked to:

- Explore their inward knowledge about sustenance—different preferences

- Choose sustenance that please and support their bodies

- Accept explicit sustenance inclinations without judgment or self-analysis

- Practice familiarity with the indications of their bodies beginning to eat and quit eating.

General Principles Of Mindful Eating

One methodology to careful eating depends on the core values given by Rebecca J. Frey, Ph.D., and Laura Jean Cataldo, RN: tune in to the internal craving and satiety signs of your body Identify private triggers for careless eating, for example, social weights, amazing sentiments, and explicit nourishments.

Here are a couple of tips for getting you started.

- Start with one meal. It requires some investment to begin with any new propensity. It very well may be difficult to make cautious eating rehearses constantly. However, you can practice with one dinner or even a segment of a supper. Attempt to focus on appetite sign and sustenance choices before you start eating or sinking into the feelings of satiety toward the part of the arrangement— these are phenomenal approaches to begin a routine with regards to consideration.

- Remove view distractions place or turn off your phone in another space. Mood killers such the TV and PC and set away whatever else —, for example, books, magazines, and papers—that can divert you from eating. Give the feast before your complete consideration.

- Tune in your perspective when you start this activity, become aware of your attitude. Perceive that there is no right or off base method for eating, yet simply unmistakable degrees of eating background awareness. Focus your consideration on eating sensations. When you understand that your brain has meandered, take it delicately back to the eating knowledge.

- Draw in your senses with this activity. There are numerous approaches to explore. Attempt to investigate one nourishment thing utilizing every one of your faculties. When you put sustenance in your mouth, see the scents, surfaces, hues, and flavors. Attempt to see how the sustenance changes as you cautiously bite each nibble.

- Take as much time as necessary. Eating cautiously includes backing off, enabling your stomach related hormones to tell your mind that you are finished before eating excessively. It's a fabulous method to hinder your fork between chomps. Additionally, you will be better arranged to value your supper experience, especially in case you're with friends and family.

Rehearsing mindfulness in a bustling globe can be trying now and again; however, by knowing and applying these essential core values and techniques, you can discover approaches to settle your body all the more promptly. When you figure out how much your association with nourishment can adjust to improve things, you will be charmingly astounded — and this can importantly affect your general prosperity and wellbeing.

Formal dinners, be that as it may, will, in general, assume a lower priority about occupied ways of life for generally people. Rather, supper times are an opportunity to endeavor to do each million stuff in turn. Consider having meals at your work area or accepting your Instagram fix over breakfast to control through a task.

The issue with this is you are bound to be genuinely determined in your decisions about healthy eating and eat excessively on the off chance that you don't focus on the nourishment you devour or the way you eat it.

That is the place mindfulness goes in. You can apply similar plans to a yoga practice straight on your lunch plate. "Cautious eating can enable you to tune in to the body's information of what, when, why, and the amount to eat", says Lynn Rossy, Ph.D., essayist of The Mindfulness-Based Eating Solution and the Center for Mindful Eating director. "Rather than relying upon another person (or an eating routine) to reveal to you how to eat, developing a minding association with your own body can achieve tremendous learning and change."

From the ranch to the fork — can help you conquer enthusiastic eating, make better nourishment choices, and even experience your suppers in a crisp and ideally better way. To make your next dinner mindful, pursue these measures.

The Most Effective Method to Start Eating More Intentionally

Stage 1: *Eat Before You Shop*. We have all been there. You go with a rumbling stomach to the shop. You meander the passageways, and out of the blue, those power bars and microwaveable suppers start to look truly enticing. "When you're excessively ravenous, shopping will, in general, shut us off from our progressively talented goals of eating in a way that searches useful for

129

the body," says Dr. Rossy. So, even if you feel the slightest craving or urge to eat, get a nutritious bite or a light meal before heading out. That way, your food choices will be made intentionally when you shop, as opposed to propelled by craving or an unexpected sugar crash in the blood.

Stage 2: *Make Conscious Food Choices*. When you truly start considering where your nourishment originates from, you're bound to pick sustenance that is better for you, the earth, and the people occupied with the expanding procedure portrays Meredith Klein, an astute cooking educator, and Pranaful's author. "When you're in the supermarket, focus on the nourishment source," Klein shows. "Hope to check whether it's something that has been created in this country or abroad and endeavors to know about pesticides that may have been exposed to or presented to people who were developing nourishment." If you can, make successive adventures to your neighborhood ranchers advertise, where most sustenance is developed locally, she recommends.

Stage 3: *Enjoy the Preparation Process*. "When you get ready sustenance, instead of looking at it as an errand or something you need to hustle through, value the process. You can take a great deal of pleasure in food shopping for items that you know will help you feel better and nourish your body.

Stage 4: *"Simply eat"*. This is something we once in a while do, as simple as it sounds, "simply eat." "Individuals regularly eat while doing different things — taking a gander at their telephones, TVs, PCs, and books, and mingling", claims Dr. Rossy. "While cautious eating can happen when you're doing other stuff, endeavor to' simply eat' at whatever point plausible." She includes that centering the nourishment you're eating without preoccupation can make you mindful of flavors you may never have taken note of. Yum!

Stage 5: *Down Your Utensils*. When you are done eating, immediately put your dishes and utensils away. This is a way of signaling to yourself that you are done eating (it tends to be much a bit tough to accept). "You're getting a charge out of each chomp that way, and you're focused on the nibble that is in your mouth right now as opposed to setting up the following one", Klein says.

Stage 6: *Chew, Chew, Chew Your Food*. Biting your sustenance is exceptionally fundamental and not only for, you know, not to stun. "When we cautiously eat our sustenance, we help the body digest the nourishment all the more effectively and meet a greater amount of our dietary needs", says Dr. Rossy. Furthermore, no, we won't educate you how often you've eaten your sustenance. However, Dr. Rossy demonstrates biting until the nourishment is very much separated – which will most likely take more than a couple of quick eats.

Stage 7: *Check-In With Your Hunger*. You frequently miss the sign that your body sends you during the supper when you eat thoughtlessly, for example, when supper time turns into your prime time to make up for lost time with Netflix appears or when you have your supper in a rush. At the end of the day, the one that illuminates you when you begin to feel total. Dr. Rossy proposes ending dinner and taking some time with your craving levels to check-in. "Keep eating in case no doubt about it", she proposes. "In case you're not ravenous yet, spare the nourishment for some other time, manure it, or even discard it." Those remains can make the following day an incredible dinner of care.

Last but not least, we get it; life does not always allow sit-down, completely tuned-in mealtimes. So if you don't have time for all seven steps, attempt to include one or two in each dinner. "If you have only a little window of time, just try to devote yourself to food", suggests Klein. "Set down your phone, get away from the screen, just be there–you can do that regardless of how much time you have."

Tips in Mindful Eating that Transform how you Relate to Food.

We lose ourselves in regular daily existence designs each day. Our propensity vitality pushes and pulls us to and from, and we are left with minimal opportunity to encounter life in a way that, for this very time, we are completely present.

Sometime in the not so distant future, to-day tasks get more from this autopilot state than others. There are a few things we do so regularly in our lives that we become like automatons, doing them all day every day thoughtlessly and commonly. These exercises incorporate strolling, driving, specific sorts of occupation, and (among others) eating.

Yet, these exercises additionally loan themselves to the activity of care, because while these examples are speaking to the draw of propensity vitality, they are likewise the perfect thing to snatch on when in any predefined time we need to turn out to be completely present in our life.

Consideration is both the quality and the activity of getting to be (and remaining) completely present at this very time in our life. It's mindfulness that empowers us

132

to break these standard examples and make a move for a progressively alert and present life.

Eating might be more than whatever another movement that fits the activity of cognizance. This because we discover the flavors we experience when we frequently devour fascinating and various just as the pleasurable demonstration of eating. Thus, it is through the simple exercise of careful gobbling that we can wake up to our life and discover more harmony and joy all the while.

On occasion, we can likewise identify poor practices with nourishment and eating. These poor propensities can cause us a ton of torment, some even respected issue.

The act of eating mindfully can spark a light on our standard eating and sustenance related propensities. What's more, in doing as such, we can ease a lot of the agony on our plate identified with the nourishment.

- **Simply eat mindfully**. Take a minute before eating to see the nourishment's smell, visual intrigue, and even surface. Appreciate the various vibes that go with your feast. This concise minute will help open up your cognizance with the goal that you become all the more completely dynamic in the eating demonstration.

- **Take your time.** Remember to lift your hand/fork/spoon and bite the sustenance itself. Give close consideration to each flavor in your mouth and notice how the nourishment you eat feels and scents. Be completely present for the biting go about as your central matter of (light) focus during cautious eating.

133

- **Recognize thoughts, feelings, and sensations.** When in your general vicinity of awareness, thoughts, feelings, or different sensations emerge, just be aware of them, recognize their reality, and after that, let them go as though they were gliding on a cloud.

- **Eat (once more).** Then give back your concentration to the biting demonstration. In the beginning, you will continually lose your mindfulness. Try not to stress; this is typical for any sort of activity of good faith. Simply rehash the procedure from stages 2-4 and attempt to eat mindfully for however much as could be expected of your supper.

- **Pay attention.** While eating mindfully, stay open to any idea, feeling, or feeling that goes into your cognizance field and doesn't attempt to push it away. Acknowledge freely whatever happens, and after that, reclaim your core interest.

The act of eating mindfully is simple. However, there are numerous little tips and deceives that you can take advantage of to help upgrade your ability to eat mindfully and proceed with your routine with regards to mindfulness.

Chapter 16. Learning To Avoid Temptations And Triggers

While telling a person to adopt the traits of the mentally strong is a good way to develop mental toughness, it may not always be enough. In a way it's a bit like telling a person that in order to be healthy you need to eat right, exercise, and get plenty of rest. Such advice is good and even correct, however it lacks a certain specificity that can leave a person feeling unsure of exactly what to do. Fortunately, there are several practices that can create a clear plan of how to achieve mental toughness. These practices are like the actual recipes and exercises needed in order to eat right and get plenty of exercise. By adopting these practices into your daily routine, you will begin to develop mental toughness in everything you do and in every environment you find yourself in.

Keep your emotions in check

The most important thing you can do in the quest for developing mental toughness is to keep your emotions in check. People who fail to take control of their emotions allow their emotions to control them. More often than not, this takes the form of people who are driven by rage, fear, or both. Whenever a person allows their emotions to control them, they allow their emotions to control their decisions, words, and actions. However, when you keep your emotions in check, you take control of your decisions, words, and actions, thereby taking control of your life overall.

In order to keep your emotions in check you have to learn to allow your emotions to subside before reacting to a situation. Therefore, instead of speaking when you are

135

angry, or making a decision when you are frustrated, take a few minutes to allow your emotions to settle down. Take a moment to simply sit down, breathe deeply, and allow your energies to restore balance. Only when you feel calm and in control should you make your decision, speak your mind, or take any action.

Practice detachment

Another critical element for mental toughness is what is known as detachment. This is when you remove yourself emotionally from the particular situation that is going on around you. Even if the situation affects you directly, remaining detached is a very positive thing. The biggest benefit of detachment is that it prevents an emotional response to the situation at hand. This is particularly helpful when things are not going according to plan.

Practicing detachment requires a great deal of effort at first. After all, most people are programmed to feel emotionally attached to the events going on around them at any given time. One of the best ways to practice detachment is to tell yourself that the situation isn't permanent. What causes a person to feel fear and frustration when faced with a negative situation is that they feel the situation is permanent. When you realize that even the worst events are temporary, you avoid the negative emotional response they can create.

Another way to become detached is to determine the reason you feel attached to the situation in the first place. In the case that someone is saying or doing something to hurt your feelings understand that their words and actions are a reflection of them, not you. As long as you don't feed into their negativity you won't experience the pain they are trying to cause. This is true for anything you experience. By not feeding a negative situation or event with negative emotions you prevent that situation from connecting to you. This allows you to exist within a negative event without being affected by it.

Accept what is beyond your control

Acceptance is one of the cornerstones of mental toughness. This can take the form of accepting yourself for who you are and accepting others for who they are, but it can also take the form of accepting what is beyond your control. When you learn to accept the things you can't change, you rewrite how your mind reacts to every situation you encounter. The fact of the matter is that the majority of stress and anxiety felt by the average person is the result of not being able to change certain things. Once you learn to accept those things you can't change, you eliminate all of that harmful stress and anxiety permanently.

While accepting what is beyond your control will take a little practice, it is actually quite easy in nature. The trick is to simply ask yourself if you can do anything at all to change the situation at hand. If the answer is 'no,' simply let it go. Rather than wasting time and energy fretting about what you can't control adopt the mantra "It is what it is." This might seem careless at first, but after a while you will realize that it is a true sign of mental strength. By accepting what is beyond your control, you conserve your energy, thoughts, and time for those things you can affect, thereby making your efforts more effective and worthwhile.

Always be prepared

Another way to build mental toughness is to always be prepared. If you allow life to take you from one event to another you will feel lost, uncertain, and unprepared for the experiences you encounter. However, when you take

137

the time to prepare yourself for what lies ahead, you will develop a sense of being in control of your situation at all times. There are two ways to be prepared, and they are equally important for developing mental toughness.

The first way to be prepared is to prepare your mind at the beginning of each and every day. This takes the form of you taking time in the morning to focus your mind on who you are, what you are capable of, and your outlook on life in general. Whether you refer to this time as mediation, contemplation, or daily affirmations, the basic principle is the same. You simply focus your mind on what you believe and the qualities you aspire to. This will keep you grounded in your ideals throughout the day, helping you to make the right choices regardless of what life throws your way.

The second way to always be prepared is to take the time to prepare yourself for the situation at hand. If you have to give a presentation, make sure to give yourself plenty of time to prepare for it. Go over the information you want to present, choose the materials you want to use, and even take the time to make sure you have the exact clothes you want to wear. When you go into a situation fully prepared, you increase your self-confidence, giving you an added edge. Additionally, you will eliminate the stress and anxiety that results from feeling unprepared.

Take the time to embrace success

One of the problems many negatively-minded people experience is that they never take the time to appreciate success when it comes their way. Sometimes they are too afraid of jinxing that success to actually recognize it. Most of the time, however, they are unable to embrace success because their mindset is simply too negative for such a positive action. Mentally strong people, by contrast, always take the time to embrace the successes that come their way. This serves to build their sense of confidence as well as their feeling of satisfaction with how things are going.

Next time you experience a success of any kind, make sure you take a moment to recognize it. You can make an external statement, such as going out for drinks, treating yourself to a nice lunch, or some similar expression of gratitude. Alternatively, you can simply take a quiet moment to reflect on the success and all the effort that went into making it happen. There is no right or wrong way to embrace success, you just need to find a way that works for you. The trick to embracing success is in not letting it go to your head. Rather than praising your efforts or actions, appreciate the fact that things went well. Also, be sure to appreciate those whose help contributed to your success.

Be happy with what you have

Contentment is another element that is critical for mental toughness. In order to develop contentment, you have to learn how to be happy with what you have. This doesn't mean that you eliminate ambition or the desire to achieve greater success, rather it means that you show gratitude for the positives that currently exist. After all, the only way you will be able to truly appreciate the fulfillment of your dreams is if you can first appreciate your life the way it is.

One example of this is learning to appreciate your job. This is true whether you like your job or not. Even if you hate your job and desperately want to find another one, always take the time to appreciate the fact that you have a job in the first place. The fact is that you could be jobless, which would create all sorts of problems in your life. So, even if you hate your job, learn to appreciate it for what it is. This goes for everything in your life. No matter how good or bad a thing is, always appreciate having it before striving to make a change.

Be happy with who you are

In addition to appreciating what you have you should always be happy with who you are. Again, this doesn't mean that you should settle for who you are and not try to improve your life, rather it means that you should learn to appreciate who you are at every moment. There will always be issues that you want to fix in your life, and things you know you could do better. The problem is that if you focus on the things that are wrong you will always see yourself in a negative light. However, when you learn to appreciate the good parts of your personality, you can pursue self-improvement with a sense of pride, hope, and optimism for who you will become as you begin to fulfill your true potential.

PART 2: HYPNOSIS AND GUIDED MEDITATIONS FOR DEEP SLEEP AND RELAXATION

Introduction

Sleep is often one of the greatest parts of our day! From the moment we wake up and prepare for the day ahead, many of us are already thinking about going back to bed. We dream of our bed when we're at work, and it looks good right when we get home. There's nothing more comforting than crawling back into bed after a long and exhausting day.

For some people, however, sleep can also be a time of disruption or a source of stress where they spend hours tossing and turning before finally being able to drift off. One way to get better sleep naturally is through the use of hypnosis and meditation.

When you can unlock your body's own secrets to falling and staying asleep, you will start to see that you have the ability to get the good night's rest that you deserve. We are going to start these readings off with hypnosis for sleeping better. The more relaxed you are, the easier it can be to stay asleep all night, and this hypnosis is designed to get you to that relaxed state.

An important part of better sleeping habits is not feeling so tired all of the time. Feeling fully rested during the day will make it easier to stay asleep at night and to avoid taking naps throughout the day, which mess up our natural sleep rhythms. Finally, affirmations and the final meditation will help you to develop the best sleep habits so that you are always going to be centered on becoming more and more relaxed.

Make sure that you don't do these anywhere you aren't comfortable falling asleep, especially if you haven't practiced meditation or hypnosis before. Never do these while driving or operating any other vehicle.

Chapter 17. The Importance Of A Good Sleep

We in general consider sleep when our mind and body shut down. Instead sleep is a functioning period wherein a great deal of significant handling, reclamation, and reinforcing happens. Precisely how this occurs and why is still fairly a secret. In any case, we do know the importance of benefits of sleep, and the reasons we need it for ideal well-being and prosperity.

One of the indispensable jobs of sleep is to enable us to cement and combine memories which we gather during the day. As we approach our day, our mind takes in a lot of data. Instead of being straightforwardly logged and recorded, these actualities and encounters first should be handled and put away; and a considerable lot of these means occur while we sleep.

Medium-term, odds and ends of data are moved from progressively provisional, transient memory to more grounded, long haul memory—a procedure called "solidification." Researchers have demonstrated that after individuals rest, they are able to hold more information and perform better on memory errands. Our bodies require bedtimes to reestablish and revive, to develop muscle, fix tissue, and combine hormones. Yet we ignore sleep for other things.

Proper rest is basic for everybody, since us as a whole need to hold information and learn aptitudes to sail through everyday life. Be that as it may, this is likely piece of the reason youngsters—who procure language, social, and engine abilities at a stunning pace all through their advancement—need more rest than grown-ups. While grown-ups need at least 8 hours of sleep for each night, one-year-olds need 17 hours, school age youngsters somewhere in the range of 9 to 11, and adolescents somewhere in the range of 8 and 10. During these basic times of development and learning, young individuals need a substantial portion of sleep for ideal advancement and readiness.

Unfortunately, an individual cannot simply amass lack of sleep and after that log numerous long periods of rest to compensate for it. The best rest propensities are steady, solid schedules that permit us all, paying little heed to our age, to meet our sleep needs each night, and keep over life's difficulties consistently.

According to the US Department of Health about 35% of the adults in United States sleeps less than 7 hours a day. Meanwhile sleep deprivation can have severe consequences on our health and lifestyle: adults who were short sleepers were more likely to report chronic health problems, obesity and physical inactivity compared to people who got enough sleep.

Although how long you sleep each day is very important, healthy sleep has more to do with quality of rest than quantity of hours. A good sleep quality is essential and contribute to your health and well-being.

Inadequate sleep affects both how we feel and how we function. Short-term effects can include sleepiness or drowsiness, reduced alertness, irritability, attention and reaction problems, poor motor skills. Regularly sleeping less than seven hours increases the risk of developing diabetes, heart disease, mood disorders, unhealthy eating habits that can lead to other chronic illnesses. Chronic sleep problems can link to depression, anxiety, and mental distress.

What Keeps People Up at Night?

At some random time, most of the individuals are experiencing issues related to peaceful resting. Difficulty in sleeping, non-getting enough rest, constantly worrying about insomnia, and the build-up of stress and frustration as a result is what has seeped into the modern lifestyle. Practically everybody encounters times of restlessness sooner or later in their life.

Many people lament they experience sleep problems. It is a term that describes several different sleep issues, including:

- Not getting enough sleep (sleep deprivation or insufficient sleep).

- Not sleeping well.

- Not spending enough time in certain stages of sleep.

- Having a sleep disorder (such as insomnia, sleep apnea, narcolepsy and others).

There are many possible reasons for sleeping difficulties, including lifestyle, sleeping habits, and medical conditions. Generally, decreased rest stem from an overactive routine, from a stress feeling, or even from a physical condition. Similarly, emotional wellness issues can prompt poor rest. A sleeping disorder can be activated or propagated by your practices and erratic sleep pattern. Irregular ways of life and rest propensities can give rise to a sleeping disorder (with no fundamental mental or medical issue).

There are some other reasons which keep people up at night. Too warm room temperature, not dark enough room, external sounds - all of that can disturb you. The stress of job, the addiction to be online all the time on mobile phones, tablets and laptops, relationship problems, financial issues, irregular food habits, drinking caffeine or smoking before bedtime, and many more are the reasons why people find it hard to get a deep restoring sleep. Overthinking, clockwatching, getting up to watch TV until one feels sleepy, talking on phones - everything contributes to a bad sleep pattern.

Nowadays, many people attend gym after work; sadly, it doesn't help to sleeping properly. Also, weekend parties where drinking alcohol too late has become a norm, mess up with the regular sleep cycle. If not addressed on time it will snowball into a bigger problem resulting in physical and psychological problems.

One of the biggest contributors of sleeplessness is the technology, keeping aside the health issues and everyday problems. Our mobile phones, tablets, PCs and other electronic devices have turned out to be such a gigantic piece of our day by day experience that it's regularly difficult to put them down—even at sleep time. Keeping your smartphone or other devices on your end table may not appear to be a major deal, yet innovation influences your rest in a larger number of ways than you understand.

Wanting to sleep but not getting to sleep is the cycle which can be ceaseless. The realization about sleeplessness doesn't help either. The more time is spent on worrying about it, the farther goes its solution. Sadly, our fast-paced lifestyle is full of roadblocks, so it is very important to pause and contemplate on our surroundings and actions which lead us to becoming restless, thus contributing to our poor sleep.

A healthy mind is crucial to healthy functioning of your body. Our bodies are biological machines which need to rest at appropriate intervals. Effective techniques are to be followed to code and train our mind in such a way that sleep comes naturally, without minimal efforts. Worrying about lack of sleep is going to drive it away further. What is needed is to seek solutions and keeping your mind clear of stressful energy which hinders peaceful rest.

Chapter 18. Guided Meditations For Deep Sleep

Guide Meditation to Improve Insomnia

Sleep has been a significant issue in the whole world. Many people have insomnia, and this affects their average productive level. Insomnia is a condition feared by many. People who practice mindfulness meditation can fight off this condition. They can fall asleep sooner and stay for long in bed.

Meditation can also reduce pain. It has the power to control any discomfort, be it emotional or psychological. People have perceptions connected to their state of mind. Attitudes like these elevate in the presence of stressful conditions. When you meditate, you will have more activities going on in the part of the brain that controls pain. You will also have less pain sensitivity.

Lastly, meditation is essential in weight loss since it directly involves the mind. The mind will then form perceptions to a particular food as well as start releasing positive thought to healthy food since a healthy mind means a healthy body and soul. Through guided meditation, you can change your eating habits, lifestyle, and even healthy health choices like exercise.

Deciding to stop your bad eating habits is not a onetime thing but can be done gradually by incorporating healthy foods in the diet. The brain triggers the mind to eat, and food cravings also come from the mind. If the mind can accept that there is a need to eat healthily and live positive, so will the brain be triggered towards healthy eating. Weight loss is necessary for healthy living and can keep you away from the many lifestyle diseases, many of which are not curable.

There is a lot of patience involved since it is not the easiest and fastest step towards weight loss but workable none the less. Meditation will help you clear your mind and reduce dependence on food that makes you feel beautiful yet not healthy. This is because the mind is cleared of negative emotions that can be an element of distraction or stress. It is like a painless stress reliever without medication or therapy. It brings weight loss naturally over the long term and creates a very positive and acceptable self-image and self-view.

Guided meditations are not all the same: it depends on the purpose you want to achieve through this practice. Do you just want to relax? Fight insomnia? Become more resilient? Accept a major change? Lose weight?

In most guided meditations, it's essential to try to use as many senses as you can: the smells, the lights, the sounds, the textures. Usually guided meditations have a musical background that invites the mind and body to relax: sounds of nature such as rain, rainforest, sea waves or the sound of a waterfall; or more traditional music like that of the Native American characterized by the sound of flutes, tubes and rattles.

Choose the musical background you prefer, what is important is to create the best condition to relax. To start, you can do a very quick guided meditation for beginners. The basic principle is to pay attention to what you do, always keep it in mind from the beginning to the end of the practice. Close your eyes and start taking three deep breaths, inhaling through your nose and exhaling from your mouth.

When you breathe in you are full of positive energy and when you exhale all kinds of negative energies, such as stress, tension and worries, abandon you. Find your breath and feel your body. Simply observe it (Headspace, n. d.).

Guide Meditation for Super Motivation

At times we need to find the cause of motivation for us to keep doing some things. Take, for instance, an individual who works for long hours. They have to find things that motivate them to get up each morning.

If you are asked what your reason for living is, what would you have to say? What is that one thing that makes you want to try harder without giving up? There is some power that results from motivation. It allows us to want to do better in the activities that we undertake.

It makes us have meaning in what we go. One of the best ways to stay motivated is to have goals that you want to accomplish. In this case, the goal is to lose weight.

As an individual, you have to ensure that you are focused on that goal for it to be effective. If you wish to cut off some extra weight, get something that inspires you. For instance, you can be inspired to weigh a certain amount. In that process, you can be evaluating how much you way daily and how far away you are from getting to your goal.

Hypnosis is a great way to help those in need of weight loss. There are various reasons a person may be overweight. Some may range from behavioral issues or underlying conditions that will require to be addressed to lose weight successfully. We will take you through a guide for a weight loss program through hypnosis as well as how to lose weight through meditation. After losing weight, a person needs to maintain it. We shall further discuss how hypnosis can help one maintain their new weight and avoid becoming overweight again.

A person needs a lot of help and motivation to succeed. With the help of hypnotherapy, one can easily stay the course and watch the pounds melt away. Following the guide above and with a credible hypnotherapist or mastering self-hypnosis will help you in achieving your goals.

For any get-healthy plan to work, it begins with shaping an association with nourishment. When they must be aware of how they eat, why they eat, and the health benefit of what they eat. The motivation behind trance for weight reduction is to empower an individual to be aware of their eating examples and nourishments to have a fruitful adventure in weight reduction.

At times fear motivates us into doing certain things. For instance, you might fear to get obese or acquiring some lifestyle diseases. Such fear ensures that you stay focused on losing weight. You ensure that you strictly follow your diet plan or that you exercise regularly. Instead of fear motivating you negatively, it motivates you in a positive way. Another case example is the fear we have before taking tests or exams.

The fear of potentially failing can make you burn the midnight oil to ensure that you do not fail in the tasks that you have engaged in.

You find yourself trying to do your best in the various tasks that you are undertaking. Eventually, you may pass in your test, with fear as the motivating factor of success. All you need to do is ensure that you convert that energy into something useful and helpful in your life. At times the fear of failure in life makes us work hard towards making a better living. This makes you wake up very early each day, determined to make that day better than the previous day. It ensures that you give your best in life for you to live well.

We, at times, find our motivation from other people. At times you find that you may not be able to inspire yourself enough, but you feel inspired by other people. When you are unable to walk alone, you can always seek help from individuals that are more inspired than you are. They ensure that you are always working hard towards achieving your goals and that you do not deviate from other things.

This type of motivation is positive and useful in your life. It ensures that you give your best in the activities that you undertake. Walking alone can, at times, be challenging.

Anytime you feel like giving up, and there is no one to remind you why you started the journey in the first place. You are prone to making wrong decisions that you will end up regretting.

One needs to have individuals that encourage them in the journey they take. As you start your weight loss journey through meditation, you can look for an individual with the same goal. You get to keep encouraging each other to accomplish certain things, and it becomes easier to achieve the set goals.

Guide Meditation for Boost Positivity

You need to shed off any unimportant attachment.

Unimportant attachments are things that no longer have any effect on your life.
These are things that will only let you down, thus derailing your life goals of achieving a mind-set full of

happiness. Your future success depends heavily on this, and for you to get at that position, you will need to detach yourself from anything that might let you down. You must note that anything might also mean any person.

We have people in our lives that always try very hard to put us down. These types of people are afraid of your success in life.

They will try their best to pull you down, no matter how hard you try to embrace only positivity in your life. It is time to get yourself going and void them like the plague. Remember, you must live and not only live but choose a pleasant experience.

It will only be possible if you manage to refuse anything or anyone that is holding you back. Since I have said this, it is now my wish that you may practice this affirmation and use it as your routine daily. Practice makes perfect, and you will only realize that when you train.

You are enough just as you are. You must release that demonic notion of having comparisons between you and others. For you to stay specific, you must have some success standards. After developing all these, set your own goals and ambitions. Your vision should relate to your mission in life. After all these, you can now judge yourself using the basis of your success.

Those rules and regulations you created in your success standards should enable you to judge yourself accordingly. Just know you are just enough the way you were born. You are a complete soul, and no part of you is lacking. So never try to make a comparison with others.

You should note that affirmation helps in the realization of worthiness. Within a short period, you will be able to control your body image. Also, it will be of a great deal

153

as it helps you in achieving some of the personal goals in life, and having a sound body is one of them.

You must be in a position to fulfill your purpose. The world should know your existence, and you must be ready to show your achievement. Showing your accomplished goals will need some positive deeds that lead to a successful life. On most occasions, people who trend are our trendsetters.

They trend because of having done something positive or negative. They are then known all over the world. However, in this motivational affirmation, you need to focus on positive things.

You need to be a trendsetter in showing the whole world what you are capable of offering. If you have been employed somewhere to sweep, you must clean until the country president cuts short his journey to congratulate you. Achieving your best is always one decisive way to be successful and lead a happy life free from stress and distress. Remember, this affirmation reminds you that no one has that power to stop you from doing or rather fulfilling your purpose in life. Sharing this thought every morning when you wake up will eventually get you somewhere. You must now stay focus and have this habit of telling yourself that no one can prevent you from achieving.

You must be results-oriented. In your daily life, you need to stay focus in life. Your primary focus should be on your results. It is through this that you will be able to realize your productivity.

To achieve this, you must be able to create some space for success. Get more success in your life. Avoid any derailing excuses that will only demean your reputation, thus lowering your success rate. Offer yourself these phrases every morning, and you will be in great joy for the rest of the day. You need not hold on excuses for failing to achieve something. Be yourself and have the ability to struggle until you reach that success in life. It is through this that your mind will have settled, giving you peace of mind. Peace of mind will enable you to lead a stress-free experience. It will reflect in your body image.

Be control of your won happiness. Happiness is an aspect of life that will initiate your feelings and moods towards a positive experience.

It is like a gear geared towards your prosperous life. Staying positive here will be of great importance, and for you to realize this, you must take control of your happiness. Responsibility is a virtue, and being responsible will make you bold enough to face all kinds of situations. Your joy is your key to success, and no one should tamper with it. Make happiness your priority and be responsible for it.

You must let no one make you angry. Angriness will only induce you with emotional feelings that will eventually affect your life more so your body image. Having seen this, you must now be in an excellent position to embrace this affirmation. Take it as an opener to your morning and employ it entirely in your life.

To achieve much in this process of weight loss, you need to embark on areas that give you a clear view of affirmations. Remember, affirmations are just phrases that are highly powerful and lead to positivity in life. By applying these affirmations, be sure that you will be able to stay focus, positive, and relaxed. There are several affirmations that you need to choose from. Try picking the ones you can manage and start your daily routine of making them permanent. Your weight will reduce tremendously.

This book also aims at making you stay positive about yourself. That's, it indulges you in the world of motivation.

Motivational affirmations, therefore, help you in achieving this ultimate goal, thus resulting in a more positive life with lots of happiness and relaxation. Stay tuned once more to these phrases. I hope you do prefer a perfect body image full of pleasure and positivity. Imagine a life full of happiness just because you have followed and fully implemented the principles in this book.

It is now very essential for you to lead a perfect life, free from negativity and obesity. This vital life involves life filled with happiness and morale to live happily and positive. All these results in peace of mind, thus making sure that your inner soul is having elements of blessings. For you to experience all these, you need to get affirmative self-control actions. It will enable you to control everything surrounding you.

Last but not least, this book consists of various aspects of life that you should follow no matter what. It is through this that you can stay put and straightforward about your personal life and keep at bay every detail of obesity. The book offers the correct guidelines that you need to follow. You can also do meditation for weight loss, especially by following hypnosis exercises. Why can't you grab this book and start as quick as possible?

Meditation for Weight Loss is, therefore, a manuscript that acts as a guideline in reducing your weight. Your work is to follow it very keenly so that you achieve every detail written here. You should know how best you can make smart goals that can be easily achievable. Without this, then your world is doomed, and you will end up living a life full of frustrations and pain. So, the best way you should follow here is to handle this book with great care in fulfilling your dreams of losing weight.

Having a strong belief that this book has helped you well, it is my humble request that you can do on it in several sites.

Don't hesitate to note its importance or significance to the readers who are looking for easy ways of losing weight.

We think about symbolism a lot when it comes to our pattern of thought. If you're hungry, you think "I am starving," "I am sick," "I am not myself." These are dramatic statements, but they are themes that pop into our head because that's how our brains are wired. We consistently connect thoughts to try and better figure things out. We also make absolute statements as a way to figure things out. You might fail once in a diet and think "I can't do this." We create these assumptions because that's how our brains come up with a solution.

We need to turn that thinking around and instead, wire our brains to think positively. To create your own affirmations, speak in "I can," "I am," "I will," "I have." statements. Use "I" in every affirmation you do, because this is all about increasing your positivity and creative thinking, not doing so for another person.

After you use the "I" phrases, next move onto making a positive statement. Never describe what you lack, and try to avoid pointing out your flaws, even if you are doing it positively. Speak in strong absolutes. Whichever area you struggle with the most is the one you should include the most affirmations from.

Chapter 19. Meditations For Better And Deeper Sleep

Sleep is so incredibly important for our health. Often times, it's something that is overlooked. When you think about it, sleep truly does determine how your next day is going to go. Meditation can grant you the ability to unwind from a busy day and fall asleep quickly and deeply. By calming your mind, meditation can help you drift off into a deep and healthy sleep. You will be provided with a few different scripts. Whether you are looking to relax into sleep, help yourself fall back asleep in the middle of the night, or are just looking to take a quick nap during the day; you can test one of the following out and see which will work best for you!

Basic Sleep Meditation Script

When it comes to falling asleep and staying asleep, there a few things you will need to keep in mind.

If you are like most people, your head is probably filled with thoughts and issues that are keeping you awake. If your mind continues to race around, you will never be able to fall asleep! While this sleep meditation should help a bit, you will also need to put in some work of your own. Much like you have learned to quiet your brain during times of stress, you will need to teach your mind how to pipe down when you are ready to finish out your day.

I always suggest creating a routine when you are ready to go to bed. One exercise you can try to help quiet your mind is to keep a notepad on your nightstand. With this close by, you can write down any important thoughts you have that you would like to hold onto. This way, you can remind yourself of whatever it is tomorrow. You will want

158

to tell yourself that these thoughts will do nothing but disrupt a nice, peaceful night's rest. Simply write down your thoughts and forget about them!

When you feel it's ready for bed, set yourself up for success. Take care of everything you need for the next day; whether that means making your lunch or choosing out your outfit. Brush your teeth, put your most comfortable pajamas on, turn out the lights, and crawl into bed.

If comfortable, I would like to invite you to start by lying on your back. Once you find a position that you are comfortable in, allow your legs and arms to fall where they're most comfortable. If at any time you feel uncomfortable during this meditation, you can always shift and change positions. For now, try getting comfortable on your back and then we can begin.

As you get settled in, go ahead and begin to practice your body scan. Remember to allow any thoughts to pass without judgment. In this moment, we are simply becoming aware of our bodies. There is no need to change anything right now. Scan for areas of tension and bring your focus on releasing the areas that feel they are tenser. As you become more aware, notice how your mind if becoming more peaceful. You are creating a beautiful connection between mind and body. You are in control of your thoughts; you have the power to quiet your mind so that you can be well-rested for tomorrow.

When you are ready, take a nice deep breath in. Allow the air to fill you with life and relax into the sense of calmness that is beginning to wash over you. Exhale, let go of any of that tension you have noticed. As you continue to breathe, thoughts of today may come rushing into your mind. Perhaps thoughts of everything you need to get done tomorrow are clouding your mind as well. If there is anything super important, write it down. These thoughts mean nothing to you now. When you are mindful of the moment, yesterday and tomorrow aren't important. Right now, you are calming down, and you are looking forward to a nice rest.

Allow all thoughts to pass without judgment. All you need to focus on right now is how your body feels. Breathe in and breathe out. Allow all thoughts to leave your mind. For the next few moments, I invite you to begin to count each breath, and you breathe in and breathe out. Gently count each breath and feel as you become more relaxed with each passing number. Count from one to ten and allow yourself to fall deeper and deeper into your bed.

If you would like, try counting with me as you drift off into a nice, pleasant sleep through the night. Allow your mind to drift as needed. There is no need to focus on anything. Simply relax and clear your mind.

One...softly focus on the number one...take a deep breath in and let it all go.

Two...sense the tension leaving your whole body. Your bed is so comfortable and warm and inviting you to fall asleep safely.

Three...you are feeling more and more relaxed. You are looking forward to a nice, deep sleep to help set you up for success tomorrow.

Four...your mind is getting very quiet. Only thoughts of sweet dreams are filling your head.

Five...you are drifting now. Feel how heavy your body feels against the bed. Your mind is ready to rest for a while. Your body is ready to take a break.

Six...you are feeling wonderful and safe. You are comfortable and drifting off...

Seven...so calm. So happy. So relaxed.

Eight...heavy. Calm. Relaxed.

Nine...breathe softly, you are ready to drift off and float away into dreamland...

Ten...

If you are still slightly awake, continue counting each breath. Feel how heavy your eyelids feel. Your body is warm and safe in bed. You are drifting...

Drifting...

Drifting...

Sleep...

Guided Meditation to Get Back to Sleep Script

We have all been there; you're enjoying a nice sleep after a long day, and suddenly, you wake up! You try to go back to sleep, but all you can seem to do is toss back and forth for a few hours. If you have ever experienced insomnia, you're not alone!

The key here is to teach yourself how to relax after you wake up. Often times, we just become annoyed that we have woken up when it's so important to sleep, especially if you have a busy day ahead of you. Through meditation, you will be able to relax your mind, relax your body, and fall right back asleep! If you have difficulty falling back asleep, try the following script.

If you are already in bed, try your best to get comfortable again. Whichever way you sleep, settle back down into that position so you can get right back to sleep. Allowing

161

yourself to become relaxed will help settle your mind, and before you know it, you will be sleeping restfully as you deserve to be.

As you settle back into bed, bring your focus back to your breath. I want you to go ahead and breathe in as deeply as comfortable and allow yourself to push that breathe out slowly. Do it again and count each number that you are able to breathe in and breathe out. Be mindful and take nice, slow, calm breaths in. Feel how each breath you take relaxes your body. Feel yourself begin to drift as sleep washes over you like a wave.

Each time you release a breath, your mind is getting calmer. There is nothing but the sweet sense of sleep and your breath right now. Simply focus on each breath being drawn in and allow that air to release just as naturally. Notice now how there is no effort behind each breath as you take it. Your body knows exactly what you need. Just relax into this moment and allow yourself to be at peace.

Notice now how much easier everything is getting in this moment. Your shoulders are beginning to relax into the bed, your legs and arms are still and heavy. Your feet are nice and warm, and you can feel yourself sinking deeper and deeper into the comfort of your bed. Your mind if beginning to drift away, you are looking forward to a full night of restful sleep.

If you can, try to blink your eyes a couple of times. Notice now how much heavier your eyelids are becoming. You may find that it even feels good now that you are trying to close your eyes. Relax into this feeling and imagine now how all of the tension is slipping from your body. So, what if you woke up for a few minutes. You are now able to relax further and focus on your breath. Allow sleep to come take you until you are ready to wake up fully rested.

If you would like, bring your focus softly back to your breath. Feel how comfortable you are, and begin counting down to sweet sleep.

Ten...

Nine...

Eight...feel how natural your breath is settling you back into sleep.

Seven...

Six...

Five...breathe softly.

Four...

Three...

Two...

One...
You're feeling very sleepy...your mind is drifting...you are ready to sleep...Keep counting your breaths until you are no longer able to focus...everything is blending together...my voice is fading away into your dream world...you are too sleepy to think of anything...count again until you drift off...

Sleep.

Nap Time Meditation Script

Sometimes, nap time can be the best part of the day. If you find yourself needing a short nap during the day whether it be to keep you up through a night shift or you just didn't sleep well last night, this nap time meditation can help you fall asleep quick and restful. When you are ready, you can start off by getting comfortable in bed or on the couch, and then we can begin.

Once you are settled in, I want you to go ahead and allow for your thoughts to begin to settle. As your mind becomes more and more quiet, try to become mindful of your body. Begin at your head and gently allow your muscles to relax all the way to your toes. Take a few moments and imagine what true relaxation feels like to you. Perhaps relaxing feels like or a warm blanket or maybe it's a tingly sensation that radiates through your body. However it feels, allow it to wash over your whole body and fall into this sense of comfortability.

As you begin to breathe in, allow your muscles to relax into the bed. Take a gentle note of where you are tense and send your relaxing energy to these areas. Remember to relax your jaw, drop your shoulders, and allow for your hands to hang loosely at your side.

When you are ready, I now invite you to draw your attention to your chest. As your chest rises and falls with each breath, allow yourself to feel how relaxing this moment is. Each time you take a deep breath in, feel as your chest rises and falls again with each breath you take. Every time you breathe, the tension is being released from your body, and you are completely comfortable in this moment.

As your mind begins to drift, gently remind yourself that any sleep you can get is beneficial. Even if this nap only lasts for twenty minutes, it will be the perfect refresher to get you through the day. Allow yourself to be at peace for a few moments, even if it's just closing your eyes for a few minutes. A nap is a perfect time to relax your mind and to relax your body. Allow yourself to restore peace into your day to help you carry on.

Feel yourself begin to drift further and further into sleep. You are completely relaxed and happy in this moment. When you wake up, you will awake perfectly rested, alert, and refreshed. Your body will know when you need to wake up. That is not something you will need to worry about in this moment. Allow yourself to give in to the heaviness of your eyelids. You are ready to drift off to sleep.

Now, I would like to invite you to picture a peaceful place. Perhaps you are relaxing on the nice, warm beach or maybe even in a quiet cabin in your favorite meadow. Wherever you are, imagine yourself relaxing in this calm place. Paint a full picture for yourself and picture yourself relaxing deeper and deeper here.

Imagine yourself as a feather in the wind. You are drifting further and further into sleep. You feel light and carefree as the wind carries you in the breeze. Picture yourself floating, drifting, so peaceful in the wind. You have never felt this relaxed in your life.

Feel now how much heavier your body is feeling. The pillows and blanket are securing you into the bed. You are safe and supported here. There is nothing that can bother you as you sink into the soft mattress. You are getting sleepier. You are ready to nap. You are relaxed. You will wake up rested.

Allow yourself to drift...it's time to sleep...

Breathe in...and out...

Softly count yourself into a nice nap...

Continue counting until the numbers begin to blur...

You are very tired...

Sleep now...

Sleep...

Chapter 20. Meditation Scripts

Relaxing into Sleep Meditation

For these next few moments, I want you to settle yourself into bed. Now that it is time to sleep, I invite you to say goodnight to your loved ones, shut down the laptop, turn off the phone, and set yourself up for success. From this moment on, there is no need to worry about anything that happened today or will happen tomorrow. It is time to be present in this moment and allow yourself the time to settle into a full, restful night of sleep. You deserve this. Go ahead and get comfortable in bed.

(PAUSE)

Now that you are ready for bed, I want you to yawn. As you yawn, take a nice deep breath in and become mindful of slowing down your breathing. As you exhale, feel as your body begins to relax into your bed. It may feel silly at first, but yawning allows oxygen to enter your system and lengthen the muscles in your jaw all at the same time.

(PAUSE)

Go ahead and try to yawn again. Allow for your mouth to open wide and let that yawn out with a long sigh. If you want, you can gently stretch your arms above your head and yawn again. Stretch your arms gently and feel the relaxing pull along your shoulder and back muscles. You may notice that there is tension here, and that is perfectly okay. Allow any judgmental thoughts to pass through your mind and spend some time releasing the tension from these areas with each breath you take.

(PAUSE)

As your body begins to relax under your blankets, continue to focus on your breathing. In the next few moments, I would like to work on quieting your mind. When it comes to falling asleep, it can be hard for some of us to stop our thoughts. Our minds are going every single minute of the day, getting tasks done, staying organized, and keeping you on track. While this is very helpful throughout the day, it is now time to quiet your mind and focus on getting to sleep. If you feel comfortable with it, I would like to work through some guided imagery to help your mind relax. Remember that at this moment, there is nothing to worry about. All I want you to do is focus on slowing your breathing, allow your body to relax, and softly listen to these words.

(PAUSE)

If you would like, I now invite you to close your eyes gently. As you begin to find your peace, begin to form an image in your head. I want you to begin to picture a comfortable room that is dark. This is a comfortable darkness where you feel safe and warm. As you settle in here, begin to picture a candle sitting in front of you. The candle is glowing warm and flickering gently around you. Go ahead and breathe as you watch the light from the candle dancing across the wall and the floor around you.

(PAUSE)

As you watch this candle, feel yourself relaxing into the patterns of the light. The soft light is relaxing your mind and relaxing your body. Imagine now that your tension and stress is melting away like the wax on the candle. As it burns, feel as the relaxation washes over the crown of your head to the tips of your toes. Allow yourself to gently ease into a deep rest as you watch the candle. Feel yourself melting away, completely relaxing into your bed, your thoughts slowing, and your eyes becoming heavier with sleep. Take a few deep breaths on your own time and allow the sleepiness to take over your mind. When you are ready to fall asleep, blow out the mental candle, and simmer in the new sensation of relaxation.

(PAUSE)

(Meditation Time: about 10 Minutes)

Sleep Body Scan Meditation

Now that your mind is rested, it is time to take a few moments to relax your muscles. By getting rid of some of that final tension, you will wake up tomorrow morning feeling well-rested and energetic. In the next few moments, we will work together to release the tension that typically builds in a few focused areas. As you hit the reset button, your body will be able to rest fully and be ready for tomorrow with full strength.

In the following meditation, I am going to invite you to tense and relax each muscle. When you tense the area mentioned, it is vital that you never feel pain as you complete each task. If you feel any discomfort, discontinue this meditation and continue on to the final meditation for the night. This is meant to benefit you, not harm you. When you are ready to begin, take a deep breath, and we can get started.

(PAUSE)

Now that you are settled in bed take a few moments now to take note of how you feel. There is no need to change anything right now. All I want is for you to be aware of your own body and where you hold onto your tension.

168

There is no right or wrong when it comes to this task, just be mindful.

(PAUSE)

To begin this exercise, we are going to start with your shoulders and your neck. These two areas are pretty common to hold your stress. When you think about it, many of us work desk jobs and spend the whole day typing. It is all too easy to hold our shoulders up close to our ears and build up the tension. Right now, I invite you to create this movement on purpose. Go ahead and gently raise your shoulders up to your ears and tighten your muscles. As you hold this position, feel how the tension builds up. After a few beats, release and allow for your shoulders to drop back into a comfortable position. Do you feel how much better this sensation is? Now that you are aware, you can practice throughout the day. Go ahead and do this again. Take a few deep breaths and let all of the tension here go for the night. Feel how wonderful it is to relax your neck and settle into the comfort of your pillow.

(PAUSE)

With your neck and shoulders relaxed, I would now like to bring your focus up to your head. Let's go ahead and start out with your forehead. First, gently raise your eyebrows. As you do this, become mindful how the tension that is created in your forehead. Now, scrunch your eyes closed and furrow your eyebrows. When we are frustrated or stressed, you do this without even thinking about it. As you move through raising and furrowing your eyebrows, take note of how this tension feels. When you are ready, allow your eyebrows to return to a neutral position and allow for your forehead to relax completely. Breathe and relax. You are doing a wonderful job.

(PAUSE)

When you are ready, slowly bring your focus down to your jaw. Before we do anything, what position is your jaw in right now? Is there tension here? Are your teeth clamped together? If they are, this is okay. The point is being aware. If you are tense here, it is time to relax and let that tension go.

To start off, clamp your jaw shut even tighter. Your lips should feel tight and tense across your teeth as you complete this action. Hold...and then relax. Allow for all of the tension to leave your mouth and let your jaw fall loose. Breathe deep and enjoy the comfort of letting this tension go. Throughout the day, many of us clamp our jaws without even realizing it. As you lay here in bed, gently wiggle your jaw back and forth and let go of any lingering tension. Take a deep breath and allow yourself to settle into bed even further. As you relax, your eyes will probably begin to feel heavier. This is your body accepting the relaxation. You deserve a full night of sleep. Allow for this to happen naturally. Take a deep breath and let it all go.

(PAUSE)

For these next few moments, I just want you to focus on your breathing. As you become mindful of your breath, gently slow it down. Breathe in deep through your mouth and hold the air in your lungs for a few beats. Do this again on your own time, and just concentrate on how this breathing makes you feel.

(PAUSE)

Now that your mind and your body are relaxed, it is time to move onto our final meditation for the night. Your body should be loose, and your mind should be at peace. If not, take a few more moments to settle into your practice and just breathe until you feel okay. When you are ready, we will move onto the sleep count down so you can settle into a nice, deep sleep for the night.

(Meditation Time: about 15 Minutes)

Sleep Countdown Meditation

To finish your meditation for the night, it is time to count down to a peaceful night of rest. When you wake up in the morning, you will feel well-rested and full of energy. In order to set yourself up for success tomorrow, you have to put in the work now. When you are ready to fall asleep, be sure all of the lights are off and that you are as comfortable as possible. Take a deep breath in, and we can begin.

(PAUSE)

Take a deep breath in. As you draw your focus to your breath, become aware of how warm and safe your body is feeling right now. You have released all of the tension, and your muscles are relaxed and loose against your bed. Your mind is at peace, and you are feeling wonderful. The only thing left is to fall into a nice, deep sleep for the night. When you are ready, close your eyes and begin to imagine that you are at the top of a staircase. Below you, there are ten steps, and at the bottom, the most comfortable mattress you have ever seen. As you gently gaze down at this mattress, you are already feeling tired. Your mind and body are both ready to fall asleep and feel the comfort of this bed.

(PAUSE)

Take another breath and take a step down toward the mattress. All you need to do right now is focus on your breath and allow yourself to make your way down these stairs. With each step, you are becoming sleepier. You are safe and comfortable in this moment, completely

171

relaxed, and ready to sleep. Just breathe and count down with me as you make your way down the stairs. At each step, inhale deeply and exhale. If you yawn, that is okay. Enjoy the gentle stretch, and snuggle down further into your covers. If you would like, you can count along with me.

(PAUSE)

Ten...

(PAUSE)

Nine...

(PAUSE)

Eight...

(PAUSE)

If your thoughts begin to wander, allow for your mind to unwind. There is nothing to think about right now; just look forward to sleep. All you need to do right now is to breathe and continue to count down with me. Outside of this moment, there is no need to worry about tomorrow. Right now, there is only sleep to look forward to. When you are ready, take another deep breath and keep counting down with me.

(PAUSE)

Seven...

(PAUSE)

Six...

(PAUSE)

Five...

(PAUSE)

Sleep is coming soon. Just continue to breathe and enjoy this sensation of calmness and relaxation. Allow for these feelings to wash over you as you step closer and closer to the comfortable bed.

(PAUSE)

Four...

(PAUSE)

Three...

(PAUSE)

Two...

(PAUSE)

One...

(PAUSE)

Now that you have reached the bottom of the stairs, it is time to crawl into the comfortable bed. Your eyes are heavy with sleep, your body gently melts away into the mattress, and your mind is wandering off into rest. For these next few moments, just breathe gently and allow your thoughts to drift off into sleep. You are safe, warm, and comfortable. Allow sleep to take over now as you continue to drift away, the sound of my voice becoming distant as you get sleepier. You will fall asleep at any moment. Just breathe and sleep...sleep...goodnight.

(PAUSE)

(Meditation Time: about 15 Minutes)

(Total Meditation Time: about 40 Minutes)

Chapter 21. Sleep Scripts

Now that you are ready to fall asleep take a deep breath in. Exhale slowly and expel any tension that may have built up during the last few exercises.

As you settle in for sleep, you may begin to have thoughts about what you have done today or things you need to get done tomorrow. Take another deep breath and let those thoughts go with your next exhale. At this moment, all you need to do is clear your mind. Today is over and tomorrow will come whether you worry about it or not. For now, clear your mind so you can wake up strong and healthy for your duties tomorrow.

For now, I want you to draw your attention to your body. Where did you store your tension today? I invite you to focus your attention on the tension and let it go as we practiced earlier. Feel now where your body is relaxed. Take a few moments to appreciate the sense of relaxation your body is feeling at this moment and allow it to spread through your whole body from head to toes.

Before you drift off to bed, let's fill your mind with peaceful images. By promoting positive mental images, this will help you relax and can help avoid nightmares. As we begin, I would like you to visualize a place where you feel safe and comfortable. Take a few moments and imagine how the place would be.

When you have your safe place in mind, I would like you to start to relax your body again. In order to get rid of nightmares, you will need to release all tension from your body. When we are fearful, this can create tension in our body. Try to pay special attention to your shoulders, hands, back, neck, and jaw. Often times, these are areas where our tension can creep in.

If you feel any of these areas tensing up, focus your attention here. Breathe in...and breathe out...choose to relax and soften these areas. As you breathe, imagine the air bringing total relaxation to these areas and allow the tension to leave your body. I invite you to continue this pattern until your breathing becomes deep and slow again.

Notice now how your body has become more relaxed than it was before. Feel as your muscles sink into the bed as you relax further and deeper. Your jaw is becoming loose. Your mouth is resting, and your teeth are slightly apart. Now, your neck is relaxing, and your shoulders are falling away. Allow this to happen and let your muscles become soft.

I want you to return to your safe place. Imagine that this place is spacious, comfortable, and filled with a positive light. In this place, you have nothing to worry about, and you have all the time in the world to focus on yourself.

In this safe place, I want you to imagine the sun streaming in. The light fills you with warm and positive emotion. There are windows where you can see the beautiful nature outside. Your space can be wherever you want it to be. It can be by the mountains, by the ocean, or perhaps even on a golf course.

Return your focus back on your safe place. Imagine how warm and comfortable the room is. Walk over toward the comfortable bed and imagine how wonderful it feels to sink into the sheets. The sun is shining down on you, and you feel relaxed and warm. The bed is so soft around you, and you feel so at peace at this moment.

Notice now how these peaceful thoughts begin to fill your mind. They are filling your conscious and are clear. Any other thoughts you had before are drifting away. Your mind is falling into a positive place as you feel yourself drifting away. The space around you is safe and peaceful, and beautiful.

Any other thoughts you have at this moment, pass through your mind and drift off like clouds drifting by. Allow these thoughts to pass without judgment. There is no sense in dwelling on them when you are in such a safe place. All you have at this moment is peace and quiet.

Any time a worried thought arises, you turn your focus back to your safe place. In this location, you can get rid of any stress you may have on a daily basis. You are here to relax and enjoy this moment. There is nothing that can bother you. You are free from stress and responsibilities here.

When you are ready, you feel your body begin to drift off to sleep. You are beginning to slip deeper and deeper toward the land of dreams. As you feel your attention drift, you are becoming sleepier, but you chose to focus on counting with me. As we count, you will become more relaxed as each number passes through.

We will now take a few breaths, and then I will count from the number one to the number ten. As you relax, your mind will drift off to a deep and refreshing sleep. Ready?

Breathe in...one...two...three...and out...two...three.

Breathe in...one...two...three...and out...two...three.

Breathe in...one...two...three...and out...two...three.

Wonderful. Now, count slowly with me...one...bring your focus to the number one...

Two...you are feeling more relaxed...you are calm and peaceful...you are drifting deeper and deeper toward a wonderful night of rest.

Three...gently feel as all of the tension leaves your body. There is nothing but total relaxation filling your mind and your body. At this moment, your only focus is on quietly counting numbers with me.

Four...picture the number in your mind's eye. You are feeling even more relaxed and at peace. Your legs and arms are falling pleasantly heavy. You are so relaxed. Your body is ready for sleep.

Five...you are drifting deeper. The sleep begins to wash over you. You are at peace. You are safe. You are warm and comfortable.

Six...so relaxed...drifting off slowly...

Seven...your mind and body are completely at peace. You have not felt this calm in a while...

Eight...everything is pleasant. Your body feels heavy with sleep.

Nine...allow your mind to drift...everything is floating, and relaxing...your eyelids feel comfortable and heavy...your mind giving in to the thought of sleep.

Ten...you are completely relaxed, and at peace...soon, you will be drifting off to a deep and comfortable sleep.

Now that you are ready to sleep, I will now count from the number one to the number five. All I want you to do is listen gently to the words I am saying. When I say the number five, you will drift out of hypnosis and sleep comfortably through the night.

In the morning, you will wake up feeling well rested and stress-free. You have worked on many incredible skills during this session. You should be proud of the hard work you have put in. Now, it is time to sleep so you can wake up in the morning feeling refreshed.

Chapter 22. Sleep Talkdown Script

Sleep Talkdown (30mns)

Good evening and welcome to the sleep talkdown meditation. In this guided meditation, you will go on a journey of deep relaxation after a long day of work when you just want to unwind and you will be sent off into a deep and peaceful slumber.

To begin, make sure that all distractions are as minimal as possible. As you progress, anything holding you back from fully relaxing will slowly start to fade away. Lay in a position that is comfortable for you. Allow yourself to go deeper and experience a willing openness the sleep that you should be getting.

Please leave all thoughts about yourself behind and anything that has caused worry or stress. It may be easier said than done but just place it to the back of your mind for now. Focus on my voice and the words that you hear will give clarity to unfold your mind for sleep.

If you are ready and willing to be present at this moment, your journey into a deep relaxing and pleasing sleep will begin. As you lay there in a gentler awareness of observation, noticing how your body is laid, sense and feel any areas soften to a looseness that promotes a more sleepier state.

Now, breathe in deeply and exhale fully.

Breathe in deeply...

And exhale fully...

Allow the sound of your breathing to soothe and calm your mind and soul.

Breathe in deeply...

And exhale fully...

You may notice that thoughts and internal mental chatters are happening inside your mind.

This is fine.

This is completely normal.

These thoughts will begin to quiet down as you concentrate on listening to your breathing. As you listen to your inhale, you will find your mind gently begin to quiet down.

So, breathe in deeply, taking in the cool and refreshing air. And exhale fully, pushing out hot and tense air.
You may feel your body starting to loosen up and relaxing as you allow the sound of your breathing to soothe your soul, taking in the infinite source of energy within you.

Just through breathing alone, you allow yourself to be in total peace with your surroundings. Now, take the time to scan your entire body, noticing any areas of tension. Focus your breathing on those areas, starting from your toes and moving up to the top of your head. Work on one area at a time.

Breathe deep and slow, allowing your breath to soothe any tension in your muscles.

(Pause 5mns)

Now that your entire body is fully relaxed, take another breath to allow your body to slip more and more into a relaxed state. Feel how at ease your mind and body are. Feel the relief and benefit of letting go of any worries that were on your thoughts...

Going into an even deeper, sleepier, and more relaxed state, let the visualization of any thoughts begin to fade off in the darkness behind your eyelids, drifting deeper into a transitioning positive dream and sleep...

As you sleep, your body rests, healing as you recuperate and regenerate positive energy in every muscle fiber and cell of yourself.

Sleeping keeps your mind and body muscle memory to remember that when you sleep well, you can do it again. Let go of anything holding you back and truly allow yourself to relax through letting go.

Your mind has the space to rationalize every thought to a groundedness of truth and ones that only benefits you as the person you are on the inside.

Allow yourself to be more at ease with each and every thought that passes your mind. Any tension from this moment on that is caused by our worry or a stressor in your life is quickly brought to a reasonable place. See it for what it truly is before manifesting itself in your body.

What you did this morning, what you ate, your interactions with others, the wide scope of emotions and experiences you might have had, the things you accomplished, and perhaps the things that you didn't.

You must realize that today is exactly what it was. The good or bad, whatever you think happened is over now and all is well. Tomorrow, when you wake up, you are the creator of a brand new day. Today will be left behind and you can start fresh however you decide.

So, with this in mind let's introduce our mantra the centering thought for this meditation. Repeat after me...

"I move forward and leave today behind. I move forward and leave today behind..."

Repeat this message as you sink deeper into your meditative state. With each inhale, fill yourself with gratitude and fulfillment of what you accomplished today. With each exhale, let go of any negativity or self-judgment that you feel that may be lingering in your mind.

Let it go. You did your best and tomorrow is a fresh new start. Staying present with your breath.

Inhale... and exhale...

Allow each part of your face and body to sleekly let go and release... Again, chant with me...

"I move forward and leave today behind. I move forward and leave today behind. I move forward and leave today behind."

And now silently in your mind, it's time to release the mantra. Slowly begin to deepen your breath moving each finger, wiggling each toe at your own pace. Slowly begin to open your eyes or if you're ready for sleep to keep them closed and move to a lying down position.

Remember we are the creators of our own lives. We direct the flow of energy in our lives based on our thoughts.

You are not the manifestation of any worrying thoughts, so dismiss them with positive self-love that only nourishes your mind and body better. As you begin and continue to let go of anything negative, you will find that you become more relaxed, more calm, and more at peace within everything.

Now, imagine seeing a boat before you. I want you to place your worries, fears, frustrations, expectations, struggles, and any negativity on that boat and know that it's about to start up and move away.

It's about to drift away out into the sea, so let it take your troubles with it. Again placed your troubles on that boat let the boat take them away out of your field of energy.

As you do so, repeat the mantra: "I release and let go." You can repeat this mantra in your mind silently or you can say it out loud.

"I release and let go."

Notice how the boat is taking away all of your negativity, anxieties, and anything that you don't need in your life right now that's not serving you. Just allow it to leave.

"I release and let go."

Continue breathing slowly and deeply. Even breaths...

(Pause 2mn)

Peaceful relaxed in the present moment...

(Pause 1mn)

"I release and let go."

Now let your breathing get a little bit deeper as you bring your awareness back into your body. Open your hands to the sky take a deep breath. Chant one more time: "I release and let go."

Breathe in... and out...

Remember that you can always return to that beautiful mantra to find peace and calmness.
Knowing that you have more control over how you reason with your mind allows you to go deeper into the state of relaxation, no sound from the outside can be heard, no light except the positivity inside you that shines, and a feeling of touch is but now a softness of comfort.

Resting, heavily breathing deeply, you just let go. The touch of the sheets beneath you begin to fade away. The sensation of your vibrations and internal energy are the only things you can sense.

Everything is being replaced with a positive and healing feeling of peace inside. There is no need to think about anything right now. Now is a time for sleep and only sleep. It's the one thing that will replenish you every night as you lay there.

Feel the vibration of positivity growth around your whole body. You may see it as a distant colored light behind your eyelids or a feeling of tingling in your hands or toes, warmer and heavier with each and every noticeably relaxing breath that you take, every inhalation of oxygen only sends you deeper into a space of contentedness and peace. The sense of relief is immense and far-reaching into the deep thoughts of your mind.

Healing any bad feeling you have of yourself. Only positive thoughts can be experienced in this moment and every moment onwards allowing you to drift heavier and warmly into it refreshing deep sleep.

As you sleep the defense mechanism only grows to protect you from negativity you feel it as a glowy warm feeling around your heart or chest area growing in strength as you sleep feeling more positive with every second that passes from this moment on you only sleep a positive slate you only rest and relax more easily and from this moment on you find it easier to drift off feeling the relief of letting go of every aspect of today leaving it all behind to be nourished and filled with only positivity in every sense of your inner being.

As we come to the end of this meditation, I will start to count to 5. As I count, you will feel yourself sinking deeper and deeper into the state of relaxation...

1...

2...

3... Sinking deeper and deeper...

4... Rest now...

5... Relax, and just let go... Thank you and goodnight.

Sleep Talkdown (2) (20mns)

Begin by getting into a comfortable position and taking a deep breath through your nose, then breathing out slowly through your mouth.

Now, let us go through a thorough body scan starting from the tips of your toes to the top of your head. Starting at your toes, imagine them in your mind's eye. Each individual toe that could be holding tension and stress, I'd like you to let it go...

Tensing and relaxing each individual toe...

And as you imagine your toes relaxing, that feeling is transferred to your foot the underneath of your foot, the top of your foot, and finally to your ankle. Start to feel limp and very loose and also very heavy as if it was sinking into the bed.

As they start to happen, that feeling flows up to your shin and your calf muscles from your knees down to the tips of your toes. Your legs start to feel as if they are sinking into the bed.

Like the warmth from a fire, your knees start to unwind and relax more. Again, feel like they are sinking into the bed and falling asleep themselves. This drowsing sensation works its way up to your thighs, where you can feel your legs relaxed and you sink deeper into the bed.

Your back also descends into the bed. Your abdomen feels free and loose. Your back unwinds and lets go. With all these sensations going on, your breathing becomes deeper and longer in length.

Thoughts start to disperse and your mind feels clearer your chest becomes free and loose as you start to relax. Loose and free your shoulders, letting go, unwinding... Now, feel your neck and throat where your breathing becomes deeper longer and heavier.

Feel in your face, cheeks, jaw, and mouth...

Your tongue peels itself away from the roof of your mouth, becoming heavier. As you start to drift off, the last feelings of tension can be felt in your forehead. Let go... As you do, your arms, wrists, and hands flop and feel heavier as you start to sink into sleep.

From this moment on, I would like you to concentrate on the sound of silence around my voice. As my voice starts to disappear into the background, you start to slip away into sleep.

The only feeling you have is comfort.
Your toes have descended into the bed, sunken deeper, sleepier. Your ankles and feet have found their place in the bed where your legs have followed your pelvis and your abdomen feeling heavier, sleepier, and dreamy...

As you drift deeper and deeper into sleep, all sight and sound start to fade away...

The more you relax, the less you can see or hear.

All sound seems to fade off into the distance...

As you drift in and out of sleep, any feelings drift away as you just let go.

There's no need to do anything as you automatically fall.

You are safe, secured in a sleepy slumber.

Your mind is free as it wanders on its path automatically as your breathing becomes deeper. With every breath that you take, your chest becomes more and more relaxed. Any thoughts that come into your mind leave as quickly as they have appeared.

You are consumed with the darkness of your eyelids. The comfort of your bed can be felt but seems to feel vaguer as you start to slip away. No one can disturb you. No worries here. Only sleep...
You feel relaxed as you sink deeper and deeper into sleep...

The more you drift off, the lighter you feel as your whole body is relaxed, ready for sleep. Your toes feel light. Your feet and ankles feel loose. Your legs fill limp. Your knees have let go. Your thighs sink.

The rest of your legs sink into the bed. Your back unwinds. Your abdomen is free and loose. Your chest is relieved. Your shoulders are loose and relaxed. Your breathing becomes deeper and deeper.

Your eyes only show you darkness and only show you sleep. Any worries about the day can be left here right now. There's no need to worry about anything at all. No one will worry you here. You will awake, refreshed from a good night's sleep.

Sleep is a strange feeling. You can feel heavy and light at the same time. Heavy as in sinking into the bed, where is comfortable safe and secure and light as a feather as all the worries of the day just drift away...

Relaxing your body more and more, deeper and deeper. Just lay there and sleep will take over. Sleep will relax you. Sleep will refresh you. Your head feels limp and loose and is sunken into the pillow. Your mouth slightly opens as you breathe deeper and longer breaths.

Your hands and wrists have now found their place in the bed where they are most comfortable. Your back has settled into position and so have your feet and toes. There are no worries, no interruptions. It is safe here.

Nothing can be more comforting than sleep. Anything there has been a worry for today can be left for tomorrow. All you need to do is sleep, relax, and awaken refreshed and ready for the day.

You are a positive person and you need your sleep. You have to be energized. To do this, you need to sleep. You are an amazing person. You are positive and you are relaxed and you couldn't feel sleepier if you tried.

As you drift off deeper and deeper, sleepier and sleepier as you relax more and feel sleepy... Let go and let yourself drift into a deep, peaceful sleep.

Thank you, goodnight, and sweet dreams.

Chapter 23. Hypnosis For Sleeping Better

Although you might be tired, you may still struggle to actually fall asleep because you aren't able to become fully relaxed. Going to bed doesn't mean just jumping under the covers and closing your eyes. You will also want to ensure that you are keeping up with incorporating relaxation techniques into your bedtime routine so you can stay better focused on getting a complete rest, not one that is constantly disturbed by anxious thoughts.

The following meditation is good for anyone who is about to go to bed. You will want to include this for getting a night of deep sleep, or one that will last for several hours. Keep your eyes closed, and ensure the lighting is right so that there is nothing that will distract you from falling asleep. No lighting is best, but if you do prefer to have some sort of light on, ensure that it is soft yellow or purple/pink. Always choose small lights and nightlights instead of overhead lighting.

Better Sleep Guided Hypnosis

You are in a completely relaxed place, ready to start the process of falling asleep. You are able to stretch your body out, feeling no strain in any limb, muscle, or joint. You are not holding onto any stress within your body. Your eyes are closed, and there is nothing that you need to be worried about in this present moment. You have given yourself permission to fall asleep. You are allowing yourself to take time to relax. You have granted your soul the ability to become completely at ease before falling asleep.

Become aware of your breathing now. Feel how the air moves in and out of you without any effort on your part.

Every move that you make is one that helps you to bring in clean, healthy air. In everything that you do throughout the day, your lungs are always working hard to push you through. Everything that requires more strain means making your lungs work harder. Now, we are going to give them a bit of rest, as well. They can never fully stop, but we are going to give them the long, deep, clean, and relaxing breaths that they need now.

Counting while you breathe will help you to become even more relaxed. Breathe in for one, two, three, four, and five. Breathe out for six, seven, eight, nine, and ten.

Once more, this time breathing in through your nose and out through your mouth. Breathe in for ten, nine, eight, seven, six, and out for five, four, three, two, and one. You are feeling refreshed. You are focused. You are centered. You are at peace.

As thoughts pass into your head, allow them to simply float away. When you think of something that does not pertain to this moment, simply push the thought away. Imagine that you are in a pool and a bug is on the surface of the water. What would you do? At the very least, you would push it away. Gently push your thoughts in another direction and allow them to float away.

Think of your thoughts as if they were sheep jumping over a fence. Imagine them escaping from the pasture in which they are held, only to jump away and go somewhere unknown. Watch as your thoughts hop over the fence. They are passing from your mind out into the world. You are simply releasing them, doing nothing more.

Your thoughts are the stars burning brightly above. They are scary, they are beautiful, and they will always eventually burn out. You will never rid yourself of your thoughts. They will always be dotting the sky. They are so distant, however. They are slow burning. Do not reach for the stars, simply let them be. Let your thoughts slowly burn out now. You only need to be focused on relaxing and becoming more and more at peace.

Feel how you are becoming more and more relaxed. You are letting go of tension in every part of your body. You are becoming more and more focused on centering yourself. You are becoming closer and closer to sleep. You are getting this rest to prepare for the day tomorrow. What happens tomorrow will happen then. There is nothing that you can do about it now. Worrying and stressing isn't going to help you whatsoever. What will help you the most at this moment is drifting deeply into a heavy sleep. Give your body the rest that it needs.

The earth is all asleep now as well. Don't just feel how you are becoming more relaxed. Feel the way that the earth has been tucked into bed as well. Feel how it is now dark and how others are sleeping restfully just as you are. There are some just waking, and some still awake, but they will eventually rest just as you are now. It is time for you to become a part of this whole peaceful earth.

Nothing about the future is scary. You have survived thus far. You are not worried about what is going to happen tomorrow, or the day after, or the day after. Even the bad things that might happen will eventually fade just as well. Nothing is going to keep you from sleeping at this moment. No amount of anxiety will keep you awake.

Everything tomorrow will be unknown. You can prepare but never predict. You are prepared. The best way to ensure that it will be a good day is to get some rest. Allow yourself to get this sleep. Give yourself permission to enjoy this deep and heavy sleep as it exists at this moment.

You are completely comfortable, all throughout your body. You feel relaxation everywhere and you exude peace and serenity.

You are feeling more and more relaxed from the top of your head to the bottom of your toes. You feel your mind start to fade into a dreamlike state. You are feeling as though there is nothing that will keep you awake.

Feel your jawline relax. You hold onto so much tension that you don't even realize. Not now. Not at this moment. You are releasing yourself from all physical strain.

Allow your ears and forehead to be as still and as relaxed as possible. These are heavy and can hold a ton of tension. At this moment, you are letting them become as relaxed as possible. Nothing is going to keep the muscles in your head so tense.

Be aware of the way that we hold our muscles throughout the rest of our bodies. Allow yourself to become relaxed. And even further. And even further. Even when we try to relax, we don't let go of our bodies all of the way. Give yourself to rest. Devote yourself to sleep. Marry the idea of being peaceful.

Allow every bone to become still, relaxed, and serene. You are tranquil from the inside out. You are rested from the outside in.

Let your shoulders relax as much as possible. Feel how they become heavy on your pillow. Your shoulders can hold the weight of the world. It can feel like everything in your body is pressing onto them. Let these shoulders drop deeper and deeper, further and further.

Let your hips be relaxed as well. Your waist, your abdomen—all of this will also hold tension. Release those

192

feelings. Let your body become calm and still. Allow yourself to be relaxed all over your entire body.

Feel the calm spread from your mind down all the way to your toes. The peace is like butter, you are the warm toast. Spread it throughout and allow it to melt into you. Let your body fade away, slowly becoming more and more peaceful.

Feel your stomach rise as you are breathing. You are breathing slower and slower, keeping your heart rate low as well. This will make it easier to fall into a deep and healthy sleep.

You are becoming more and more relaxed. You are starting to feel your body become completely calm. Not one single part of you is still holding onto any tension.

Nothing about the past or the future scares you.

It is time now to fall asleep.

You are going to get the deepest sleep by letting everything go. You are not carrying any fear, anxiety, stress, or pain. You are at peace. You are content. You are calm. You are complete. You are tranquil.

Don't allow thoughts to keep you at the surface of your sleep. Become more and more tired, getting closer and closer to falling all the way asleep.

We are going to count down from ten. When we reach one, you will be fast asleep.

Ten, nine, eight, seven, six, five, four, three, two, one.

Chapter 24. Deep Sleep Hypnosis - Sleepy Ocean Visualization

It is going to be a really nice sleep tonight...before you fall asleep, I will take you to the most beautiful beach you've ever seen. This place will relax you and calm you to your very soul.

First, take a nice deep breath, getting into a very comfortable position. Rest your head upon your soft pillow and take another deep breath...relaxing into the bed, loosening all muscles.

Breathing deeply, letting your legs relax and sink into the bed...breathe fully, letting your torso melt into the mattress...breathing, completely let go the muscles in your neck and shoulders, letting you head be cradled by the pillow...take one last deep and relaxing breath, as you exhale let your eyes gently close.

Good...

Relax your body even more by letting go of any areas of tension...breathe in again slowly... release the air with a whooshing sound, like a wave crashing on the sand...

Become more and more relaxed with each breath...

Breathe in again very slowly...pause for a moment....and let it go...

Feel your body giving up all tension...becoming fully relaxed...enjoying every moment of this calm and peaceful breathing...

There is a gentle wave of relaxation flowing through your body...down and up...up and down...just like the waves of the great ocean...

It flows from the tips of your toes, through your feet, up your ankles, and lower legs... through the knees, thighs, hips and pelvis...the relaxation flows through your abdomen, chest, back and shoulders...down each arm, relaxing any tension...all the way to the hands and each fingertip...it flows up your neck, relaxing you deeply...the back of your head fully relaxes, your facial muscles let go completely...and the very top of your head, including your brain, becomes deeply relaxed...

Breathe in slowly and deeply again...releasing the air with a whooshing sound...and as you do bring into your mind the thought of a white sand beach.

The sand is warm...and as soft as velvet under your feet...

The waves of the turquoise ocean in front of you is making that gentle whooshing sound, just like your breath...

This beach is surrounded by tropical forest. You can hear the song of beautiful birds being carried through the air...you notice the leaves on the palm trees are moving with the wind, making a soothing rustling sound...you can hear crickets and tropical frogs enjoying their life in the rainforest.

Notice the different greens of the nature, the beauty in the way that each leaf reflects the sunlight.

You can feel the gentle warmth of the sun on your skin, relaxing you. This place is the definition of tranquility. The ocean water is shallow for a distance, then far out along the horizon you can see the water gets deeper and is therefore a deep sapphire blue.

There are white fluffy clouds in the sky that resemble the blossom of cotton in its raw form...drifting by, slowly in the sky. The sun's rays alternate between warming your skin and being hidden behind the passing clouds.

The beach sand turns into giant rocks to your left, that soar into tall caves along the water's edge. As you walk towards these caves, you feel the sand moving under each footstep...you gaze behind you and see a long strand of your footprints trailing behind you. The rock formations get more massive as you draw closer... as you draw near the cave, you find yourself under the shadow of its cliff, and the air becomes cool from the shade.

There is a large opening in the rocks... it is a welcoming entrance.

As you go inside the cave, you can hear the sounds of the ocean waves become amplified as they bounce off the rock walls. This cave is magnificent. You can hear the sounds of trickling water, so you follow it to find its source. Along the interior wall of the cave, fresh water is springing from rocks, making the most relaxing sound of moving water you've ever heard. This water seems to glow, although there is no sunlight reflecting in the cave, it shimmers with light before your eyes.

You cup your hands together and gather some of this water, bringing it to your lips for a drink. It is the purest and refreshing water you have ever tasted. It nourishes and replenishes you... hydrating every part of your being with its beauty.

The tropical birds know of this water source, and make their way flying into the cave, chirping their beautiful song. There are all different types of birds, large and small. They land on the floor of the cave and drink the fresh water that is collected in various puddles below. Bringing their beaks down, scooping the water, then raising their heads high to allow the water to trickle down their throats. They are not afraid of you; it is almost as if you are part of their flock.

These magnificent birds are co close, you can clearly see the beautiful rainbow of colors that make up their feathers... bright reds... yellows... greens... and turquoise blues that match the water of the ocean.... Their eyes are surrounded by the crisp white of their skin, and they look directing at you with kindness and curiosity... After getting their fill of hydrating water, they fly out of the cave and back into the rainforest.

You take a moment to sit down in this cave, there is the perfect shape rock protruding from the ground that almost resembles a bench. Have a seat and close your eyes for a moment, tuning into the sounds around you....

The waves... the distant birds... the tricking fresh water... the breeze... each sound soothes you to your very soul... take a deep breath in and hear the sound of the air going in and out of your lungs... you can smell the clean salt water...

(pause)

Open your eyes and see the cave towering above you... What a beautiful spot.

You are ready to go back out and explore the beach, because it has gotten a little cool for you here...

As you make your way out of the cave, the cool rock under your feet turns back into sand... you pass into the sunlight and feel the sunrays begin to nourish your skin. The water is so clear and inviting that you decide to go for a little swim. The sand becomes firmer under your feet because it is saturated with sea water... a waves comes closer and catches your feet. At first, the water seems cool, but it's actually the perfect temperature. The waves rush up to your ankles, and your feet are being buried in the sand as your weight presses you down into the earth.

You make your way into the water and can see that it is shallow for a long distance. It goes to just above your waist. Curious to see what's going on below the surface, you decide to dip your head under the water.... As you do, you find that allowing yourself to become weightless in the ocean is one of the most serene experiences in your life.

Without hesitation, you open your eyes underwater to find that you can see perfectly clear, without any discomfort.

In front of you, there is an immaculate reef, teeming with fish. You swim closer, finding that you don't have an urgency to go up for air. It is almost as if you are a tropical fish in this ocean.

As you swim closer to this city of underwater life, you see that the colors are more brilliant that anything on land. It's as almost as if you are witnessing the rainbow manifesting as life. Everything you see is alive... moving in the ocean's gentle current...

A few small yellow fish with black stripes notice your arrival... they look at you with curiosity in their eyes, and excitement in their swimming. Then they travel back down into a giant pink sea anemone... you can see that this is their home. Several yellow fishes pop in and out of the living home, dancing about... it's almost as if they are showing off their place of residence.

A large purple fish with bright glowing green spots catches your eye... swimming slowly by with confidence and grace... They notice you, but don't seem to be phased by your appearance...

You are witnessing every color you can possibly imagine in your view of this reef... from the blackness of the pupils of the swimming creatures, to the shimmering white light of the sun cascading through the water like a diamond prism.

Everything is peaceful here at the shallow reef.

You are about ready to head back to the shore to enjoy a walk through the sand... then you suddenly see a mighty sea turtle coming close by... the way their arms and legs push them through the water makes the turtle weightless, though you know he could easily weigh more than you. The sweetness in their eyes comforts you to the soul...

Just when you thought this experience couldn't get any better, you see there is a trail of baby turtles following behind... you thought by the size of this sea turtle, it was a male, but now you can see the gentleness that could only be embodied by a caring mother. Her hatchlings have made the daunting journey into the expansive ocean. They are vibrant and ready to take on life. This is only the beginning of a long lifetime along the reef.

You are grateful for this experience in the reef, and it's time to head back to the beach. Getting out of the water is effortless because the waves are gentle, and the water is shallow.

The sun begins drying your skin.... the clouds are passing by ever so slowly... you are beginning to feel tired from taking in all the beauty around you, and just so happens that a plush beach recliner is positioned facing the water, with a large white umbrella providing just the right amount of shade...

Have a seat and position yourself on the chair so that all of your muscles can let go... you are fully ready to take a long nap in this paradise. Inhale deeply the sweetness of the air... exhale into complete tranquility... hear the nature behind you.... The ocean in front of you... and the breeze all around you....

You see the cave you were exploring earlier in the distance and can remember the crisp taste of the fresh spring water...

You can feel the cushioned beach chair supporting you... Every part of your body and mind are at peace, and deeply relaxed...

Gazing out upon the big blue, you notice the horizon, and how it is the only perfectly straight line in the landscape... You enjoy the precision of how the ocean meets the sky.

Take in a few more deep breaths as you lazily keep your eyes open enjoying the sights of this beach paradise.

Breathing in deeply... relaxing more and more... exhale into serenity...

Breathing in fully... let your body sink down, melting any last bit of tension away... exhale into tranquility...

Continue breathing slowly... Allowing the breath to lull you into a deep sleep... slowing down more and more....

You can hear the sounds of the waves gently crashing on the sand... in and out... as the waves come and go, just like your breath...

Allow your eyes to gently close as you rest on your beach chair...

You sleep deeply and soundly... fully rejuvenating as the hours pass by... sleeping this well comes easily to you... you let everything go, so that you get the restful sleep you deserve...

Letting each breath relax you even more... taking you into a deep, deep sleep.

Good.

Allow your mind to drift and wander to wherever it takes you... into the dream world... where there are endless possibilities for you to learn and grow...

Allow my voice to fade into the distance now as you drift off to sleep...

Goodnight...

Chapter 25. Principles For Self-Hypnosis For Sleep

For this meditation, make sure that you have become relaxed enough to fall asleep. You will instantly fall asleep at the end, so you must ensure you are in a safe and comfortable place. Complete pitch-black darkness is preferred, but if you must sleep with a light on, ensure that it is dim. You can include a noise machine or sound effects machine as well if that will help you become more relaxed.

As I count down from ten, start to let your body feel free and focus on hearing the thoughts that I say as if they were your own.

Ten, nine, eight, seven, six, five, four, three, two, one.

I am feeling more and more relaxed right now.

There is nothing around me.

I am alone, and this is OK. I see nothing but pitch black and darkness. As an image starts to burn into my vision, I quickly dissolve it.

I start to focus on nothing. No thoughts from the previous day are coming into my brain.
Each time I start to think about something that causes me stress, I focus only on nothing.

There is nothing to focus on, but that is enough to keep me distracted from anything that might keep me awake.

As an image burns into my vision again, I push it away. There are no images that I will see that will keep me distracted long enough.

My vision is trying to make something out in front of me, but that is just how my eyes work.

They are so tired now, so I need to keep my lids closed so that I can fall asleep.

All day, my eyes are looking at different things around me. Sometimes I have to squint to see things in the distance, and other things are in plain sight.

Sometimes I look past the things I do not want to see, and other times I move my vision away fast when I'm sneaking a peek and do not want others to know.

My eyes are tired now, so I need to rest them. I have so much left to see as I go throughout my day. I do not need to see anything right now. I need to keep these eyes focused on rejuvenation.

My eyes are done for the day, just as my mind is. When I start to think about what I have to do tomorrow, I push that thought away. Nothing that I will encounter is something that I need to be stressed about right now.

I am prepared. I am ready. I will conquer, and I will succeed. Right now, I need to focus on getting very deep sleep.

Though I can hear some things in the background, it is all silent in my mind. I hear nothing but what is going on around me right now.

Each sound is one that pushes me further and further to sleep. It is like a piano lullaby that slowly lulls me to a drowsy stupor.

I feel the nothingness throughout my body. The lack of sight and sound and everything else around me makes me feel so much lighter.

When my body is free, my mind is free. When my mind is free, my body is free.

When I can be relaxed, it will be so much easier to fall asleep.

I will not even have any nightmares or other vivid dreams to keep me up. There will be nothing to prevent me from going to sleep, and I will get exactly the right amount of sleep.

I realize now that there is nothing around me. Everything is black. Everything is dark. Everything is far.

This does not scare me. This fills me with peace. This reminds me that I have nothing to worry about. I have nothing to think about. I have nothing to do.

The only thing I need to focus on right now is myself. I am focused on my breathing.

I am tired, and I am starting to fall asleep. This is exactly what my body needs.

This nothingness, this black state of space is the perfect solution to my need for a deeper sleep. This is what will bring me closer to being rejuvenated and refreshed tomorrow.

I feel nothing above me, next to me, below me, or around me. It is just me, and my mind. I can feel my eyes, I can feel my breathing, and I can feel my head. All of these are perfectly relaxed, helping me to focus on what is more important than anything in this world right now – falling asleep.

As nothing surrounds me, I become more aware of my breathing. I can feel the air fill my lungs and leave through my body.

Air is always around me. This will always soothe me. The only thing I need is air. Whether I am trying to wake up or fall asleep quicker, air is what will help me. It is my body's rhythm. When I am breathing, I am creating something. I have created life within me.

I can feel the air enter my body now. It comes in slowly as I start to fall asleep. Even though I am trying to get a deeper sleep, I need to make sure my breathing is right.

If I fall asleep without regulating my breathing, it can keep me from getting a deep sleep.

I breathe in for five as I feel the air come into my body. I breathe out again for five more as it exits.

Breathe in. One. Two. Three. Four. Five.

I hold it for a moment, feeling it spread relaxation from my chest to my fingers, and down to my toes.

I breathe out for one, two, three, four, five.

I continue to do this, each time, my breathing getting a little slower and slower. This is helping me to relax, become calm, and feel my body become air itself.

I am not someone who needs to be working right now.

I am not someone who needs to be anxious right now.

I am not someone who needs to be awake right now.

I need to go to sleep, and my breathing, and my eyes, and my mind, and everything else around me is going to help me fall asleep. I am doing exactly what needs to be done right now, and it will help me get a good night's sleep that I thoroughly deserve. I am focused on nothing but giving my body the exact thing that it needs to power me through tomorrow.

I can spend my night worrying, my sleep dreaming of the future, and my morning anxious about waking up. None of this will help me do better tomorrow, however. What

204

is going to be the most beneficial to me includes getting a good night's sleep and repowering my body for what is to come tomorrow.

I can feel my eyes getting heavier and my breathing getting slower.

There is still nothing around me, and that doesn't scare me. There is no one that is going to hurt me, and not a soul will disturb my peaceful slumber.

I am not above ground or below it. I am the air that exists everywhere. I am drifting into the nighttime sleep that everyone else is in right now. The only thing that matters is that I feel this sleep heavily.

The biggest concern I have at the moment involves falling asleep.

Even if I do not fall into a heavy slumber at first, that's fine. I am relaxing my body, giving it the rest that it needs to carry me throughout the day.

When my sleep is right, so is everything else. Even if I am getting to sleep too late, any sleep is better than none at all.

When I focus on getting deep sleep, it helps me to get the most out of my time as I lay unconscious.

I still feel my body expanding into the dark space around me, my sight getting deeper and deeper. Each time something passes in my mind, I let it drift off without giving it a second thought.

If I feel like there is something to be afraid of, I remember that is not the case. I am safe. I am focused. I am not afraid. I am not anxious. I am not stressed.

Each time something pops into my vision and wants to take my mind's energy, I push it out. Everything dissolves around me into the blackness.

That is where I am going now. Into the dark. There is no turning back for today. I will wake up tomorrow, ready and energized. As I count down from twenty, I continue to breathe in for five, and out for five.

Chapter 26. Induction Techniques To Get Self-Hypnosis

At this point in the audio, I invite you to make yourself as comfortable as possible in your bed. Please have all the light's turned off and distractions put away. You have already put in a full, hard day of work. Think of sleeping sound and comfortable through the night as a reward for working so hard.

How was your day today?

Were you productive?

How did you feel?

I want you to think about these questions as you settle further into the bed. Gently tuck yourself under the cover, and we will begin our journey. Ready?

Inhale deeply. Hold onto that breath for a moment, and then let it go. To begin, I am going to lead you through an induction script for self-hypnosis. By allowing yourself to slip into this state of mind, it will help you let go of any stress you may be holding onto, even if it is in your subconscious. I am going to help you tap into these emotions so you can let them go and sleep like you never have before.

All of us are stressed. Honestly, who can sleep when they are worried? In this state of mind, you probably feel too alert to even think about sleeping. When you are stressed, the adrenal glands in your body release adrenaline and cortisol. Both of these hormones keep you awake and stop you from falling asleep.

In the audio to follow, we will go over letting go of your worries, even if it is just for the night. You are in a safe place right now. Anything you need to get done can wait until tomorrow. It is important you take this time for yourself. We all need a break from our responsibilities at

207

some point or another. I invite you now to take another deep breath so we can focus on what is important right now; sleep.

To start, I would like you to close your eyes gently. As you do this, wiggle slightly until your body feels comfortable in your bed. When you find your most comfortable position, it is time to begin breathing.

As you focus on your breath, remind yourself to breathe slow and deep. Feel as the air fills your lungs and release it in a comfortable way. Feel as your body relaxes further under the sheets. You begin to feel a warm glow, wrapping your whole body in a comfortable blanket.

Before you let go into a deep hypnotic state, listen carefully to the words I am saying at this moment.

Everything is going to happen automatically.

At this moment, there is nothing you need to focus on. You will have no control over what happens next in our session. But you are okay with that. At this moment, you are warm and safe. You are preparing your body for a full night's rest and letting go of any thoughts you may have. There is no need to think of the future or the past. The only thing that matters right now is your comfort, your breath, and the incredible sleep you are about to experience.

Now, feel as the muscles around your eyes begin to relax. I invite you to continue breathing deeply and bring your attention to your eyes. They are beginning to feel heavy and relaxed. Your eyes worked hard for you today. They watched as you worked, they kept you safe as you walked around, and they showed other people you were paying attention to them as you spoke. Thank your eyes at this moment and allow them to rest for the night so they will be prepared for tomorrow.

Your breath is coming easy and free now. Soon, you will enter a hypnotic trance with no effort. This trance will be deep, peaceful, and safe. There is nothing for your conscious mind to do at this moment. There are no activities you need to complete. Allow for your subconscious mind to take over and do the work for you.

This trance will come automatically. Soon, you will feel like you are dreaming. Allow yourself to relax and give in to my voice. All you need to focus on is my voice.

You are doing wonderfully. Without noticing, you have already changed your rate of breath. You are breathing easy and free. There is no thought involved. Your body knows exactly what you need to do, and you can relax further into your subconscious mind.

Now, you are beginning to show signs of drifting off into this peaceful hypnotic trance. I invite you to enjoy the sensations as your subconscious mind takes over and listens to the words I am speaking to you. It is slowly becoming less important for you to listen to me. Your subconscious listens, even as I begin to whisper.

You are drifting further and further away. You are becoming more relaxed and more comfortable. At this moment, nothing is bothering you. Your inner mind is listening to me, and you are beginning to realize that you don't care about slipping into a deep trance.

This peaceful state allows you to be comfortable and relaxed. Being hypnotized is pleasant and enjoyable. This is beginning to feel natural for you. Each time I hypnotize you, it becomes more enjoyable than the time before.

You will enjoy these sensations. You are comfortable. You are peaceful. You are completely calm.

As we progress through the relaxing exercises, you will learn something new about yourself. You are working gently to develop your own sleep techniques without even knowing you are developing them in the first place.

On the count of three, you are going to slip completely into your subconscious state. When I say the number three, your brain is going to take over, and you will find yourself in the forest. This forest is peaceful, calm, and serene. It is safe and comfortable, much like your bed at this moment.

As you inhale, try to bring more oxygen into your body with nice, deep breaths. As you exhale, feel as your body relaxes more and more into the bed. Breathing comes easy and free for you. As you continue to focus on your breath, you are becoming more peaceful and calmer without even realizing it.

As we continue, you do not care how relaxed you are. You are happy in the state of mind. You do not have a care in the world. Your subconscious mind is always aware of the words I am saying to you. As we go along, it is becoming less important for you to listen to my voice.

Your inner mind is receiving everything I tell you. Your conscious mind is relaxed and peaceful. As you find your own peace of mind, we will begin to explore this forest you have found yourself in, together.

Now, I want you to imagine you are laying near a stream in this beautiful and peaceful forest. It is a sunny, warm summer day. As you lay comfortably in the grass beside this stream, you feel a warm breeze, gently moving through your hair. Inhale deep and experience how fresh and clean this air is. Inhale again and exhale. Listen carefully as the stream flows beside you. A quiet whoosh noise, filling your ears and relaxing you even further.

It is becoming less and less important for you to listen to me. Your subconscious mind takes hold and listens to everything I am saying. All you need to do is enjoy the beautiful nature around you. The sunlight shines through the trees and kisses your skin gently. The birds begin to sing a happy tune. You smile, feeling yourself become one with nature.

Each time you exhale, I want to imagine your whole body relaxing more. You are becoming more at ease. As you do this, I want you to begin to use your imagination. You are lying on the grass. It is located in a green meadow with the sun shining down on you. The sun is not hot, but a comfortable warm.

Imagine that there are beautiful flowers blooming everywhere around you. Watch as the flowers move gently in the breeze. Their scents waft toward your nose as you inhale deeply and exhale.

When you are ready, I want you to imagine that you begin to stand up. As you do this, you look over your left shoulder gently, and you see a mountain near the edge of the beautiful meadow. You decide that you would like to take a trip up to the top of the mountain to see this beautiful view from a different angle.

As you begin to walk, you follow the stream. Imagine gently bending over and placing your hand not the cool, rushing water. As you look upon the water, imagine how clean and cool this water is. The stream flows gently across your fingers and it relaxes you.

When you are ready, we will head toward the mountain again. As you grow closer to the mountain, the birds begin to chirp. Inhale deep and imagine how the pine trees smell around you. Soon, you begin to climb the mountain at a comfortable pace.

You are enjoying the trip. It is wonderful to be outside with this beautiful nature, taking in all the sights and sounds. Now, you are already halfway up the mountain.

The meadow grows smaller as you climb higher, but you are not afraid. The scene is beautiful from up here, and you are happy at this moment.

As you reach the top, take a deep breath and give yourself a pat on the back for your accomplishment. Take a look down on the meadow and see how small the trees look.

The breeze is blowing your hair around gently, and the sun continues to shine down on the top of your head. Imagine that you are taking a seat at the very top of the mountain. You close your eyes in your mind's eye and take a few moments to appreciate this nature. You wish you could always be this relaxed.

When you take your life into your own hands, you will be able to. This is why we are here. Of course, you may be here because you want to sleep, but you can't do that truly unless you learn how to let go of your stress. Through guided meditation and exercises within this audio, you will learn how to become a better version of yourself. I am here to help you every step of the way.

Soon, we will work on deepening your trance. You are beginning to relax further into the meditation and are opening your heart and soul to the practice. Remember that you are safe, and you are happy to be here.

Chapter 27. Deep Sleep Hypnosis Script

Welcome.

This is going to be a thirty-minute guided hypnosis session to help you drift off into a deep and relaxing sleep. The most important thing to do while listening to this session is to keep an open mind. You must go with the flow, listen to my voice, and remember to breathe. Remember, it is not always possible to enter a light hypnotic state on the first try, but we are going to try as I guide you gently and smoothly into this state so you can fall asleep. Please bear in mind that you are not going to enter any sort of deep catatonic state. Nothing is going to be physically altered within the realm of your mind. The process of hypnosis and this guided meditation is extremely safe, and you are in control of it.

Now, I want you to get comfortable. Because you are trying to achieve a deep sleep, you should be lying down, your head resting on your most comfortable pillow and you are warmed by your softest blanket. Lie back and let your shoulders go slack, relaxing against the cushion of your bed. Gently close your eyes and release all the tension from your muscles. Release the tension in your arms, then your legs. Let go of the tension in your chest and in your back. All of the muscles in your body begin to feel looser and looser and your body is feeling light.

Recognize that this is a time for only you. You have set aside all of your day's activities and are now ready to fully embrace a beautiful and peaceful sleep. Breathe in this moment of relaxation, where nothing else matters. There is only you in the warmth of your bed.

As you lay, I will ask you something very simple. In your mind's eye, imagination a kind of ruler or some sort of measuring device. Imagine something which can measure the depth of your own relaxation. Imagine this ruler in the front of your mind. Perhaps it is your favorite color, smooth with small painted tick marks and numbers.

Take a moment to notice where you are on your current level of relaxation. Out of a scale of 100 down to 0 being your most relaxed state. Understand that there is no right or wrong measurement to begin with. Explore your state, be honest with yourself as you measure your relaxation. What tensions do you still have left in your body? What anxieties, sadness, or pain still lingers? Very soon you are going to increase your relaxation and melt away this negativity and drift off into a peaceful sleep.

Perhaps are currently at a 60 on your scale of relaxation. Even though you may actually be lower down than that, imagine yourself moving the marker in front of you. With each deep breath, you slide the marker further down along this ruler closer and closer towards zero, towards immense relaxation. As you breathe and the marker slides down, you feel your muscles release in your arms then your legs, your back relaxes, and your chest opens like a flower, welcoming in big and tranquil breaths.

You may be aware that your sense of relaxation has expanded inside of you. Perhaps all the way down to 40 or 30. You see the marker slowly glide downwards along the scale. You feel that a wave of warmth has washed over you and you are beginning to feel your whole body becoming engulfed in the warmth of peace. As you feel your body releasing its tension even more now, you feel calmer. You have now reached a ten on your scale and gently, you take a deep breath through your nose. Let it fill your stomach until it is like to burst. Then release it.

You reach nine...You enter a peaceful, calm environment. You reach eight...You can feel the warmth of the sun on your face. It is a reminder that you are loved.

You reach seven...Each sound that you hear, you do not deny. Instead it lulls you further and deeper into a deep state of relaxation.

You reach six...You inhale through your nose and fill your belly. You inhale all of the good things the world has to offer.

You reach five...Gently, through your nose, you release your breath. You expel any negative feelings that remain.

You reach four...You feel your body becoming lighter. Your arms and legs feel weightless and free.

You reach three...You feel your chest brimming with warmth and light.

You reach two... You accept the peace that has enveloped you. This peace welcomes you into a deepening serenity as your mind quiets.

You reach one... You feel yourself drawn towards the warmth of peaceful sleep, so close you can almost graze it with your fingertips.

You reach zero... You feel a comfort deep within you that starts in your chest and radiates outwards like a blooming flower. This comfort fills you with security and you remember that you are safe. You have released your worries and concerns, and in its place, there is warmth, light, and comfort.

Gently you are lulled by this wave of serenity. You feel yourself beginning to drift beyond zero, into a realm of warm colors. Billows of reds and pinks, yellows and oranges undulate around you in soft embraces until you float down onto a plush, cool surface.

With only your fingertips, you detect that you have landed on a grassy field. Around you, you can smell the sweet fragrance of wildflowers that have populated this clearing. Your body and mind have quieted to listen to the soft rustle of the breeze through grass and flower petals, and you remember the beauty of the earth. You breathe in through your nose a deep breath that fills your stomach. Through your nose, you slowly release it.

You recognize the warm colors from before, now painted in the sky. The reds fade into pinks seamlessly as though crafted by a painter's brush. The hues swirl into the setting sun and exude a warmth that you feel throughout your body. You are existing in this space with only beauty. You are existing without concern for time or worry. There is only you in this space and all of the tranquility it shares with you.

The pinks give way to magentas, then onto violets and dark blues. The sun sets and reveals an endless sky, sprinkled with thousands of twinkling stars. You see dustings of silver and purple in the sky. The bright sliver of moon casts its beam upon you, cascading you in comfort.

Your muscles seem to melt, going slack and welcoming sleep. The stars above you dance, twirling through the vast stretch of sky, but you are still. You allow this positive energy to enter your mind. It swells within you until you feel peace exuding from every pore. You have reached a depth of serenity that exists on the brink of sleep. Allow yourself to accept rest.

Underneath the moon, you accept rest. Soon, you begin to notice a new pleasing sensation that arrives at your arms and spreads to your legs and your back, your neck, and forehead. You recognize this sensation as a sublime floating energy entering your body. You feel a delicate tingle throughout your body, ushering in lightness and calmness. This sensation is like a soft white linen, cleansing you from the inside out. It is a warm touch of healing energy, of love and passion.

These soft vibrations rid you of tension. Anxieties are expelled. Sadness and fear no longer exist here. All of the leftover stress is now dissolving entirely, turning into dust carried off by the wind. It is melting away under the power of this healing energy. In its place there is safety and the knowledge that you are loved by whom you love. It is merely you, the stars, and the moon.

The lightness you feel swells, as if tiny balloons are attached to different parts of your body. You feel your body beginning to rise and drift upwards in the direction of the stars. Peacefulness and serenity are lifting you higher into the air into the welcoming embrace of the expansive night sky. For a brief moment you understand that you exist in the space between the earth and the sky, a realm that belongs to you and is safe from anxiety. You claim this realm as yours in which to dream. This is your dreamscape, where you float towards rest and sleep. Your realm is one of peace that connects the heavens with the ground. It is yours alone to govern, to allow only positive energy and love. You roam over the tops of trees, drift across the width of lakes, and coast above others, sleeping in their warm beds.

Your entire body now is floating higher and higher in this realm as you feel such elation inside as you realize you are now gliding through all of space. You are drifting and roaming here, no longer bound by gravity. You are now soaring like a hot air balloon, ascending higher and moving towards infinity of this welcoming expands. As

217

you float you are letting go of everything that you no longer need. You toss away unwanted negativity. You hold on to the comfort that peace grants you.

Your entire body now is floating higher and higher in this realm as you feel such elation inside as you realize you are now gliding through all of space. You are drifting and roaming here, no longer bound by gravity. You are now soaring like a hot air balloon, ascending higher and moving towards infinity of this welcoming expands. As you float you are letting go of everything you no longer need. You toss away unwanted negativity. You hold on to the comfort that peace grants you. As you become just like the pure brilliance of the stars, a beautiful shining light, you feel your spirit break free and finally you are able to float out through the entire universe. You reach out further and further into the purest wisdoms, and the most loving embraces of all of the celestial beings that surround you. They are calling you to rest, to dream, to sleep, to heal. You feel yourself realigning from within.

You feel yourself moving with tranquility and mindfulness, further and further. As you wade through the stars, you feel yourself gently feeling heavier. You understand that you are drifting towards rest.

You drift through the cosmos, feeling gravity's kind tug towards the ground. Gently you float towards the earth like a leaf falls from a tree, eager to meet its rest on the ground below. You feel completely relaxed and slipping away into a restful sleep. Before you escape into your dreams, you return to your bed where you are warm and protected. Your body softly nestles under the blankets and your head snuggles into the pillow. You notice your arms and legs still feel weightless and there is a residual warm vibration throughout, a pulsing that beseeches sleep. You happily oblige.

218

I am going to count down from five. When I reach one, you are going to fully embrace the peace that has engulfed you and lose yourself in sleep. You will feel yourself slipping into a calm and serene rest.

Five... You think of the night sky and its expansiveness. It melts away every remaining tension until your body and mind are relaxed. It is summoning your sleep.

Four... You feel the warmth of peace move from the top of your head and down your neck. It moves through your shoulders, radiates through your chest and stomach, and finally glazes over your legs.

Three... You feel your body become heavy and you softly sink in a little deeper to your consciousness. You are safe and protected.

Two... You feel yourself drift away, like a leaf on a still pond. You float away, quietly into the night.

One... You are now asleep, resting and at peace.

Breathe in, Breathe out. Breathe in, Breathe out. When you wake, you will be refreshed and ready to take on the day. You will be ready to conquer the stresses of your life now that you have conquered sleep.

Chapter 28. Relaxation And Stress Scripts

Now that you are completely relaxed, I want you to take note of how you are feeling as a whole. How are you doing at this moment? How does your body feel?

Take a few moments and scan your body. There is no need to judge yourself right now. All I want you to do is notice is how your body is feeling from your head to your toes.

Scan through your body from your feet...to your ankles...all the way up your legs...and into your hips. At your own pace, scan your body through your stomach, chest, hands, shoulders, neck, head, and face.

We worked on relaxing before to help deepen into your practice, but you may notice certain areas where you are still tense. You have noted where you are stressed. Now, gently take note of where your body is most relaxed.

As you focus on your body, notice how it begins to relax with no conscious effort. As you scan your body, feel as the muscles become looser and less tense on their own. All you need to do is lay quiet and remain relaxed. You feel happy that this is happening naturally. With each passing moment, your body falls more relaxed, even more, ready to fall asleep.

Now that you are feeling more relaxed, I want to talk about your body image. Many of us move through the day, uncomfortable, simply because we are not happy with our self and the way we look. But what is body image? Are you thinking about what your body looks like? Perhaps you are thinking about the ideas you have about your body. How are you feeling about your physical self at this moment? What does body image mean to you?

Inhale...and exhale...

As you continue to focus on your breath, I invite you to take a few moments to consider the thoughts and ideas you have about your body. How do these thoughts make you feel as you scan over your own body image? For some, you may feel comfortable and content. For others, you are unhappy, unaccepting, or dissatisfied. Perhaps, there is a combination depending on how kind you are to yourself. However, you feel, accept the emotions you are feeling at this moment.

Stay with me for a moment. I invite you to ponder how it would feel to accept your body the way it is? How would it feel to be okay with your physical self? Take a few moments now to breathe, and picture in detail how this would feel.

Breathe in...and breathe out...wonderful.

Now, try to think of a moment in your life when you accepted your physical self. Whether it be your whole self or a part of your self that you really enjoy, think of a moment.

Which part of your body do you accept?

Imagine now, how it would feel to accept your whole body as opposed to thinking of yourself as a collection of separate parts. If you are beginning to feel stressed out over these thoughts, allow us to take a few steps back to return to relaxation.

Notice certain parts tensing up at this moment. Make a note of these locations and focus positive energy to return these body parts to total relaxation. Inhale...and exhale...you are safe and loved at this moment. You are calm and relaxed...inhale...and exhale...

When you have returned to a state of total relaxation and calmness, I invite you to repeat the following body image affirmations after me. If you don't feel like repeating these, try to listen and relax as I speak. As you work on a positive body image, you may feel yourself less stressed through the day. When we love ourselves, it grants us the ability to spread that love to others. Perhaps if you loved yourself more, you would take the time to release stress and enjoy a peaceful night's rest. Who knows, perhaps your body image has been bringing you down more than you ever imagined.

When you are ready, repeat after me. Each affirmation I am about to say is completely true. Even if you don't believe it, you will work through your negative thoughts until you believe them to be so. Let's begin.

I am perfect the way I am.

(Pause)

I choose to accept the way I am.

(Pause)

My body is acceptable the way it is at this moment.

(Pause)

I choose to accept the body I am in.

(Pause)

I am a wonderful person as a whole.

(Pause)

There is no reason to be perfect.

(Pause)

I have imperfections, and that is okay.

(Pause)

I love the person that I am.

(Pause)

I am human, and I have flaws.

(Pause)

I choose to accept these flaws.

(Pause)

I will stop judging my body.

(Pause)

I am in love with who I am.

(Pause)

I choose to accept myself.

(Pause)

I love myself so that I can love others.

Wonderful. Feel free to repeat these affirmations as often as you need. Now that we have gone through some, how are you feeling? Whatever you are feeling at this moment is perfectly acceptable. Perhaps you believe every word I have told you, and perhaps you don't. As you practice positive body image more, you may find yourself becoming less stressed and much happier.

Take a few moments now to return to relaxing. Any tension or stress you may have after thinking about your body can be let go with each breath you take. Remember what I taught you about deep breathing. I want you to continue to breathe deep and natural. Ready?

Inhale...one and two...and three...and four...and (pause) one...two...three...and exhale...two...three...four...five...

Inhale...one and two...and three...and four...and (pause) one...two...three...and exhale...two...three...four...five...

Inhale...one and two...and three...and four...and (pause) one...two...three...and exhale...two...three...four...five...

Inhale...one and two...and three...and four...and (pause) one...two...three...and exhale...two...three...four...five...

Inhale...one and two...and three...and four...and (pause) one...two...three...and exhale...two...three...four...five...

You are doing a wonderful job. Now that we have gone over the emotions of your body image, I would like to go over a progressive muscle relaxation exercise to help your body heal itself. This is a vital exercise to help you get the most out of the sleep you are soon to slip into. When your body is relaxed and comfortable, you will sleep deeper and wake up feeling more refreshed.

As you continue to focus on your breath, I invite you first to release the tension from the bottom of your feet. Imagine how it would feel to step into a nice, warm bathtub. How does this sensation feel to you? Does the warm water tingle? Feel as your feet fall loose and imagine this feeling of total relaxation washing from your feet and up into your ankles.

This sensation rises gently over your ankles and flows up your lower legs until it begins to kiss your knees gently. At this point, you allow the sensation of relaxation spread through your whole body. It rises around your hips and through your pelvic areas.

You gently give into the sensation as it washes over your stomach, hugs around your lower back and continues to

224

rise over your chest. As this happens, relax your upper arms, lower arms, and wrist. The sensation flows over the palms of your hands. Imagine the sensation flowing to each finger. Your hands feel pleasant, relaxed, and warm.

Bring your focus back to your breath, and the relaxation spreads through your collar bones, across your shoulders and washes down your entire back again. Sink into the bed further and take a deep, cleansing breath in...and let it go slowly.

Now, allow the sensation up even further as it spreads across your chin, through your mouth, your cheeks, it gently caresses your nose and up to your eyes. At this point, your eyelids feel peaceful and heavy with relaxation.

Allow the relaxation to wash over the top of your head. Feel your eyebrows relaxing. Your forehead is smooth and cool. The relaxation has washed over your whole body, and you can feel it flowing from your head to your feet.

You are completely relaxed now. Feel as this sensation flows down your spine. It starts at the top, down your neck, into your upper back...middle back...lower back...and gently makes it way down your tailbone in the very bottom of your spine. Feel as every muscle relaxes around your spine. Breathing is coming so easily and naturally for you; you aren't even thinking about it.

As you continue to breathe, complete another body scan. Are there any areas of tension left? If so, direct the flow of relaxation into that area. This energy has the ability to lift and carry the tension away. Imagine the air you are breathing as the energy to cleanse your body. Each time you breathe in, picture the tension leaving your body every time you breathe out.

When you are ready, I want you to create an image in your head. I want you to picture your current state of being. Are there any physical ailments that have been bothering you? Perhaps you have an injury, an illness, or just overall pain you have been dealing with. It does not matter if this is something that has been diagnosed just yet. Whatever the problem is, imagine this problem in your mind, and we will work on healing it through this guided meditation.

With this specific location in mind, I want you to picture this area being dark. Truly picture this area in detail. What does it look like? How does it feel? Create a clear mental image in your mind, and we will begin.

Now, picture healing relaxation as light. Imagine this light flowing through your whole body, and then direct the light toward the dark area. When we put forth the effort, our body has a wonderful way of healing itself.

This healing light has the ability to promote strength, it can support your immune system, and promotes the growth of healthy tissue in our body. This healing light can also clean your body and help you to remove any waste, bacteria, or toxins that are hanging out in you. It also has the ability to remove any unhealthy matter from your body so that you can be the healthiest version of yourself.

As you picture the light moving through you, imagine that it begins to swirl and focus on the dark area. Notice how small pieces of this area begin to be carried away by the light. Notice this and allow the dark pieces to leave your body. Gently breathe in the healing energy and breathe out any tension or illness you have been holding onto.

You have the power to allow this light to heal the problem areas you have in your body. Imagine the dark area in your body become completely enveloped by the healing light. Slowly, the dark area becomes lighter and lighter. Your immune system is working hard to heal you, and the light travels to any area you truly need it in.

Now, the healing light courses through your whole body. It fills you with complete health and relaxation. Any problem areas in your body, the light seeks and makes healthy again. It is carrying away your discomfort and healing you to the best version of yourself.

Allow this to happen. Continue to take cleansing breaths in and breathe out any negative matter you have been holding onto.

Breathe in total relaxation...and breathe out the old...

Now, I invite you to take a few moments to relax and enjoy this healing process. Feel as your confidence begins to grow now that you have worked on improving your body image and healing your body. You feel as your body grows more relaxed and readier to fall into a restful night's sleep. You feel wonderful, happy, and completely stress-free.

You are doing wonderfully. In a few moments, we will be moving onto exercises so you can fall asleep. Before we get there, I want you to turn your focus inward. Take a deep, truthful look inside to find your authentic self.

As you do this, begin to reflect on your values. What is important to you? What do you value most in life? Why is it that you chose this audio to help release stress so that you can sleep better at night? For the next few moments, I invite you to focus on your breath and ask yourself these very important questions.

(Pause)

Breathe in...breathe out...

These values you have been thinking about are a major part of what makes you who you are. If you are being true to your core values, these beliefs are what drive your behavior. When you live true to your values, you will be much happier.

I now invite you to think of your values and think how you can incorporate them into your day-to-day life. When you are ready, I want you to now think of what else makes you the person that you are.

When we find out authentic self, this gives us the ability to learn who we really are. Our authentic selves are the person we are meant to be. When we try to be who we are not, this can hold you back and create a lot of stress.

If you are telling yourself that you are not being your authentic self, I want you to imagine the type of person you want to be. Take a deep breath and imagine observing yourself. How are you acting? Is this the person you are or who you want to be?

Now, I want you to picture yourself standing in an empty room. Imagine that you are stripping away everything that is holding you back from your true potential. Your self-doubt begins to dissolve, and, in its place, confidence takes over. This person you are picturing lets go of anything that stands between you and success. You let go of illness, baggage from the past, and lack of resources. When you are your authentic self, there is nothing to stand in between you and your goals. Watch as all of these problems disappear and go away for good.

What is left when you strip all of these problems away? This person is who you are at the core. All of your character traits and personality makes you who you are, and that is all you can ask of yourself. You work hard.

228

You are a committed person. You are in love with your life.

We all have issues to work through, what is important is that you work on them every day. There is always room for improvement, and that is why you are here. You are letting go of the stress, finding yourself, and learning how to become the best version of yourself.

With all of these positive changes you have made in just one night, it is time to put your mind to rest. You have done a wonderful job of working on your well-being. At this moment, you are feeling calm and relaxed. You have let go of your worries, explored your true self, and found your authentic core. When you are ready, take a deep breath in and let it go.

At this moment, you should feel completely calm and at peace. Your body begins to gently tell you that it is time to fall asleep. In the next few moments, we will begin to place your mind and soul at rest. You will sleep peacefully and deep through the night. In the morning, you will awaken feeling calm and well rested at the time you need to wake up.

When you fall asleep, you will automatically fall out of your trance. Your subconscious will do all of the work for you. All you need to do right now is focus on your breath and allow yourself to fall asleep for the night.

Chapter 29. Positive Affirmations For Better Sleep

An affirmation is an affirming statement that you make to yourself in order to reiterate the importance of an idea. Throughout the day, you might think of negative affirmations that validate your perspective. These can include things like, "I'm not good enough," or "Nothing is going right in my life." These statements aren't necessarily the whole truth, but they might have a certain element that can help solidify one perspective.

These affirmations are going to help you focus on what's most important and remember the ideas needed in order to get your best night's sleep possible. Repeat these back to yourself, write them down and make notes around your home, or simply remember them in your mind when you need them the most.

Affirmations For Falling And Staying Asleep

The best way to include these affirmations in your life is to repeat them daily. They will help retrain your brain to think more positively rather than the negative ways that you might be thinking now.

In order to reiterate the importance of affirmations, including physical activity can help you to remember them even more. When you integrate a physical exercise with a mental thought, it helps make it more real. It will be easier to accept these affirmations in your life when an emphasis is put on truly believing them.

The first movement that you can do in order to remember these exercises is to physically hold an item. It can be something as small as a stone that you keep in your pocket, or you can pick out a special pillow or blanket that you choose to use with each affirmation.

As you are saying these affirmations, physically touch and hold these items. Let it remind you of reality. Stay focused and grounded on remembering the most important aspects of these affirmations.

Alternatively, try implementing new breathing exercises that we haven't tried yet. The method of breathing in through your nose and out through your mouth is important, but as we go further, there are other ways that you can include healthy breathing with these positive sleep affirmations.

One method is by breathing through alternate nostrils. Make a fist with your right hand with your thumb and pinky sticking out. Take your pinky and place it on your left nostril, closing it so that you can only breathe through one.

Now, breathing for five counts through that nostril.

Then, take your right thumb, and place it on your right nostril, closing that and releasing your pinky from the other nostril. Now, breathe out for five.

You will notice that doing this breathing exercise on its own is enough to help you be more relaxed. Now, when you pair it with the affirmation that we're about to read aloud, you will start to put more of an emphasis on creating thinking patterns around these affirmations.

An alternate method of breathing is to breathe in for three counts, say the affirmation, and then breathe out for three counts. You can do this on your own with the affirmations that are most important to your life.

It will be beneficial for you to have a journal that you keep affirmations in as well. Have one handy to write these affirmations down as they apply to your life. Writing about them will help you remember them and keep a note of the things that are most effective in your life.

When you are having a bad day, you can visit these affirmations. When you need a little confidence booster, or some motivation, use these affirmations.

We will now get into the reading of these. Remember to focus on your breathing as we take you through these, and if you are not planning on drifting off to sleep once they have finished, taking notes can help as well.

Healthy Sleep Dedication

1. I am dedicated to making healthy choices for my sleeping habits.

2. The things that I do throughout my day will affect how I sleep; therefore, I am going to make sure to focus on making the best choices for all aspects of my health.

3. I will do things that aren't always easy because it will be in the best interest of my health overall.

4. When I am well-rested, everything else in my life become easier.

5. I am more focused when I have slept an entire night, so I know that falling asleep is incredibly important to my health.

6. Developing healthy habits is easy when I dedicate my time towards a better future.

7. It feels good to take care of myself.

8. I deserve a good night's sleep; therefore, I deserve everything else that will come along with this benefit.

9. I am naturally supposed to get rest. It is not wrong for me to be tired and to choose to do healthy things for my sleep cycles.

10. Dreams are normal, and I am focused on embracing them and avoiding nightmares.

11. I choose to go to bed at a decent time at night because it is best for my health.

12. Whatever is waiting for me tomorrow will still be there whether I get a full night's sleep or not, so it is best to ensure I am getting the proper amount of rest.

13. I take care of my body because I know that it is the only one that I will ever have.

14. I allow discipline in my life to guide me in the right direction to make the choices that are healthiest for my individual and specific lifestyle.

15. I nourish my body and make sure I get the right amount of nutrients to keep me energized throughout the day.

16. I am strong because I get the right amount of sleep.

17. Getting the right kind of sleep is good for my mental health.

18. I am happier when I am well-rested. I am in a better mood and can laugh more easily when I have had a good night's sleep.

19. I am grateful for my opportunity to be healthier and to get better sleep.

20. I am thankful that I have the ability to make the right choices for my health and overall well-being.

21. Having habits is not a bad thing, I just need to make sure that my habits are healthy ones.

22. I am less stressed out when I am able to get a better night's sleep.

23. I am the best version of myself when I am healthy. I am healthiest when I am well-rested and focused on getting a better night's sleep.

24. Everything else in my life will fall into place as I focus on getting the best night's sleep possible.

25. I love myself, therefore I am going to put an emphasis on dedication to better sleeping habits so that I can feel better all the time.

Relaxing

1. I am feeling relaxed.

2. Relaxation is a feeling I can elicit, not a state that I have to be in depending on certain restrictions.

3. I can feel the relaxation in my mind first and foremost.

4. As I feel my body becoming relaxed, I can feel that serenity pass through the upper half of my body.

5. All of the tension that I might have built throughout the day is now starting to fade away.

6. I am focused on myself and centered within my body.

7. I can tell that my muscles are becoming more and more relaxed.

8. There is nothing that is concerning me at the moment.

9. There will always be stressors in my life, but right now, I do not have to worry about any of those.

10. As I focus on being calmer, it is easier for my mind to relax.

11. I do not have to be afraid of what happened in the past.

12. I cannot change the things that are already written in history.

13. I don't need to be fearful of the future.

14. I can make assumptions, but my predictions will not always be accurate.

15. I can focus on the now, which is the most important thing to do.

16. As I start to draw my attention to the present moment, I find it easier to relax.

17. The more relaxed I am, the easier it will be for me to fall asleep.

18. The faster I fall asleep, the more rest that I can get.

19. I have no concern over what is going on around me. The only thing I am concerned with is being relaxed in the present moment.

20. I exude relaxation and peace. Others will notice how quiet, calm, and collected I can be.

21. I am balanced in my stress and pleasure aspects, meaning that I have less anxiety.

22. I am not afraid of being stressed.

23. Stress helps me remember what is most important in my life.

24. Stress keeps me focused on my goals.

25. I do not let this stress consume me.

26. I manage my stress in healthy and productive ways.

27. I have the main control over the stress that I feel. No one else is in charge of my feelings.

28. It is normal for me to be peaceful.

29. I allow this lifestyle to take over every aspect, making it easier to have a more relaxed sleep.

30. When I can truly calm myself down all the way, it will be easier to stay asleep.

31. I let go of my anxiety because it serves me no purpose.

32. I am excited for the future.

33. I am not afraid of any of the challenges that I might face.

34. It is easy for me to be more and more relaxed.

35. There is nothing more freeing than realizing that I do not have to be anxious over certain aspects in my life.

36. I will sleep easier and more peacefully knowing that there is nothing in this world that I need to be afraid of.

37. Staying Asleep

38. Nothing feels better than crawling into my bed after a long day.

39. My bedroom is filled with peace and serenity. I have no trouble drifting off to sleep.

40. Everything in my room helps me to be more relaxed.

41. I feel safe and at peace knowing that I am protected in my room.

42. I have no trouble falling asleep once I am able to close my eyes and focus on my breathing.

43. I make sure all of my anxieties are gone so that I can fall asleep easier.

44. When bad thoughts come into my head, I know how to push them away so that I can focus instead on getting a better night's sleep.

45. I am centered on reality, which involves getting the best sleep possible.

46. It is so refreshing to wake up after a night of rest that was uninterrupted.

47. Any time that I might wake up, I have no trouble knowing how to get myself back to sleep.

48. Whenever I wake up, it is easy to get out of bed within the first few times that my alarm clock rings.

49. The better night's sleep I get, the easier it is for me to wake up.

50. I release all of the times that I have had a restless night's sleep.

51. No matter how many times I have struggled with my sleep in the past, I know that I am capable of getting the best night's sleep possible.

52. My sleep history doesn't matter now. I want to get a good night's sleep, so I will.

53. The more I focus on falling and staying asleep, the fresher I will feel in the morning.

54. Getting a good night's sleep helps me look better as well. My hair is bouncier, my face is fresher, my eyes are wider, and my smile is bigger.

55. Sleep is something that I need.

56. Sleep is something that I deserve.

57. No matter how little work I got done in a day, or how much more I might have to do the next day, I need to get sleep.

58. There is no point in my life where sleep would be entirely bad for me. It's like drinking water. I could always at least use a little bit of it.

59. I am alert when I am focused on sleeping better.

60. It is easier to remember the important things I need to keep stored in my memory when I have been able to have a full night's sleep.

61. I can focus on what is going on around me more when I have been able to sleep through the night.

62. There is nothing about getting sleep that is bad for me. As long as I am doing it in a healthy way, it will improve my life.

63. I know how to cut out bad sleeping habits.

64. I understand what is important to start doing to get a better sleep.

65. As soon as I start to lay down, I am focused on drifting away.

66. I do not let anxious thoughts keep me awake anymore.

67. I will sleep healthy from here on out because I know that it is one of the most important decisions for my health that I can make.

Conclusion

You have learned a lot of things in this guide. You know how to release your anxiety, how to lose weight, how to meditate properly, what the most efficient affirmations are. You can do miracles if you use these techniques properly.

Experiencing weight loss success

I wish you a wonderful experience on your way to losing weight!

But pay attention not to overcompensate and not to create another addiction: undereating instead of overeating. Bonnie has fallen into this trap, but as soon as she understood the very root of her problems, she could find her own correct way. Now she is healthy, 54 kilos (119 lbs.) and she has been maintaining her weight for five years. She is married to a smart, generous, loving man. Her husband is not Tony, but her true love! Tony was a wonderful and useful story in her life. Without him, she would have probably never learned to see and appreciate her own real value.

Hypnosis and meditation will not only help you in weight loss but will guarantee your general wellbeing.
One of the good things about meditation is that you can practice it anywhere and at any time you find convenient. You can also do it at no extra cost. This is a good way to rejuvenate your mind and to focus on the things that matter. It also ensures that you improve your performance levels on the activities that you chose to undertake. With the poor eating decisions that we are making nowadays, we are having increased cases of lifestyle diseases. Obesity is now a huge challenge among the majority of individuals. It is about time that we step up and make better and more informed decisions

regarding our lives. Some of these decisions include changing our eating habits and ensuring that we take good care of our health. Meditation helps us to maintain discipline in that which we do. It ensures that we stay focused on the plans and decisions that we have chosen to make. With the right attitude, meditation can transform your weight loss journey.

If you wish to lose weight or maintain a healthy body, you can begin your meditation journey. It is an easy process that you can easily follow up as long as you are determined. All you need to do is decide to start. The journey of a thousand miles begins with a single step. At times you have to go past tapping the waters and get in it completely. In the beginning, you might find it challenging to do so, but it's the encouragement that you keep giving yourself that will ensure you manage to utilize meditation in your weight loss journey successfully.

Experiencing deep sleep and relaxation

Sleep is something that we need, and there are healthy and natural ways that you can better find the habits needed to improve your overall sleep cycles. Like any other habit, hypnosis and meditation is something that should be consistently practiced to get the best results.

Ensure that other parts of your life are healthy and balanced as well, as this will help play into how much healthy sleep you might be able to get. Check out other meditation books on similar topics, and more specific issues as well, in order to keep your entire mind, body, and soul cleansed and healthy.

Take a few moments to notice how heavy your eyelids are. As you continue to breathe gently, they become heavier and heavier. It feels wonderful to rest your eyes as they remain relaxed and closed. All of the tension you had earlier has left and drifted away without a care in the world. Each breath you take allows the tension to slip through your fingers and your toes. All that you have left at this moment is total relaxation.

Now, allow your mind to drift away. There is no need to focus or think in these final moments before you drift off to sleep. Your mind is relaxed. Your body is relaxed. Your whole body feels warm, soft, and totally relaxed.

So, thank you for reading. I hope you enjoyed this book and found it helpful. Now your journey starts! Always remember to love your body and your soul, because this is the only way to harmonize them.

POSITIVE THINKING AFFIRMATIONS

AND

GUIDED MEDITATIONS FOR ANXIETY

LEARN HOW TO ATTRACT SUCCESS, MONEY AND PROSPERITY.

MANAGE YOUR EMOTIONS, FIND THE STRESS SOLUTION, STOP WORRYING AND OVERTHINKING

Awakening Transformation Academy

PART 1: POSITIVE THINKING AFFIRMATIONS

LEARN HOW TO ATTRACT SUCCESS, MONEY AND PROSPERITY

Positive thinking affirmations: introduction

Positive thinking can transform your life. Learning strategies to change the way you view situations and people can help you to look on the bright side. As you begin to look towards positive things and release the negative thought patterns, you will see that you are happier and better able to accept when bad things happen in life.

Positive thinking can completely reshape and reform the life that you live. Allowing yourself to embrace the positive will bring about change that we could not even have imagined.

Positive thinking can be the fuel in the tank that propels individuals on to reach heights greater than anyone else ever thought possible. Someone who believes in themselves and is not afraid to reach for the things they want in life, no matter how big their goals may be, will have an infinitely better chance of success then someone who does not believe in themselves. Negative thinking on the other hand can be the barrier that prevents otherwise capable people from achieving the things they want in life. It can be the prison that confines you, separating you from your goals that may be so close and yet seem so far away.

Positive thinking is based on certain ideas and perceptions that we have about ourselves and our abilities. The importance of each different factor (or "building block") varies a little bit from one individual to another, but for virtually all of us the factors that most significantly influence our natural daily thoughts include some combination of: the activities one participates in, the friendships and relationships a person has with others, a person's state of mental health, a person's state of physical health, and how a person understands the perception that other people have of him or her. Extensive research has shown that these are the most important factors in determining one's level of positive thinking, which means that a big part of building positive thinking is creating and following a plan to improve each of these factors. We'll go through these factors one by one and discuss how you can make positive changes in each area that will increase your positive thinking.

Thinking positively is influenced by the way you feel about your day to day activities. Note that the activities themselves tend to be less important than how one feels about them. There are plenty of wealthy and outwardly successful people (many working in law firms, accounting firms, and investment banks) who feel miserable and unfulfilled by the work they do and they pay a price in the form of scathing and intractable negative self-talk

They can also help you improve your behaviors and reach your goals.

More importantly, they can help you undo the damages caused by negative scripts, which you repeatedly tell yourself and cause you to have a negative self-perception.

Chapter 1. Positive Thinking and the Law of Attraction

Ever wondered why the whole world seems so crappy when you are feeling down? It feels like everybody is being mean to you for no reason. Similarly, when you're feeling great, everything around you feels amazingly friendly and warm. It feels like nothing in the world can bring you down. You're in the, "oh yes you can go ahead if you are in a hurry" nice person mode. Here's a reality check – the world is the same on all days, your attitude makes the difference.

What is the Law of Attraction?

The Law of Attraction is a theory popularized by Rhonda Byrne's book The Secret, published in 2006. The essence of it is, we actually bring about or create what we think. It is based on the powerful principle that we have the ability to attract anything we desire into our reality simply by visualizing those desired goals, using visualization techniques, positive affirmations, showing appreciation, and directing inspired action.

The law of attraction when combined with quantum physics states that we are all functioning as tiny particles within a large Universe that is directly responding to our thoughts with a corresponding frequency to create our reality.

The Universe is reacting to your thoughts with a matching frequency to manifest your dreams. It simply means that whether we are actually aware of it or not, the Universe is responding to our positive and negative thoughts to create our reality. This means we are responsible for inviting both positive and negative circumstances in our life.

One of the most crucial aspects of using the Law of Attraction is placing your focus on what you want rather than what you do not want. What you think about has a direct impact on how your life actually unfolds.

The most powerful thing about the Law of Attraction is that it puts the power of your life in your hand. You operate the remote control of your life to experience the life of your dreams. When you find yourself being held down by negative or self limiting thoughts, all you need to do is flip channels to something more positive. Thus, the Law of Attraction gives you the freedom to determine the course of your life through the power of your thoughts. Your destiny can be shaped based on how you choose to visualize it.

Ever wondered why people who always operate from a 'lack of' point of view seldom seem to live a desirable and fulfilled life? Their thoughts are forever functioning with a sense of scarcity, which leads to even greater scarcity. Remember, the universe cannot distinguish between the good and the bad. It doesn't know what you want or what you do not want. On a quantum physics level, it is simply responding to your thoughts with a matching frequency to manifest what you are thinking.

If you are consumed by thoughts of how you never have enough money to pay your bills, travel and enjoy the good things in life, you are only attracting more of no money to pay bills, travel or enjoy the good things in life. This will again lead you to think about your haplessness, which again manifests more of it. You see what is happening here? It is a vicious cycle. Until we break free from negative thoughts and replace them with more positive thoughts, we really cannot lead a life of our dreams.

Now that you understand the Law of Attraction, how can you apply it in everyday life to transform your destiny? Here are some quick and fabulously effective tips.

Clarify Your Goals

If there's one single tip to achieve the most out of the Law of Attraction, it is to keep your goals highly specific. Make them as detailed and precise as you can. Don't simply write you want to start a popular blog and earn money from it in the next six months. Be clear. How many readers do you want your blog to reach in six months? What is the revenue you desire to earn in the next six months from the blog? How many Twitter, Instagram and Facebook followers do you wish to earn in the next six months?

Replace your goals with the description of your outfit, and the sales assistant with the Universe. When you describe exactly what you want, it becomes easier for the Universe to give it to you. Similarly, when you are vague about your goals like, "I want to be rich soon", the Universe is unclear about the message, and responds with equal vagueness by giving you an amount that is certainly not "rich" for you.

When you want a dream house, simply do not focus or write, "I want a new house." If you want to boost your chances of manifesting a new house, describe it in explicit detail. What is the color of the walls and curtains in your house? How does the furniture look? How does the front porch of the house or apartment entrance look? How do the doors and windows look? How does the upholstery look? What are the electric and hardware fittings like? What are the picture frames adorning your walls? You get the gist, right? Being as detailed and descriptive as possible increases your chances of manifesting exactly what you desire.

Cultivate Gratitude

However much we try, we all have that mental list of everything we don't want. The best way to get rid of it is by being thankful for all the good things we have. Next time whenever you find yourself waiting at the doctor's or taking the train to work, utilize that time to create to list of things you are truly grateful for. It can be anything from your nieces/nephews to your limbs to the house you live in. Your best friend's terrific sense of humor when you are feeling low and your dog' warm welcome each time you get home from work count too. These are all the little things that make your life more meaningful.

When you are thankful for everything you have, you only create a cycle of goodness. By showing gratitude for your gifts, you are opening the opportunity to receive even more of those gifts. So when you express gratitude for having money, irrespective of the amount, you are inviting or attracting even more money into your life.

Keep a gratitude journal. Documenting your blessings is a great way to grow more of them in your backyard. The more tangible and concrete you make these blessings; the higher are your chances of experiencing more of it. Make it a habit to write a minimum of five things that you are grateful for. Let the happy feelings connected with thankfulness overcome you when you fall asleep.

Gratitude unlocks positive vibes for opening our minds to all the good things we deserve. Get into the habit of creating a list of things you are thankful for at the end of each day. Include each little thing that adds value to your life. Over a period of time, you'll notice how this simple habit can transform the way you live. You will attract more of what you are truly grateful for, and lead a life of your dreams.

Aligning with a strong positive and gratitude filled energy helps attract greater positive energy your way. Building a gratitude attitude isn't tough. Pro tip – be thankful for even those things which we do not have but wish to receive.

Practice Positive Self-Talk

How and what you say to yourself will be more powerful in determining your reality than what anyone says to you, because you are always listening to self-talk. Most of us fall into the trap of concentrating self-talks on what is wrong about our lives or what we do not want.

For instance, when we wake up, we grumble about another boring day at work or when we catch a cold, about how we are tired of being ill at ease. We seldom say, "I am so glad to feel better with each passing day." How many times have you told yourself that you are open to fresh opportunities rather than complaining about how abysmally low your salary is? Notice how different you feel by brining even a slight change in the words and perspective you use while tackling challenging situations. Practice this consistently and you will notice how you actually attract the desired results.

Create new statements that are relevant to your situation and keep repeating them to feel more positive and in control of the situation. These can also be general statements about how good you are feeling or how fabulous your life is or how you are a money magnet. If you are experiencing a tough breakup it can be something like, "I am in love with myself and I absolutely approve of how wonderful I am." Similarly, if you are attempting to lose weight, "I love my body and I treat it with respect. I feel wonderful about myself." Keep repeating. If you are growing your income, try saying, "Wonderful/fantastic new job opportunities are on their way."

The affirmations can be put up just about anywhere from your phone screen to bathroom mirror (where you can see it the first thing each morning) to wake up alarms to work desk. Place it prominently at different places where you can spot it throughout the day. This way, you will keep repeating these positive affirmations, and exposing your mind to it.

There may be some predominant presumptions or beliefs which may be holding you back. Positive affirmations simply restructure these destructive beliefs to promote greater optimism, focus and consistency to create a future we actually desire.

When you say something repetitively, it gets embedded into your subconscious mind as reality. You are feeding your mind the desired results, and your mind plays along by influencing your actions in the direction of these desired results. So when you keep repeating, "I am a money magnet" or "I attract wealth", you will be open to and identify several money making opportunities that come your way or even create those opportunities. It will be easier to synchronize your actions with the fulfillment of your end goal. When your subconscious mind is constantly fed with an idea, it works endlessly to see that idea to fruition because the mind believes the idea to be your reality.

Visualize Your Dreams

Visualizing your dream is another great way to trigger the power of your subconscious mind. Create a virtual

253

board with Pinterest or a real one using images from your favorite magazines. Pick images that best reflect your goals, and inspire yourself to achieve it. Allow yourself to absorb these images and feel them like you are actually experiencing them. Let these images act as powerful motivators and visual stimulants to fulfill your goals. The images should move you and stir you into action for creating the desired result.

Images have a far greater impact on the subconscious mind than simply words. It gives more clarity and tangibility to your dreams. If you want to travel, include images of your dream destination. If you want to create a blog, include image of blogs you really love. Make it interesting, detailed and fun. Use positive slogans, motivating quotes, sketches, comic strips – just about anything to make your vision board a highly potent catalyst in manifesting your dreams. Again, constantly looking at a visual stimulus embeds these images in your mind.

Another visualization technique is to explicitly visualize everything in life like its actually happening in the present. A few minutes before you go to bed, visualize everything that you want to achieve, and experience it as if it is actually happening. For instance, if you want to be a confident public speaker, imagine yourself on stage, addressing a crowd of several hundred people.

Visualize everything from your body language to the pace of your breath to the tone of your voice to the sound of applause. What are you wearing? What are you saying? How is the audience responding? When they said "God is in the details", someone must surely be referring to positive thinking and the law of attraction because the more detailed you are, the higher are your chances of transforming visions into reality.

One of the most important aspects of visualizations is imagining things in the present and not future. For the law of attraction to create the desired results, act as if you are already receiving everything you are envisioning. Not in future but right now. You should act, speak, think and behave like the vision is already fulfilled. Your visions should reflect that the universe has already granted you everything you've ever desired.

Write down your wishes or goals. When you construct your wishes, always begin with "I am so glad and grateful that..." and complete the sentence by asking the universe for exactly what you want. Write these wishes or dreams in the present tense as if you have already received them.

Always Focus on the Positives

We all have the tendency to focus on the not so pleasant things about people and situations. Next time you find yourself annoyed with your partner for not turning up on time for a date, think about how they cook really well for you or get along fabulously with your friends. There is always some good in the most seemingly hopeless situations. Get into the habit of recognizing that good.

If you find yourself feeling irritated with your boss for giving you more work than anyone else, see this as indication of how they believe in your capability and trust you with greater responsibility. When you focus on the positive, you are obviously inviting more good. Do this small exercise – starting right now until the next 24 hours, think and be vocal only about the good. Avoid complaining, and focus only on the positive aspects of everything you come across throughout the day. Notice the splendid effect this simple exercise has on you after 24 hours.

Practice Random Acts of Kindness

Well, this need not be restricted to leaving a generous tip for the waitress or buying coffee for the guy in behind you in the Starbucks queue or handing over happy meal to a homeless person. It can be everyday acts of kindness such as smiling at a stranger, paying someone a genuine compliment, giving up your seat during a long commute, or holding the door open for a stranger.

These small yet powerful random acts of kindness create a positive energy circle, which invariably finds its way back to you. What you give more of, you receive more of. When you give kindness, compassion and positivity, you receive it equal measures. Similarly, when you spread happiness and cheer everywhere, it comes back to you multifold.

Pretend Play

Remember how as little kids you dressed up doctors, nurses and pilots to slip into the role of these adulthood careers. Wasn't it fun pretending to be an astronaut or store keeper? Well, connect back to your childhood and indulge in a bit of pretend play to manifest your dreams.

Write a letter and address it yourself. Receive an email from self in future mentioning about the lovely things happening in your life. It can be a year or twenty years from now. Your intentions become crystal clear, and positive vibes follow. Get yourself a princely royalty check with an exact date if you have just started writing a book. It won't just act as an inspiration but also drive your subconscious towards goal fulfillment.

Once a stand-up comedian, who performed small gigs at local businesses, was once heckled by the audience for one of his performances. Broke, dejected and depressed, he drove up a hill. He sat there looking at the glistening city of Los Angeles, where he dreamt of achieving huge success. To feel good, he simply wrote himself a check for $ 10 million mentioning "acting services rendered." The post dated check was a constant fixture in his pocket.

The stand-up comedian truly went on to make millions with movies such as Ace Ventura and Dumb and Dumber. Yes, you guessed it right. The comedian was none other than Jim Carrey, the ace entertainer who has millions of people around the world with his comic histrionics.

He was doing nothing but carrying an energy vibration in his pocket. Looking at the check every now and then made it a firm fixture in the subconscious mind, which then began to guide his actions toward fulfilling the goal of becoming a well-known entertainer.

Write yourself a check, carry a pretend account statement or write yourself a make believe degree for setting a clear intention and directing your action towards fulfillment of that intention. Life reflects back what you think and carry around you. When you surround yourself with a "can do" vibe, you often end up doing it. It's no wonder that those who consistently focus on how poor they are seldom lead a financially thriving life, while those that are thinking abundance are subconsciously always on the lookout for avenues to create wealth.

Get Busy Doing

The Law of attraction is not simply about imagining things but beginning from a point of creating in your mind what you want to manifest in real. Know exactly what you want, be guided by intuition (not external factors or negative mind talk), speak to yourself in a highly empowering manner, focus on the good things in life, be thankful for your blessings, and visualize your desires.

When you do all this, you will invariably take action in the direction of your goals to manifest a life of your dreams. You will be moved and inspired to act on those goals, guided by intuition and the power of your subconscious mind.

Chapter 2.   14 Powerful Positive Thinking Practices

Here are 10 simple yet powerful everyday positive thinking hacks that you can begin practicing right now.

Direct Your Energy and Thoughts

Our thoughts come with a frequency and a matching vibration that invariably attracts corresponding frequencies in our life. Negative thoughts attract negative energies, where as positive thinking draws positive energy. Divert your energy productively towards thinking positive outcomes and you will create the desired life.

Meditation can help in directing your thoughts from negative to positive. Try the guided visualization technique to envision your perfect life. Guided visualization or imagery is nothing but directing our consciousness towards imagining scenarios which we desire in life. This can be done with guided visualization videos/CDs or an instructor.

Directing your thoughts is a method used by psychotherapists to control negative thoughts and transform them into more positive thoughts. When you feel unhappy or anxious, create positive thoughts that put you in a happy frame of mind. Think of a happy image or show yourself some love with positive feedback.

Redirecting thoughts is a popular method used by psychotherapists to help keep your thoughts in control when you begin experiencing negative emotions such as depression, stress or anxiety. Just how can negative thoughts be controlled?

When you start feeling a compellingly negative emotion, try and consciously start generating happy thoughts about things that delight you. It can be something you are looking forward to or something funny that has happened in the past. The idea is to control negative feelings and shift thoughts from positive to negative gradually.

Create a code word, which is based on a happy memory or something that truly pleases you. For instance: cupcake, shopping, holidays, family, travel etc. Each time you find yourself besieged by negative thoughts, bring in your feel good mantra or code word and start thinking about feelings/thoughts associated with it to distract yourself from self destructive thoughts.

Forgive Yourself

Avoid beating yourself mentally over things that have not gone as expected or you've done wrong. Rising above regret and guilt gives us the power to create a more positive future. Understand that nothing will change what has happened.

Forgiving yourself for past mistakes gives you the control to create a rewarding future. Be gentle with yourself when it comes to dealing with past issues. Do not let a few past mistakes determine the course your entire life ahead. Positive thinking is not about denying those mistakes or being defensive about them.

It is about accepting past mistakes and moving on without letting them bog you down or determining your future. We all make mistakes. However, only the best of us learn to rise above them to build a future of our dreams.

Give Yourself Due Credit

How often have you felt uncomfortable receiving compliments or accepting that you are indeed fabulous? While we are quick to criticize ourselves, we rarely appreciate what we do really well. There are so many things we've done right each day.

When we move away from a general tendency to reflect only on our mistakes or what could've been done right, we experience a greater sense of accomplishment. There is greater self-confidence, self-esteem and positivity, to help overcome what we've messed up and create more of what we really want. It is easy to feel frustrated when things are not going your way.

However, try focusing on your achievements and give yourself credit for what you've always been doing well. This will automatically change your thought vibrations from negative to positive, from destructive to constructive, from self-limiting to possibilities. Instead of "I just can't do this", you will start thinking: "this is possible."

Avoid Catastrophizing and Labeling

Catastrophizing is assuming the worst outcome in any situation. It is anxiety related to underperforming or not being good enough. Catastrophizing can be combated by staying realistic about the possible consequences of any situation.

For instance, thinking we are going to fail in an examination, which will lead to failing the class and eventually dropping out of college. Some may go a step ahead and imagine themselves living on welfare. When you think realistically, you realize that even if you fail the test, you may not fail the entire course. There may be no dropping out of college or being unemployed.

Individuals with more depressive tendencies invest a lot more time tagging or labeling people around them and themselves. These labels are unfortunately more negative, and have a detrimental impact on our thoughts. For instance, you may be in your late 20s and moved back in with your parents after losing a job because you can't afford the rent. You will end up labeling yourself jobless, dependent and single rather than considering it a transition period. When we get rid of judgmental labels, we feel more liberated and positive from negative thought patterns.

Practice Mindfulness

Increasing awareness about your actions will put in greater control of your life to experience more happiness. You weren't born to lead or programmed or robotic life, were you? Mindful meditation increases your awareness about the things around you, your decisions, daily activities, choices, physical sensations and much more. You learn to focus on the present moment, and enjoy greater control of your happiness.

Practice mindful meditation to center your thoughts on an idea, and completely focus on the present in a more detached manner. Practice mindful breathing or meditation for about 15-20 minutes each day. It will help increase self-awareness and awareness of the present moment. Your thinking pattern will gain greater consciousness. Try signing up for a yoga class to be more aware of your body and breathing. Mindful meditation helps you experience greater peace and inner calm.

Meditation calms the mind and brings about a sense of stillness or balance, where there is no turmoil going on in your head. It helps you focus on the present, without worrying about your past or future. Mindfulness allows you to concentrate on living in the present moment and appreciate things around you by experiencing them to the fullest. Mindfulness is about mentally connecting with being in the present moment and focusing on the now, instead of going through life's experiences on autopilot.

Think about how little children and animals conduct themselves. There are deeply connected to their inner selves, totally immersed in enjoying the present moment (I've yet to see a worrying dog) and full of gentle curiously in experiencing things around them. This is exactly what mindfulness can help you achieve. When you approach your thoughts with a sense of mindfulness, you don't feel the need to latch on to them or push them. Instead, there is a childlike wonder in exploring them non-judgmentally.

Explore Your Creativity

Exploring your creativity is one of the best ways to practice positive thinking. Be artistic. Use your hands to create something distinct, positive and out of the box. You will learn to apply lateral thinking and explore original thoughts, which can lead to higher positivity. Even if you do not consider yourself an intrinsically creative individual, there's always something to do to express yourself and experience greater positivity.

Take a class about something you've not considered (think pottery, woodworking or collage making). Master a new craft such as knitting, sewing or crocheting. Learn a new language. Try writing a short story or poem. Take to doodling or sketching. Audition for a part in your local community theatre.

Spend Time With Positive Folks

Research has pointed to the fact that we are a reflection of the five people we spend most of our time with. These people influence everything from our thoughts to words to actions. Therefore, if you want to feel more positive and upbeat, simply surround yourself with more positive folks. These people inspire the "can do" spirit in you. Positive people help you believe in your goals and your ability to manifest them. They are constantly encouraging and inspiring you to reach your highest potential.

Whiners, complainers and critics spread a more negative aura that is likely to affect you too. We subconsciously emulate the thought patterns, speech and habits of people around us, which simply means when we surround ourselves with positive people, we are more prone to reflect the same positive energy vibrations. Isn't it tough to be negative when all those around you are infectiously positive?

Since we are so heavily influenced by the people around us, identify those who fill you with a sense of positivity. Avoid folks who drain your energy and achievement drive. If you are already a negative thinker, you may fall even deeper into the trap.

Stop Playing Victim

It is easy to play victim and blame circumstances when you encounter challenges in life. However, when you learn to accept reasonability for your behavior, you learn from your mistakes and display greater control over future circumstances. Avoid blaming other people unfairly. Admit your mistake and move on. Some things cannot be changed, which means we simply accept them and move on.

Though we cannot control each situation befalling us, we can control our reaction to the situation. Rather than playing victim, simply acknowledge the circumstances and realize that you are in control of your reaction. Control the things you can and learn to let go of what you can't. Playing victim makes you feel more helpless and less in control. Break the shackles of helplessness to take greater control of your life, which ultimately leads to increased positivity and happiness. Be the ultimate "possibilitarian" you can.

Do not wait for situations to change. Act like they have already changed even when you feel victimized by circumstances. Believe that the power to shift your circumstances doesn't lie externally but is held within you. If you are looking for love, begin loving yourself unconditionally first. If you are looking for a new job, make the most of the one you are currently working in. Understand that the process of change begins with your intention to change the circumstances surrounding you.

Practice Self Hypnosis

Self-hypnosis is a natural state of mind which is characterized by high levels of focused concentration. It can help you change thought patterns, kick destructive habits, take greater control of your thoughts/actions and experience relaxation from the stress of daily living. It is much like meditation, and can transform your life.

Self can be harnessed to break the pattern of negativity and trigger more positive thoughts. You can gain complete control over your thoughts, feelings and actions by heightening concentration levels and directing yourself towards fruitful thinking.

Stop Making Excuses

You either have a dream or an excuse. They can't co-exist. There can be a zillion excuses for not achieving something or not doing things that make you happy. What is stopping you? Quit giving excuses. Sign up for those dance lessons today.

Start saving to travel the world. Go out there and make friends if your previous relationship ended on a disastrous note. Life is about living, not coming up with a bunch of excuses for simply existing. Are you truly living or merely existing? Don't create obstacles in your path to happiness. Ditch them and go out there to live a life you've always dreamt of.

Set and Work on Goals

Keep yourself busy by setting and working on achieving meaningful life goals. Once you accomplish a single goal, you will be driven to aim for higher laurels. Be inspired and positive by constantly adding fresh and meaningful goals into your life.

No matter how small the accomplishment, your confidence will soar with each victory. Your self-esteem will increase multifold once you realize you have the power to go after anything you set your heart on. This can be a brilliant catalyst for a healthy, happy and positivity filled life.

Volunteer For Social Causes

When you lend your energy for something as positive and unconditional as social causes or charity, you feel great about being able to make a difference in the life of people. Few things are more positive than being able to add value to the lives of those less privileged than us. Giving more also opens us up to receiving more.

Volunteering allows you to meet-to-meet like-minded and positive people, who inspire you to give. It instills a sense of gratitude about how fortunate you are to enjoy the gifts not everyone has been bestowed with. You appreciate the positives in your life even more, which leads to increased positive thoughts and actions. What goes around always comes around. Like begets like. When you give you create a circle of goodness which eventually finds its path back to you.

Get Instead of Have

Did you even notice how many times you say you have to do xyz thing? I have to mow the lawn. I have to pay my bills. Replace have to with get, and witness the effect it has on your overall attitude. The perspective changes from being obligated to do something to a feeling of gratefulness for the things that are a part of our routine.

Instead of saying, I have to purchase groceries today, you say I get to purchase groceries today. This makes it sound more like a privilege than an obligation. The attitude shifts from need based to one of fulfillment. Try doing this from today, and you will be happier, more driven and less stressed.

Refuel and Replenish

When you are physically drained and hungry, it is tough to stay in a positive frame of mind. The combination can keep us negative despite best attempts. Keeping your body healthy, well nourished and well rested is a great way to support the mind in staying positive. Lack of sleep poses a threat for the smooth functioning of your nervous system, which can cloud positive thoughts.

When you sleep and eat well, you view a broader variety of vital details and possibilities. If you find your attitude and thought process consistently negative, take a close look at your eating and sleep patterns. Opt for a mid morning fat-protein combo such as peanut butter with apple, which can stabilize your blood sugar.

Chapter 3. The Spiritual Value of Positive Thinking

If you are a skeptical type of person, you may have made quite a big stretch to pick this book up in the first place.

Please don't! We're going to talk about the spiritual value of positive thinking, but that doesn't mean we're proposing any kind of religion or trying to convert you in any way. We're simply using the word spiritual to indicate a deeper dimension to the practice of positive thinking.

Self-love

Self-love is one of the basic concepts of positive thinking; you need to Love Yourself the Way You Are. Many Buddhists would say, instead, that you need to have self-compassion; that's a way you might find more comfortable to think about this concept.

Having compassion for all living creatures is a central Buddhist value, but it is normally expressed as compassion for other living creatures. However, having compassion on your own self is also important. The Venerable Amy Miller, a Buddhist thinker in the Tibetan Mahayana tradition, sometimes says "Don't beat yourself up!"

For instance, at a lecture to the Root Institute at Bodh Gaya, she spoke about the difficulties of maintaining a meditation practice. Many people start well, for instance, taking a retreat for a week or two, but when they return to the ordinary world, they find it difficult to continue regularly.

The message "don't beat yourself up" is a great help to them, for several reasons:

- You only managed to meditate for five minutes, not two hours? "Don't beat yourself up!" You still managed five minutes, and it will still do you good. Maybe you can do more another day.

- You didn't meditate today? That must mean the end of your Buddhist life; you've ruined it. You'll never be a good Buddhist now. (Do you recognize the catastrophizing going on there?) "Don't beat yourself up!" Tomorrow, it's a fresh morning and you can restart and do your meditation, and you've lost a single day, that's all.

- Meditation is intended to free the mind from worries and incessantly recurring thoughts. But if you are beating yourself up for missing a meditation session, your thoughts will keep going back to that subject, and you will be unable to free your mind.

Amy spoke about one Retreat she took during which she couldn't stop thinking about pizza. It was a fasting retreat, which made it worse! Rather than continue to obsess about the pizza, or rather the absence of pizza, she decided to imagine that pizza as richly and fully as she could. She took her time to imagine how hot the pizza was straight out of the oven, how good it smelled, how good it tasted. She actually ate that pizza in her meditation. And as soon as she had done that, the pizza stopped bugging her. The obsession was gone, and she could now meditate properly. By having compassion on her hungry thoughts instead of beating herself up for being distracted from the meditation, she was able to get back on track.

Meditation

You don't have to be a Buddhist to find meditation useful. In fact, almost all religions use meditation. Orthodox Christianity has a meditative tradition; Jewish Kabbalah followers meditate, as do Sufi Muslims and many Hindus. Plenty of agnostics and atheists also find meditation useful for clearing the mind, relaxing, and keeping themselves open to life and its endless potential.

A meditation is essentially very simple. Probably the simplest form is pranayama, in which you concentrate on your breath in order to focus the mind. Other forms of meditation use chants or mantras, such as "Om" or the name of Jesus, and some also use imagery as a focus. Although such sounds and images often have religious significance, you could meditate on the name of the Dude or the flying spaghetti monster if you wanted to, and if you did so with single-minded focus, that meditation would work just as effectively as any other.

If you want to meditate, one of your best resources is YouTube. You can download an impressive number of guided meditations for free. There are also apps you can download on your tablet or smartphone, such as Headspace and Smiling Mind. Or you could always go to a meditation class that's provided through a local yoga center, Buddhist temple, or education program.

Finding meaning in life

Positive thinking is about finding meaning in your life. Again, that doesn't have to be religious. It could be religious, and for many people it is, but it doesn't need to be.

A few examples of how people have found meaning in their lives show how they have created their own values and lived up to them. These people are not conventionally religious, but they have found a deeper meaning to the way they live their lives, and in doing so, they have also found happiness.

- "I've saved all my little cat family from the pound. They came as anxious, frightened, fierce felines, and now they are all happy, relaxed cats who know that they are loved. When life is getting me down, I look at my cats and I think, I've achieved something worthwhile."

- "I renovated this old watermill all on my own. I've saved something of our local history and I'm passing it on to the next generation. And I've got local kids enthusiastic about preserving our water-meadows. Every time I see a child smile at a frog jumping into the water, I feel great."

- "I just love painting, and I've organized my life so I can spend all the time I want at my easel. Every day I try a new way of putting my ideas on canvas, a new way of seeing the world. Every day, the world is worth seeing."

- "I've built a successful real estate business that's well respected. I know this little corner of the city better than anyone else; I've sold some houses twice or three times over the years! And I still love seeing new houses being built. I can't imagine a better way to live my life."

Like attracts like

Many hermetic traditions are based on the idea of like attracting like. At its simplest, that's how sympathetic magic works--the idea for instance that rubbing a lucky coin can attract money towards you.

I'm not proposing you carry out magic rituals as part of your positive thinking practice! But many people who have started on the positive thinking path have found in their own lives, and believe very strongly, that positive energy attracts positive energy.

If you think about it, that's not such a dumb idea. For instance, if you are in a room with a number of other people but just one of those people is full of enthusiasm and energy, that's probably the person that you want to talk to. In business, a confident presentation is always more convincing than an argument made by someone who appears more downbeat or hesitant.

Of course, that energy needs to be genuine. We've all experienced the kind of fake enthusiasm from the Charles Atlas School of self-help that says "Have a nice day" or "Wow, that's awesome," but doesn't actually mean it. What I'm talking about here is the energy that comes from positive thinking that comes from being the best you can be and living your life to the fullest. We can all tell the difference between the salesperson who just wants to sell a product and a salesperson who really believes the product is great--that's the kind of positive energy that I'm talking about here.

So, on a superficial level, you can already see that like attracts like. People whose positive thinking has transformed their lives will find other people like themselves. That may mean you can attract a fantastic mentor, it may give you access to teaching programs you'd never get on otherwise, it may lead to profitable business contacts. Or it may simply mean that in a year's time, you'll look at your contacts list on Gmail and find

273

it's full of fantastic people with great energy that you really enjoy hanging out with.

Some people take this idea of positive energy further. They look at the energy of the entire universe. There is such a huge amount of energy in the universe, and you have access to all of it to draw on for your daily needs. They believe that your positive attitude can actually bring good fortune; your own positive energy will attract wealth, health, and other good things. Certainly, the scientific studies that have been carried out on positive thinking do appear to show that as far as health is concerned, positive energy tends to have a beneficial effect on your life. Whether it will make you richer? The jury's still out on that.

You might also think about what happens when we introduce positive energy into the political arena. Very often, political battles are fought by using a negative mission statement--things that we don't want to happen. Such battles are often acrimonious, and they sap our energy, they don't put much back into our communities. On the other hand, when a political campaign has a positive purpose to make people's lives better or to improve a whole community, that can really energize people and bring them together. Whichever party you support, why not think about how to make politics a more positive space to achieve more for everyone?

Chapter 4. Being Positive In Bad Situations

As you know, it is not easy to be positive if the situation is negative. It is normal for people to feel down. Sadness is a natural emotion. However, you should not be sad for too long. If you do, you will become depressed. Depression can be debilitating. It can hinder your growth, happiness, and success. Even worse, it can affect the people around you, especially your family and friends. It can also affect your professional life.

How to Maintain Positive

Having a positive attitude is the most ideal way to overcome negative situations. However, you need to be disciplined, focused, and determined to do this.

First, you have to learn how to control your responses. This is actually crucial to staying positive during negative circumstances. You have to take a deep breath to calm yourself. You can also start counting to calm your mind. When your mind is calm and clear, you can come up with a better response.

It is never a good idea to respond to anything if your emotion is negative. In fact, you have to practice the popular saying that if you cannot say anything nice, you should not say anything at all.

If you are in a negative situation and you are in a bad mood, you are likely to say something insulting, provoking, or negative. If you open your mouth and utter these words, the people around you will also feel negative. All of you will be negative, and this can result in a much worse situation.

Some people prefer to forget the negative situations that they have been in. However, if you are a smart person, you will use these negative experiences as learning opportunities. You should view the negative situations that you have been in as something that can be helpful to you in the future.

If something happened to you in the past and your reaction did not make things better, perhaps you can change the way you react in order to change the outcome in case a similar situation occurs in the future. Rather than be ashamed of yourself for having experienced such situation, you have to congratulate yourself for overcoming it and for having the initiative to use it as a learning opportunity.

People who are positive and successful also make mistakes. After all, nobody is perfect. However, these people have no qualms admitting when they are wrong. They do not pretend to be right all the time. When they make a mistake, they own it, apologize, and make up for it. They also learn from it and move on. They do not allow their past mistakes to affect their present and future. Rather than deny their shortcomings, they strive to improve themselves.

Seeing the Bright Side

It is true that you cannot control every external factor, but you can always control the way you respond to it. How you think affects the way you act towards every situation.

If you are a novelist and a publishing company rejects your work, do you get discouraged and quit writing, or do you continue to look for another publisher who will publish your work? If your house is destroyed by the typhoon, do you sink in depression or do you pull yourself together and

276

look for solutions? If your business goes bankrupt, do you give up on your dreams or do you try again?

Successful people also have downtimes, but as you know, they always rise above. They also feel stressed out and get heartbroken due to failures. You just do not notice that because they choose to focus on the positive and continue reaching for their goals. You do not see their sufferings because they do not wallow in them. All you see are their success because that is what they focus on growing.

So, how can you see the bright side if there seems no bright side? First of all, you have to acknowledge the fact that there is a bright side. There are two sides to everything – the positive and the negative. Believe it or not, even the worst case scenarios can have some good in them.

Say, you got divorced and you lost all your money. Your initial reaction may be to get devastated. You lost a partner and you have no means to support yourself. How can there be any good side to this? Well, you have to calm yourself first. Sit down, relax, and meditate. Calm yourself so that your mind will be clear. When you are ready to analyze your situation in a more logical perspective that is when the positive changes are going to happen.

You are divorced, and your bank account is empty. You still have good health, don't you? You have family and friends who support you. You can go to your parents and talk to your siblings. You can have drinks with friends. You have to remain grateful for those people who still have your back.

Then, you have to be open to the possibility of finding someone new. You can take your time to heal, but you should not give up on love. You may not feel that you can be in a relationship again, but you will if you desire it.

Focus on yourself and the things that make you happy. Work out, pamper yourself, and indulge in your hobbies. Doing the things you love can increase your confidence.

So, you think that you have no money. You can get a job. You should muster courage and go apply for a job. It does not have to be a high paying position right away. You can start at the bottom. The important thing is that you get a job and you have a means to support yourself.

You can regain your confidence little by little. As the days pass by, you will get better and better. Eventually, you will be able to look back at your past with peace in your heart. You will no longer feel bitter or angry because you have chosen to treat your negative experiences as learning opportunities.

Chapter 5. Bring On Positivity

Optimism is not just a state of the mind; it is also shown through your actions and words. If your work gets canceled due to inclement weather, an optimistic person would enjoy the time off or work on something else to be productive. Whereas positivity is about having a positive attitude - even when challenging situations arise. One psychologist once theorized that you attract what you think about most. This is the Law of Attraction and it says that when you think of and focus on something, it will happen. Remember how you wished to not see a certain person and you did? You focused your thoughts and energy on that particular person, and there they were! Well, that's law of attraction.

This theory is true whether you are thinking negative or positive thoughts. The more you think of negative thoughts, the more you'll encounter negative things. Let's look at this scenario. Imagine you're in a taxi hurrying your way to work with a traffic jam on the street. Human nature tells you to start worrying because you might be late to work. When you do, you decide to get out of the cab and power-walk your way through the traffic jam. As you are walking, you keep looking at your watch, ticking and ticking. Twenty minutes until work became ten that rapidly became five. At this point you're stressed and sending out all types of negative energy. As you cross the street while looking at your watch, a car hits you. It may not be a big hit but you still felt the pain. And because you are very anxious and stressed during that time, you shout at the driver and confront him. Now the clock says you are late. With this scenario, you can see that a cascade of events will happen once you strongly think negative thoughts.

The same is true when you think of more positive thoughts. When you are about to enter your workplace, you started telling yourself that you can do all your tasks for the day. You greeted everyone with a smile on your face, found your way to your desk and pleasantly started working. Even if a pile of unfinished papers greeted you that morning, you did not panic. Instead, you took a look at each of them and prioritized them. You grouped all papers needing immediate attention and you did the same for the not-so-urgent ones. With a positive attitude, you gradually finish them all without undue stress.

Adopting positivity, just like other processes, takes time. You need to consciously make an effort to practice it every moment of every day, whatever comes your way, until it becomes a good habit. Again, it is believed that it takes 30-days of consistently doing something to form a habit. Adopting positivity is a commitment and you have to be faithful in adopting positivity not only in your thoughts, but also in your actions and words. Below are some strategies to begin with positivity.

Be healthy

Many people don't think they can manage their problems because they are sick or because they feel too weak to accomplish their tasks. If this is the case, the best way to counteract it is to stay healthy. Start a healthy lifestyle by eating a balanced and healthy diet – one that has the right amount of carbohydrates, proteins, and other sources that is right for you. A food regimen that contains plenty of vegetables and fruits is good because they contain vitamins and minerals that are essential for the proper functioning of your cells.

Exercise is another way of maintaining a healthy lifestyle. Exercise does not only make your body stronger and your muscles larger, but exercise is a good way of relieving stress and energizing yourself. If you exercise regularly, you'll have the zest to work the whole day. Without exercise or good nutrition, you'll often feel lazy, inadequate and weak.

Change the way you think

Though changing the way you think is as difficult as changing the way you were brought up, it is something that you can achieve over time. Emotions are things that we ultimately have control over, and we have the ability to change the way we feel about certain things. Much of it can be changed shift of perspectives or the way we view certain situations. Think of ways to turn your negative thoughts into positive ones and do not let these negative thoughts control you. Ask yourself, what is one positive thing I can take out of this negative perspective? Then, look for another positive thing, and focus your energy on those positive things instead of the negative ones.

Start positive self- talk

You don't need other people to encourage you. You can do it to yourself. A simple "Good job!" or "Congratulations!" can already do the trick. What is even better with this method is that you don't need a specific time to do it. You can do this when you are busy, or when you are not doing anything, or when you are eating. You don't need anyone to do this, either. It may sound silly but it works. Talk to yourself like talking to a friend; encourage yourself, praise yourself and always remind yourself that you are powerful enough to overcome all the challenges that you will encounter in the future.

If you are doing something for the first time, don't be afraid. A negative self-talk may sound like, "I don't know

281

how to do this," but a positive self-talk would say, "This is a new experience and I will learn new things from this." If you want to do something but you don't have the resources, a negative self-talk would say, "I cannot do it because I need this first." A positive self-talk would most likely be, "I can do it. I just need to get this first."

Always look forward to something

Every day, you get to encounter different challenges, experience various events or meet new people. When you see the things happening to you as being part of something great, then you are attracting positive things into your life.

Positivity and optimism start with a positive attitude. You can gain optimism by anticipating that something good will come out of whatever it is you are going through right now.

Chapter 6. Assess Your Way of Thinking

Have you thought about your thoughts? Does that question confuse you? Probably because you have not yet considered analyzing your own thought processes and how your mind takes you somewhere when you are confronted with unfamiliar things. Maybe you have wondered why a certain situation happened but have never asked yourself why and how you responded to that particular circumstance. A positive thinker does not only think about improving the situation but also deliberates on how to correct the attitude or the response towards it. This requires you to evaluate and later on, improve your way of thinking. Assessing your way of thinking is the first step towards acquiring a positive mindset. When you start to be conscious on how you respond to situations, you will be better in adapting and overcoming difficulties. And so knowing that you have the power to change the way you think, you would get a sense of security within yourself and would leave you unfazed no matter what you go through. Take note of a few tips to help you out in evaluating your own thoughts.

Be responsible with your attitude

A lot of people would blame their failures on everything around them when in fact, they do not realize that it is their choice right at the onset of setting up a particular goal that actually influenced the result.

Whatever your thought is, it is your reality. That is why you should always take responsibility for your attitude towards any problem. No one else has that level of control in your mind but yourself. So if you want to take hold of your thoughts, first, learn to identify it.

Keep a journal or diary to reflect on your thoughts

First, you have to catch your negative thoughts and figure out what they are. When you see that thought floating by, you have to catch it, look at it and ask "what're you doing in my brain?" Some examples of the negative thoughts are "I am not worth of wealth" or "I don't deserve to get promoted and earn higher wages". These thoughts can be so ingrained in your brains since childhood to the point that you think they are just normal. What you need to do is to look at these thoughts and ask yourself how these thoughts are there? Where do they come from?

When assessing the way you think, it is important to have a substantial evidence of your thoughts and feelings. Keeping a journal is a classic way of assisting an individual for personal growth and personality development. By journaling, you will be able to peek into your own mind, gaining insight into your moods and behaviors. At first, you will feel a bit awkward especially if writing is not your best suit but after a while, you will be surprised by how much you will be able to learn about yourself just by a single entry. All you have to do is to take a few minutes at the end of each day to write down a situation and how you reacted to it. List or write down all your negative and positive thoughts all throughout the day. By doing this consistently, you will be able to notice a pattern emerging or stimuli that somehow trigger a negative thought. By tracing your thought processes at the end of each day, you can create action plans on how to manage it and how to turn your negative way of thinking into a positive one.

When you start journaling, you need to be honest about how you felt about a certain situation and how you responded to it. If you are not a natural writer, just create a list and be a bit more detailed. You can pick your top five most predominant negative thoughts as well as positive thoughts all throughout the day.

You also need to take the time to reflect on the thoughts that you have listed down. If you had time to journal every day, be sure to have your reflection and evaluation at least once at the end of the week.

Now that you have learned how to identify your negative and positive thoughts, it would be easier for you to combat those that you need to eliminate and enforce those that you need to maintain. By understanding the way you think, you would be able to control your attitude towards any situation.

Chapter 7.   Strategies to be Happy

Who wouldn't choose happiness? No one would allow himself to be lonely when life is offering him an opportunity to live his life the best way that he can. We are born to actually to live our lives and to live it abundantly. Happiness could be elusive for most people. You can be someone who has been through a lot of suffering and disappointments and have been accustomed to expect pain and loneliness as inevitable as day and night. Because of this, we try to find happiness in the wrong places and the wrong people.

Why does it matter, anyway? Is it not enough to have the perfect job that pays a lot? Is it not okay to settle with someone who possesses great qualities but does not make you happy? Is happiness overrated?

On the contrary, happiness contributes a lot to a person's success whatever endeavor he or she is taking. According to research, doctors who are happy tend to provide more accurate and efficient diagnoses and could give patients a sense of hope. Schools that are more focused on the emotional and social well-being of students tend to acquire more academic attainment and improve students' behavior. Happier people contribute more to society positively and are more likely to be willing to reach out and help each other. They are more likely to do volunteer work, vote and create a healthy community.

Happiness matters so much because it is our ultimate goal in life. It might be pushed too often at the backseat but deep in our subconscious, it takes precedence over all the material things that we have. If you want to take that first step towards happiness, take note of the following strategies that could jumpstart your life:

Setting up your goal

The first step to finding real happiness is to know what you want and work to achieve it. There is nothing better than setting up clear goals and visualizing the steps to reach them. When you anticipate something, like the fruition of a particular dream, you will feel your blood pumped up and get you excited about all the possibilities around you. Anticipation could light up a light bulb in our brain whenever you think about all the things that you are looking to achieve. When you have a goal to look forward to, you will get a sense of purpose and meaning in your life. Setting up a goal makes you responsible and accountable with the path that you would like your life to go. Just like a compass that would always remind you where north is, a goal would keep you grounded and sane amidst all the craziness in the world.

Be specific about what you want. It doesn't matter if it's that European tour or a significant weight loss, it is important that you are specific when you are creating your goals. If you have something precise and concrete that you can focus on, it would be much quicker for you to get back on track when you feel your focus declining. When you know what you really want, you will be able to rally all your resources behind this particular goal. This means that you would make use of all that you have that is related to that goal the best way and would avoid wasting time on things that are not as important or as related to achieving it. A very simple example would be sacrificing that third Starbucks coffee of the day and instead keep the money for your dream vacation. Investing on healthy food instead of junk and processed food would definitely level up your weight loss goal.

Break down your goals into workable chunks. Avoid being too grand when you think about doing a certain task to reach your goal. If you are planning on wearing a size 6 bikini this summer, then maybe you need to focus your attention first on shedding 5 pounds a month. When you break down a goal, you will avoid getting too overwhelmed and disheartened that you will not be able to reach it. When you reach these smaller goals, you will also feel a sense of satisfaction that would motivate you to press on and go the extra mile. Maybe a little more than 5 pounds next month is an additional $10 for your dream vacation. Also, when you make a mistake, it would be easier to clean up and redo.

Vision Board and Inspirational Tool

Did you know that our brain would respond better to visual stimuli? For example, you know because you have already learned from school what red looks like. You are very much aware that the red color sets off an intense emotion be it love, anger or hate. But why is it that we feel offended or panicky when we receive an email with a subject line that is in the red font? Seeing something visually invokes an emotion that a simple thought of it could never do. The same principle can be applied to your goals. It is one thing to think about all the marvelous dreams and aspirations in your head, and another to actually see it written down. So how do you create a vision board?

Take time to visualize and write down your goals. It would motivate you to take more assured steps into reaching them. It also puts you in the right frame of mind when you get distracted by things around you.

Relax and have fun. A vision board which is also known as a life collage should be an activity that would put your mind and your spirit in the same and correct perspective. Do not put too much pressure on yourself especially when you are not a natural artist. You are not trying to magically make those images manifest in your life right now, find your flow and make this activity fun for yourself.

Go creatively crazy. When you have a specific goal written down, back it up with pictures, quotes, inspirational texts and visual affirmations. Go all out with the images, anything that inspires you to reach your goal should be pinned on your board. Let the excitement that you are feeling about achieving your dreams fuel your creativity but make sure that you are creating one cohesive board. Once done, go ahead and hang this in a conspicuous place in your room or your desk. This way, it would always remind you of your purpose when life gets in the way.

Changing your mindset

Changing your perception has a lot to do with pursuing your goals and achieving happiness. During the process of reaching for your dreams, you will find that there will be a lot of roadblocks and frustrations that would pull you down. It takes a person with a positive perspective to actually pull through and accomplish any goal. Changing one's mindset may not happen overnight, but being intentional and making a conscious effort to look at the bright side of a situation would help you get to your goal quicker.

Try to fight fear. This is the biggest enemy of true happiness. When you succumb to fear, you will sell yourself short and would settle for mediocrity. It would make you develop tunnel vision, closing yourself off from better opportunities around you.

Love yourself

This may be the most basic thing to do to acquire happiness but loving yourself is something that could be hard to attain. At times, it is easier for us to accept another person's weaknesses and flaws so long as they do not point to our own. We lavishly give gifts to other people, spend time with them and put their needs first before our own. Although this in itself isn't really bad, when you lose yourself in the process of making other people happy, then you need to re-evaluate your priorities. It is impossible to give something that you do not have an abundance of. So keep in mind that you also deserve to be loved and pampered.

Be aware of your reactions and feelings towards certain situations. Do not ignore or dismiss your natural responses and try to listen to your gut. When you are self-aware, you will gain more insight and understanding of how you are as a person and would be more effective in providing outward love.

Do not misconstrue self-love as self-worship. Loving yourself is accepting that you have flaws and weaknesses, at the same time you excel on certain characteristics and attributes. Self-love does not mean that you are above everyone else, on the contrary, it means that you fail at times and accepting that it is okay. It means giving yourself 100% respect.

Visit a peaceful place

All of us crave that one happy place whenever negativity surrounds us. It is important then that you have a spot where you can unwind and where you can look at a particular situation in retrospect. It does not have to be a faraway destination, a quiet spot at the rooftop, a park near your place, anywhere where you can have a downtime and refresh your mind. This is a great way to start turning your negative thoughts into positive. When your mind is free from all the clutter in your life, it will lead to a better and more positive perspective.

When you attain happiness, you will find that negative thoughts have no power over you. Living a more positive life would be easier and more gratifying now that you have overcome negativity.

Chapter 8. 5 Ways to Overcome Negative Thoughts

If you are a natural pessimist, you may think you have already hit rock bottom when it comes to perceiving the worst about a situation. Your mind might have brought you to the deepest, darkest and ugliest place when faced an unexpected change in your life. One simple challenge such as passing a driving exam would send you into a frenzy of anxiety due to the negative thoughts that you allow inside your head. A lot of people would find it hard to dismiss this way of thinking because they have been so accustomed to reacting this way that it is almost automatic.

Negative thoughts would come bombarding your mind and would overflow in your everyday life if you do not rein it in. You always have the power to choose which kind of thoughts you want to entertain. Here are a few tips that you can apply whenever you feel like pessimism is slowly taking hold of your mind:

Choose happiness

As with everything that we want to happen in our lives, whether it is a long-lasting relationship, or a meaningful friendship, or a way to lose those extra pounds, the key to being successful in all of these is to be intentional. Believe it or not, choosing happiness is intentional as well. Abraham Lincoln once said "Most people are about as happy as they make up their minds to be", and it is true. You have to literally take those essential steps in choosing happiness. Mind you, doing this is not a once in a lifetime event. Like when you wake up in the morning and decide that today would be a perfect day, then forgetting all about it once you step out of the room to

292

face a big pile of mess in the living room. Choosing happiness is when you decide to do it moment by moment of each day. You will find that in the process, there would still be persistent negative thoughts that would creep back up but choosing to be happy again and again is a way to combat those.

One thing that you can focus on to stay happy is to count your blessings. When you shift into this way of thinking, it would be hard to look at challenges the same way again. You will find that in spite of the difficulties, there are still a lot of things to be thankful for.

Speak affirmation to yourself daily. It is one thing to believe that you are capable of something, but you could elevate this belief if you actually hear it from yourself. Try the "I am..." statements where you can choose from a list of affirmations that you can say. Just make sure that you carefully create an honest, truthful and relevant list that you can use.

Start your day on your terms. You may have let go of your control over that alarm clock, but that does not mean that you can lose control of your entire day. Establish an energizing and meaningful routine in the morning to set your whole day towards success.

Challenge your negative thoughts

It is always important to know what is true in your life. Sometimes, we get so caught up with negative thoughts that we forget that most of them are illogical and almost always...unfounded. You might think "this has happened to me before, and it did not go well." While it is true that the premise may look familiar, that does not mean that it would yield the same result. One thing to take note of when you lean towards negativity is to think about a situation objectively. Say for example; your brain would tell you "you always fail exams." Try to evaluate it or write it on a piece of paper and challenge it. "Always? How was I able to graduate if I always fail exams?" "How can I fail something that I have spent the time to prepare for?" These are some examples of truth that you can challenge the negative thought with.

Replace negative thoughts with positive thoughts

Recognizing and testing the accuracy of a negative thought is your first step into gaining an advantage over it. Once you have learned to identify and challenge these negative thoughts, it would be easier for you to turn these into positive. Keep in mind, though, that converting your thoughts should not mean that it is something that you will go blindly optimistic about. Being optimistic is not expecting something to turn out in your favor without any grounds. If you did not bother to practice driving, then you cannot expect to pass the exam by sheer luck. Be positive about a desirable outcome if you are 100 percent sure that you have done your utmost to acquire the best possible result. Hope for the best when you have done your best.

You can also challenge your brain by asking it questions. But make sure that you carefully construct your questions in such a way that it would require a positive answer. So instead of asking "why is it so difficult to pass this driving test?" try "How did I ever get this opportunity to drive my own car?" Make a conscious effort to direct the focus of your questions to positive thoughts.

Stop blaming yourself

Most likely, they are going through difficulties themselves that is why they are acting that way. When you personalize, you would have the tendency to get paranoid and would probably just sell yourself short. When you always think that everyone is against you and that everything is conspiring to take you down, then you will never reach your full potential. Rationalize and start focusing more on your abilities and your goal. This way, you will be able to divert your attention from things that would not benefit or affect you but only on things that you have control of.

No to filter thinking

Negative thinkers are guilty of filter thinking. This is when you tend to focus on the negative side of a situation or when you only hear the bad side of a comment. When you do this, there would be no room for constructive criticism in your mind. Pessimists would never view criticisms as constructive, but only something that would limit them from progressing. This kind of thinking would annihilate all kinds of potential that could be developed, would exhaust any passion that you have, and would burn out all the hope that you might be clinging to. There is some truth in looking at the "brighter side" of life; you may not realize it but looking at both the positive and negative side of a situation would provide you a deeper insight and would help you in achieving your goals better and faster.

You are well aware now of the consequences of allowing negative thoughts in your mind and in your life. With this knowledge, you will be able to turn your pessimism into a positive mindset easily.

Chapter 9.   Affirmations

What is an Affirmation?

An affirmation is anything you believe to be the ultimate truth. According to the dictionary, to affirm anything means claiming something to be true. Usually, when you repeatedly say something to yourself, you declare it true; therefore, when you repeatedly say or do something, you affirm it to yourself.

For instance, when you keep telling yourself you are a failure and cannot become the motivational speaker you desire to be, you will start believing this statement and eventually imbed it in your mind. Similarly, if you frequently tell yourself "I can do it," and never stop believing in it, you will be 100% sure you can achieve your goals and then use that strength to actualize them. This means an affirmation is any phrase or suggestion you repeatedly state to declare it to yourself that you believe it to be the truth and nothing else.

According to some people, affirmations are similar to "fake it till you actually make it." Science proves otherwise.

Your affirmations should be visible. Remember that repetition is crucial in making your affirmations effective. If you want your affirmations to work, you need to keep them stuck in your head.

You can write down your affirmations in your journal every day. This way, you will be reminded of them upon waking up and before going to bed.

You can also meditate on your affirmations. Think about what they mean to you and what emotions they evoke.

You can also create reminder cards and leave them around your room.

You can stick one on your mirror, put one in your drawer, and leave another one in your nightstand. Each time you see these cards, you will be reminded of your affirmations.

How Affirmations Work

Affirmations work in two ways: first by activating your RAS, and second by producing dynamic tension in your body and mind. Let us discuss the two effects individually.

Activating Your RAS

The first way through which affirmations work is by activating your Reticular Activating System (RAS). The RAS system is akin to a filter that discards any information it feels you do not want and keeps all the information it is sure you will need. If it were not for this system, a plethora of information would bombard you to a point where your senses would overload and you would become massively overwhelmed.

To ensure you do not go through this situation, the RAS registers what is important to you keeping your interests, likes, dislikes, goals, desires, and needs in consideration. For instance, if you are out in the market in search of grapes, you will see tons of vendors selling grapes. If your friend is accompanying you and wants to eat hamburgers, he, or she will see eateries and food trucks selling burgers. This happens mainly because the RAS in your brain and that in your friend's brain activates and registers things based on your current needs. You want grapes so you spot them whereas your friend wants to eat burgers so his/her focus lies on them.

Whenever you repeat a suggestion frequently, you affirm it. By doing this, you tell your RAS that the particular thing is very important to you. If you say, "I want to lose weight," you tell your RAS that losing weight is very important to you and as such, your RAS turns this into your goal. Your RAS will then make you notice more gyms, weight loss products, and exercises so you can achieve your goal.

This is how you make an affirmation work for you: by making your creativity and activity kick into high gear. Your RAS makes you aware of what you want and then your mind creates similar thoughts that shift your focus to the important things thus helping you attract those things towards you through a law called the 'Law of Attraction (LOA), a universal law stating like attracts like. Your mind and its three levels have a big role to play in helping the law of attraction work but since LOA is a vast topic.

This is just one way through which affirmations work. Let us discuss the second technique.

Creating Dynamic Tension in Your System

The second way affirmations create their magic is by producing a strong tension in your system. If you are saying something that is at a higher vibration than what you believe to be true, you will experience an uncomfortable dynamic tension. If you say, "I am happy with my life because I have achieved my goals" whereas in reality, you have not accomplished any of your set goals and are not pleased with yourself, you will experience a sore incongruence between what you are chanting and what you believe to be true.

Because this tension makes you feel uneasy, you would want to get rid of it fast. There are two ways to do that: the first one is to stop chanting the affirmation altogether and the second way is to make the affirmation true by doing things and taking action. If you feel unhappy because you have not achieved your goals, you start working to fulfill them so you make your reality match the affirmation.

Now that you are aware of how affirmations work, let us see the role your mind plays in ensuring the law of attraction works.

Chapter 10. Affirmations Decoded

Ever heard about positive thinking? Have you been told that what you think about and speak about is what will manifest in your life? If you have, and someone has been telling you about the power of your words, then it means that they know a thing or two about affirmations, and that just by speaking to yourself in a certain way, you can change the course of your life dramatically.

Affirmations are statements that are said to give one encouragement or help one to tap into their subconscious mind and thus guide action. Affirmations are typically positive, meant to drive one to action or to bring something that we desire to manifestation. When you want to bring about a positive change to your life, you should use the power of affirmations.

The beauty of affirmations lies in the way that they work. They are a tool which you can use to amplify every area of your life, whether you need to work on your personal relationships, finances, career or life in general. So how do they work?

Here's a little experiment for you to try out. Think about what you think about. That is right, take a moment to consider the number of thoughts that you have had since you started reading this book. There are many different thoughts, as you will find that the mind is constantly racing, and most people can have up to 300 thoughts in just sixty seconds. This is great, except that most of the thoughts that people have are negative.

Now, it is unlikely that you are walking around and purposefully thinking about negative things. If that was the case, then your face would be a constant mask of misery. No, these negative thoughts are taking place in your sub-conscious, holding you back from achieving what you know you are capable of. They are the thoughts that tell you that you are not good enough, and that you will be a failure. These thoughts have you believing that you are incapable of accomplishing certain things.

When you begin to make affirmations, you are becoming aware of these types of thoughts, and choosing to change them by thinking positively. The interesting thing is that when you begin to think positively in this way, your circumstances in life begin to change. If you have been facing struggles, they start to clear up, and the journey you are on looks so much clearer.

The key to making the most of affirmations is to ensure that you keep them positive, and that you believe that they are true. Affirmations should speak to your soul, such that what you want to be true can come to pass. When you are firm in the way that you declare something, then you are making an affirmation. For example, you could try to say the following: -

- I am energized and ready to make the most of my day.

- Money loves me and is attracted to me

- Every move that I make is leading me to success

- I feel like I am where I need to be

- I am successful at everything that I do

- I am happy and healthy, I feel great

You probably said these affirmations in your mind as you are reading this book. Now, take a moment to say them out loud. Whether you want to or not, you will notice that you are feeling much better, and that you are beginning to believe that the words you have spoken are truth.

Creating a Positivity Base

In order for you to fully experience the benefits of affirmations, you need to create an affirmation base. This requires that you look deep within you and find you how you can radiate energy that is positive, by considering the way that you are using your mind. In addition, you will need to develop the ability to take any anxiety that you are experiencing and turn it into positivity. So what can you do to enter this state? Here are some tips to help you.

1. Take a silent moment

When you have a thousand thoughts rushing through your mind at any one time, it becomes difficult for you to focus on something as simple as being positive and using affirmations. For you to ensure that affirmations work, you need to focus on having a mind that is quiet.

A quiet mind is not plagued with negative thoughts that can throw you off balance. The mind instead focuses on the present moment and all the benefits that this moment has.

While you are working towards having a quiet mind, ensure that you are not leaning on artificial enhancers, such as drugs or any other treatments that are artificial in nature. The point is not to trick your mind into being quiet, it is to naturally achieve quietness.

2. Think Creatively

Positive affirmations will call for you to find interesting ways that you can utilize your mind. Amongst these is the ability to think creatively. You need to be able to see things in new ways so that you are able to express your affirmations with ease. When you have this ability, the words that you can use to motivate yourself are without limit.

3. Happy Attitude

Ensure that you have a happy attitude in all that you are pursuing. When you have positive energy, it will be much easier for you to see the good in every situation. This will help elevate your consciousness.

This book is all about how you can use the power of affirmations in your daily living. There is one focus that this book has, and that is to help you double your earnings by using affirmations. If all that has been on your mind is how you are going to pay your bills and make it from one month to the next, you will find that the words you speak to your situation can create lasting results for you. All that you need to do is believe.

Chapter 11. Happiness Affirmations

One of the most essential things to pursue in life is true happiness as it is the foundation of any other meaningful thing in life. If you think about it, why do you do what you do? What motivates you to strive for success? Why do you work hard every day? All these questions can be answered by one simple answer, "Happiness". Much of what we do in life is because we want to be happy but many of us are not because we lack the understanding of what true happiness means. One basic thing you should know is that it is not found in material possessions and that it lies within you, all you have to do is uncover it. Together with peace, wholeness, love and peace, happiness is considered as one of our deepest longing. Once you achieve happiness it influences other things like your relationships, work and health. It is exactly what fuels us to thrive and flourish as human beings and when happy you will live a more fulfilling and satisfying life. To be happy then the work should begin in your mind and is why I want to introduce to you the best affirmations that will allow anyone to cultivate true and lasting happiness.

1) I choose to be happy and I deserve to be happy

Every single person deserves to be really happy in life and this can only be made possible if they choose to be. This affirmation is meant to push you towards making every moment an opportunity to believe in the ability to be happy and aligning all your thoughts, actions and feelings towards attracting happiness.

2) I spread happiness to others and absorb happiness from them

Happiness shared is one that will last and you should understand that people build us and we should build them too. Whatever you do, ensure that it benefits both you and those around you. It is not only your happiness that matters but also for those in your life. With this affirmation you will know how to connect and relate with other people and will at the end live a happier and more fulfilling life.

3) Life makes me happy

You might be at a very bad point in life and may not see anything to smile about but the truth is that there is so much in life to be grateful for. Affirming to this is a way through which you will learn to be a more grateful person. This will be through overlooking the negative and focusing on the positive and this includes the fact that you are alive. There is so much in life to be happy for and the problems you may have in life are not reason enough to not live happily.

4) Happy thoughts come to me easily

Happy thoughts will come to you when you allow them to and by affirming to the fact that happy thoughts come to you easily one opens up to all the happiness that is available. Once you believe in the fact that happy thoughts can easily flow through your mind then you will and with time you end up being the happiest you have ever been. Our thoughts you should know shape a big part of our life and being in control 0fv them makes you a better person.

5) To me happiness is a journey and not a destination

Happiness keeps growing from time to time and you should never stop working towards being a happier person. As the affirmation explains, it is a journey and not a destination, just keep working on making your life better by creating more and more happiness. This way you cultivate so much self love and confidence which is what you need to make life more meaningful.

6) I have a bright and happy future

If you affirm to the fact that you will have a bright and happy future you will not have to worry anymore. All you will be left with is working towards making it as you wish, simply put, if you can think it then you can achieve it. When you keep telling yourself that you have a happy and bright future then the present moment will be one of joy.

7) Happy thoughts bring happy things in life

What many people don't know is that our thoughts have so much power and with this affirmation you will learn that with happy thoughts you could actually bring happy things in life. This therefore focuses all your energy into being happy as it will come with a reward. Everything you do will with time be for the sole purpose of being happiness as it is considered to be the foundation of greatness.

8) I am happier than I have ever been

Admitting that you are actually happy is an essential step to take as you will begin believing in happiness. Every day that you tell your subconscious mind you are happy you will gradually feel that way as every part of you gets used to the idea of being happy.

9) It is fine to be happy

Even through your darkest time it really helps to believe it is okay to be happy, this is especially in times of loss. Life can be tough at times but why waste it being sad especially when you know how limited time we have. You could have difficult experiences and situations but by knowing it is okay to be happy you will try to be.

10) Helping others bring in so much joy

This is one very important thought to keep reminding yourself because helping others is an act that can change your life forever. It will not only make you happy but will bring in so many blessings into your life. Affirming to the fact that helping others is good makes you take every opportunity you can to help. This will with no doubt bring you so much satisfaction.

11) I have the power to make myself happy

This is actually very true; every single person has the strength within them to bring happiness into their lives. Believing in your ability to make yourself happy shows that you are ready and willing to be happy. This will at the end push you to the positive things in life allowing you to manifest as much happiness as possible.

12) I am very happy with where I am in life

Many people find it difficult to accept the things they have and where they are in life which could be the reason why they lack peace. Affirming that you are happy with where you are in life makes you a more grateful person and you will never worry too much about the past or future. This is a good way of creating peace through which you will ultimately live a happy life.

Chapter 12. Health Affirmations

Whatever it is you want to attain in life you can't really be able to if you don't first work on being healthy. Being in good health should always be a priority goal and is the reason why I want you to have the best affirmations for achieving and maintaining good health. Sometimes the diseases is always just in the mind and changing how you think about your general health and wellbeing will give you a new beginning. To have the strength and ambition needed to push through life you will need use health affirmations to be healthy. The thing is that when the mind thinks health thoughts then the body finds it easier to stay healthy. Below are effective health affirmations you could use:

1) I am healthy

This is an important affirmation that helps you declare every single day that you are a very healthy person. Admitting that you are healthy is a path to becoming or maintaining your health. When you believe that you are healthy then your body agrees with you.

2) I always feel good

Affirming to the fact that you are always feeling great will not allow any kind of sickness to bring you down as you believe in feeling good. This makes you feel good at all times and no part of you objects to that. When you feel good about yourself, your health will also improve.

3) I deserve good health

Every single person deserves to be healthy and no matter how weak you feel or the amount pain you are in, you still deserve to be very healthy. This affirmation is meant to help you know that you are not a lesser person because of your health and that it is within your power to feel better. When the mind instructs the rest of your body to feel and be healthy then that is how it will be.

4) My happiness will put me in good health

You don't have to frown or feel sad about anything because your good health is dependent on your happiness. The more times you encourage yourself to stay happy the easier it becomes to improve your health. The thing is that your body, mind and heart need you to have inner peace for effective functioning.

5) Every day that passes my body becomes more energetic

When one is sick it does you no good to think that there is totally no improvement as this does you no good. Believing that you are actually making progress and that your body keeps gaining energy from time to is what you need to get well. It actually gives a peace of mind and encourages you to not give up.

6) My daily exercises will make me healthier

This affirmation acts on pushing you to maintain your exercise routine which as you may already know has so many benefits for both your mind and body. The more you believe that the exercises you do are of so much benefit then you will maintain them and in the process build a stronger and healthier you.

7) My body is strong and will fight any diseases

It is true that you are strong enough to fight all kinds of health problems and this is because you know how to take care of your body. The moment your mind assures you that you can fight whatever is trying to creep into your body then you will overcome.

8) I choose to nurture my body with healthy foods

This is where you get into the habit of eating healthy and generally living a healthy lifestyle. Using this affirmation daily will not allow you to compromise your healthy in any way just because of laziness or ignorance. We all know that what we eat matter so much when it comes to improving our general wellbeing.

9) All my thoughts are filled with health and wellbeing

Your thoughts highly influence how you feel and is the reason why you need to encourage yourself to hold thoughts that are only for your own good. What you think about yourself is what will be and is the reason why those individuals who keep complaining they are sick even if they are not end up being sick.

10) I am very grateful for my good health

Gratitude is what opens you up to the best of what life offers and this is why this affirmation comes in as very necessary. The more you thank God for your good health the more healthy you end up being.

11) I love taking care of myself

This affirmation pushes you to do things that improve your health in all ways because you tell yourself you love living a healthy lifestyle. This way you will definitely get into the habit of really taking care of yourself.

Chapter 13. Success Affirmations

We all have our definitions of success but whatever yours is I know you can achieve it by using affirmations. The understanding of success changes from person to person because we all have different goals and personalities. But what is important is believing in the fact that you can achieve your own definition of the word which is made easier by consistently using affirmations. It is said that the first and most essential step to success is having an understanding of who you are as a person and determining important factors that will push you towards success. As much as we all have unique pattern of interests and abilities we all have the potential to make our dreams a reality. A mind that believes in success will at the end of it all become successful.

The success affirmations are meant to help condition your mind for success and also get you ready because an unprepared mind can't achieve much.

Below are very essential success affirmations:

1) I am a success magnet

This means that you can attract success at any point or time in life because there is so much potential in you. Success is not limited to specific individuals and you too can be successful no matter how challenging the journey seems.

2) I always have solutions

When you are faced with any kind of difficulties it helps to believe that you always have a solution and solution will come. Nothing is impossible to conquer in life as long as one gives it their all. During hard times there is no need to panic and this gives you room to find solutions.

3) I am in charge of my life

Affirming to this is a way through which a person can start being more responsible and most importantly taking action. Knowing that you are in charge, gives you the power to always work towards creating the best for yourself. Success is dependent on your actions and you are the only person who can make a difference.

4) I understand that success comes through good thinking and hard work

Nothing good comes into life if you can't think positively and work hard to make them a part of you. Affirming to this every morning is good as one wakes up feeling enthusiastic towards working as they know good things come through working hard.

5) I deserve to be successful

You deserve to be successful and you will be if you work hard and focus all your efforts into being successful. No one should ever tell you that you don't have what it takes when you know that you have all it takes. You have all the potential to succeed and all that you need is believe in that.

6) I always have successful ideas

Your ideas are not worthless as you might think or as other people may say and this is the kind of affirmation one needs to believe in that. Those same ideas you undermine could be what you require to finally have a better life.

7) I love working hard

It is at times difficult to keep working hard but when you use this affirmation you will never quit. Through hard work a person can make so much progress and the truth is that nothing comes easy in life.

8) Goal setting is the way to go

With this affirmation you can be able to maintain the habit of setting goals as it keeps reminding you how efficient it is. Any time you think that goals are useless just because you haven't achieved yours make sure you have this affirmation in mind. With goal setting and affirmations you will have a double source of motivation.

9) I love waking up early

Individuals who wake up early every day are said to be the most successful because this kind of habit is what you need to stay focused. The more you keep affirming that you love waking up early the easier it will be for you to naturally wake up early every other day.

10) I have so much pride in myself

This is the kind of affirmation that reminds you to always appreciate yourself even if you are not where you desire to be. The thing is that you have obviously made progress and this is worth appreciating. This kind of mentality is what you need in order to stay on track.

11) I am a risk taker

Success comes when you can finally overcome all your individual fears and finally learn to take risks. This is necessary because it is what opens you up to more of life's possibilities. Getting stuck in your comfort zone means you will never change or improve in any way.

12) I have so much talent

We all have our unique talents and yours is what you need to finally have the things you want in life. What am trying to say is that no one is better than you and by believing in yourself then you can be the best at what you do.

13) There are so many possibilities in life

Life offers every person possibilities and opportunities, it doesn't have to be so much but whatever you have coming your way should be effectively utilized to achieve greatness. Don't ever think you have nothing in your life when you haven't reached out to find out what is in store for you.

Chapter 14. Affirmations and Prayer

For many people, affirmations are not enough to change the course of one's life. They need to be backed with prayer or a connection to something that is more spiritual. This connection could be to a god or higher being, or it could even be to the miraculous power of the universe. This all ties in to a premise that underlies many religions and beliefs. That is, you need to ask for what you want from your higher being, believe that your higher being shall bring it into your life, and prepare to receive it in a manifestation that is beyond what you can imagine.

Our Psychology and Prayer

Prayer in itself is one of the most powerful psychological tools that we have. Within our consciousness, it helps us to develop our faith in things that are unseen, believing that they will come to pass. When you are facing the toughest financial situation, or are looking at relationships that are not working, then you may find yourself praying for a solution, a way out or a change in your circumstances.

When you are in prayer, you give yourself up to whatever nature has to offer you, with the believe that doing so, being able to surrender, will lead to a turnaround in situations, so that you can receive all the good things that have been designed for you.

The question is how does prayer tie in with affirmations? It comes down to repetition. In many religions there are prayers that are repeated in the same way every day, the same words being said over and over again. The belief it that repeating these words makes it easier to bring what you are asking for into life. Whether you are asking for blessings, to be at one with others, or even thanking your higher power for the good things that happen in your life. The result is the same, you end up with positive thoughts.

People who pray go into states of meditation, which then raises their levels of consciousness and positively affects their thinking. To use affirmations through prayer, you need to speak positive words about who you are. Here are some examples.

I AM: -

Joy – This reveals that I am an embodiment of positivity, a person whom all want to interact with. I am able to satisfy all of those around me, and I am on the path of achieving great things.

Love – This reveals that I am highly generous and my positivity affects me and all those around me. Love means abundance, and being able to enrich experiences and people with my existence.

Unique – There is something special about me and what I have to offer the world. Others may try to imitate me, but will be unable to identify that special part of me. I have a reason for being here.

Free – My decisions in the present are not dictated by what has happened to me in past moments. This means that the world of possibility is before me, and all I need to do is grab hold of my positive thoughts.

Use affirmations in prayer with a primary goal, and that is to change your perceptions towards positivity so that you can attract more positive situations into your life. This way, you will begin to see changes happening in your life. Many people choose prayer and affirmations when they are facing painful or desperate situations in their lives. To experience all the benefits that affirmations can bring to your life, you need to use them, and praters if you wish to do so all the time, whether things are going as you want or not. When you choose challenging situations to apply affirmations and prayer to, you are coming from a place of negativity that also includes desperation, which will make it more challenging for you to get the results that you wish to achieve. Here are some affirmations that you can say which could also qualify as prayers.

- I know that everything is working out for the best in my finances.

- Thank you for all the prosperity in my finances that I am enjoying to date.

- I am happy for this situation in my life that has opened my mind and my heart.

- I appreciate being able to see my financial situation from a different light

- Thank you higher power, for helping me face and overcome this tough financial situation

When you are praying, there are other actions that you can take which will make it much easier for your affirmation to work. Try substituting the words that you use, especially when you are talking about the things that you need. Take the word have for example. When used in a negative way, such as in the sentence, I have to get more money, I have to solve this problem, you are showing a negative attitude towards your problem and your higher being.

Try using the word get instead, and accompany this word with some gratitude. For example, you can say that you get to pay your bills on time and are thankful for that. In addition, you can also say that you get to be thankful for

319

the turnaround in your life. These words transform the affirmations that you are using.

The same applies for the words always and never. There are rarely any absolutes in life, and these words refer to absolutes. Change them and speak the reality of the situation that you are facing. When you do so, you are dealing with the truth, and not expounding on a problem that can easily be controlled.

Keep in mind that the affirmations you use in prayer need to be based on solutions to any issues that you are facing. When they are oriented in this way, it is easy for you to retain your positive energy instead of focusing on the problems that you have, which may be devastating. As you spend more time praying and affirming solutions, you are helping to alleviate the way you think about the problem, which helps you feel lighter about it.

In your prayers, you need to be selfish, and put yourself in the forefront. This basically means that you should come first in every request. Affirmations are not about changing the circumstances of other people; they are for you. If you want to help others, you can use words that call for guidance, so that you can be used as a tool that benefits others. Use your prayers wisely and you will have more confidence in the possible results.

There are different ways that you can tap into the power of affirmations, and if you prefer a spiritual path, you can follow one and still benefit from amazing results.

Chapter 15. How to Use Affirmation Effectively

Believe it or not, some affirmations may cause more harm than good. For example, have you ever told a friend not to be nervous and ended up making him twice as nervous as he already was? The mind is clever, and it won't give up its disposition without a fight, so here's what we do to make effective affirmations:

- Turn declarative affirmations into interrogative affirmations – one of the most recent findings in behavioral psychology is that people are more willing to admit defeat in an argument if they were asked questions instead of being attacked by argumentative statements. For example, if you're nervous about giving a company presentation, instead of telling yourself: "I'm going to do great! I've practiced all night and I've done this man times before," you can instead ask yourself, "Last time I've presented, people were amazed at how entertaining and informative my slides were. What can I do to make this presentation even better?" By giving yourself concrete questions to answer, the brain doesn't think it needs to defend itself. Use this tip whenever positive declarative affirmations don't seem to work.

- Be specific with your affirmations – In order for your brain and the Universe to collaborate properly, you have to be clear about what you want. A lot of people have problems identifying exactly what they want but have no trouble identifying what they hate. If you're one of those people who notice the negatives more than the positives, don't fret; a simply workaround is to find the opposite of the things that you hate. For example, find a song you really hate – to the point that you cringe and squirm whenever it plays on the radio. Now find what you believe is the opposite of that song in terms of how it makes you feel. In most cases, the opposite of that song to you is your favorite song. In short, if you know something that makes you unhappy, then chances are, the opposite of that will make you happy.

Here are step-by-step instructions on probing areas of your life that need positive affirmations:

1. Write down your regular daily routine

2. Separate the things you experience into three columns:

   A. Events you enjoy experiencing

   B. Events you don't enjoy experiencing

   C. Events that don't really evoke a strong emotional response.

3. For column B, look for the complete opposite of that event and list it in column A. For example, if column B contains a statement like: "Never getting a good night's sleep and always waking up groggy and tired," it should be converted to something like: "Having a restful sleep and waking up feeling refreshed, alert, and ready to face the day!" and placed in column A.

4. For column C, look for the positive version of that event and list it in column A. For example, if column C contains a statement like: "Eating breakfast," it could be converted to something like: "Eating a healthy, delicious breakfast that'll keep me energized throughout the day" and placed in column A.

5. Column A should now contain specific events in your life that you can use as a starting point for positive affirmations!

- **Be consistent with your affirmations** – there has been a phenomenon observed wherein people who use their goals and dreams as passwords to accounts they access everyday end up achieving those goals and dreams. This has to do with the fact that they are forced to type these goals and dreams again and again, forcing it to seep into the deepest crevices of their minds. By consistently affirming yourself at least thrice a day, your mind will eventually learn to accept a better form of reality you've crafted.

- **Believe your affirmations** – telling yourself that you are calm and relaxed before an interview doesn't mean you're going to deny that you're nervous. On the contrary, you're actually acknowledging your nervousness and then positively affirming yourself to overcome it. If you notice that you're reacting in a very strong and negative manner when you try to affirm yourself, try to apply the tip regarding converting declarative affirmations into interrogative affirmations. It's extremely important that you believe what you're telling yourself otherwise you'll be subconsciously affirming the opposite.

Chapter 16. Using Affirmations to Speak to Your Finances

If ever there was a secret to gaining financial success and freedom, it is in affirmations. The words that you speak, whether you choose to say them out loud or you repeat them in your thoughts, have incredible power. When you want to use affirmations for your finances, you need a starting point. At the starting point, you should ask yourself – what are you saying about your finances now?

Take a moment and think about how you think of your finances. Some of the phrases which may easily come to mind include: -

- I am so broke right now.

- If only my money lasted more than one week after pay day.

- I wish I could afford that lovely home.

- My neighbor's car is brilliant – where does he get the money?

You will notice something that these phrases have in common, and that is they all focus on your desire to have money. In addition, this desire that you have comes from the point of lack. If your thoughts are similar to these, you are constantly acknowledging that you do not have money, and you lack some of the things that you want.

When you look at your thoughts and consider the law of attraction, it will start to become clearer, the understanding as to why you experience financial difficulty. Before you can use affirmations, and have them work to increase your finances. You need to be in the right state of mind. That state of mind is one of abundance.

Perhaps one of the hardest things that you can try to do is be positive in a situation that is potentially negative. However, if you want to benefit from affirmations, this is the first thing that you need to do.

To achieve this, you need to think of your finances in the present moment, not so much as they are, but as you would like them to be. This will call for some fantastical thoughts, which may seem unrealistic at first, but you will find that you can accomplish something using this strategy.

Here are the positive affirmations that you should be telling yourself to get the financial results you desire.

- I am so glad that I have a source of income.
- The money in my wallet is more than I need.
- I can go the whole month without experiencing lack.
- I am so glad that I can find homes which inspire me.
- My neighbor works hard to get what he wants. I will do the same and achieve something great.

The tone of these affirmations is quite different from what would normally go through your mind. These have elements of hope and expectation, and another essential attribute which is gratitude. Incorporating gratitude into your affirmations can help hasten the results that you achieve.

It is important that you understand that even with positive affirmations, you will experience ups and downs in your finances. This is not a bad thing, and you should not then decide that affirmations are not working for you. What is important is the steps that you take to deal with these situations as they arise. There are several powerful steps that you can follow to help you get back on the right track with your positive thinking and utilization of affirmations. They are as follows: -

Step 1: Practice

Affirmations require practice, each and every time that you have a moment to do so. It is so easy to slip into negative thinking because it is comfortable. After all, it is possibly what you are used to doing. When finances become a challenge, remove words like 'cannot' and 'won't' from your vocabulary. These are the words that will limit the power of your affirmations. Instead, replace them with words like I will, and I can, and I have. These are powerful and effective words, and have the incredible ability of turning your situation around.

Step 2: You're the Boss

When you want to double your finances, you need to keep in mind that the only person who is in charge is you. You are in control of what is happening within your daily experience with money and how you react to it. All you need to do is decide that every reaction you will have is positive.

Step 3: Seek out Positivity

Sometimes, it is a challenge to find those positive words within you, which you know will pull you forward. This may cause you to feel like a failure and lead you down a spiral of negativity. When it comes to your finances, this can be devastating. If you rare feeling lost, look to someone who has surpassed their financial problems and listen to their story. Within it, you will inevitably find reference to positive affirmations that they used to carry them thought the tough times. Draw some inspiration form their messages, and begin to feel good about your situation. The more you listen to these, the easier it will be to speak out some excellent affirmations, even if all you are doing is copying the words of someone else.

Step 4: Recognize your Power

Do not underestimate the power that your own words have on positivity. Think about this situation. Someone walks up to you and asks you the question, How are you doing? You can simply respond with the word fine. This would be diminishing the positivity that you can bring into your life. Instead, focus on words that pack a punch. These would include worlds like excellent, brilliant and fantastic.

Now apply this to your finances. In the middle of the month, someone asks you, How are you managing financially? Rather than moan and groan about the way that everything is going wrong, choose instead to affirm that your finances are fine. You can say something life, 'They are great thanks. I am expecting some excellent news in a few days.' Your positive outlook and powerful words will help you see something totally new in your situation.

Step 5: Look for Stimulation

Think back to a moment where you experienced blissful happiness? You never wanted the feeling to come to an end right? In fact, it is possible that you did everything in your power to extend the feeling for as long as you could. This is because you understood the power that this feeling had.

You can do the same with your finances. When experiencing periods where you have more than enough, stimulate your thinking to believe that this situation will last much longer than you expect. This will mean that in the dull moments when you do not know what you should be looking forward to, you are already stimulated for positivity.

Step 6: Be Thankful

Affirmations make it easier for you to be thankful. You can easily start your affirmations with the words, I am so thankful that….. For example, you could say, I am so thankful that I am ready to pass this test. Using affirmations to appreciate the little things in life will help you draw to you the finances you are hoping for.

Step 7: Forget about the past

Have you had some trouble with money in the past. Perhaps you have faced bankruptcy and debt and the situation seemed much worse than you could manage. Use affirmation to move away from the restrictive thinking that may have limited your past. Choose instead to focus on what you are able to accomplish in the near future. When you do this, making the commitment to remain positive becomes so much easier and you will find that you are able to bring more finance in your life.

The Results of your Affirmations

Speaking positive affirmations into your financial situation gives out the message that you have your finances under control. This opens up opportunities for you to develop your finances with positive results. Do not expect that positive affirmations will automatically result in a wallet that expands within a few days. Using positive affirmations is not the same as picking money from an endless source.

What you can expect is that your affirmations will reveal to your various ways in which you can expand your finances. These could be excellent ideas to help minimize your debts, entrepreneurial solutions for you to build your future, or even sources of money that are around you which you never thought of before.

Here is what you need to look out for. Once you start making positive affirmations, stay alert to ideas that come to your mind. Many times, these ideas may not make much sense. For example, you may have some old books within your home that you never read. One day, out of the blue, you have the thought to start a lending library where you charge people a certain amount of money each week. This may seem like something small, but you can trust it is the beginning of financial inflow into your life.

What all this means is that you need to be mindful and alert. Pay attention to thoughts that are a call to action since these are the ones that will change your finances.

Chapter 17. 10 Tips to Avoid Wrong Affirmations

To ensure that you are not making any wrong affirmations which are negative in nature, you need to move away from the mindset that is plagued by fear and doubt. Positive thinking requires your positivity and faith that things are going to go as you want them to, which is that your needs will be met as you desire.

Here are 10 tips that you can use to avoid the wrong affirmations.

1. *Catch Yourself*

As you are now conscious about the number of negative thoughts that you have in a day, you are ready to learn how to catch yourself when you have a negative thought. The moment you notice one, replace it by saying a positive affirmation. Your thoughts may not be in words alone, and could include the visualization that you have for the future. When you visualize a situation going wrong or failure, choose to see it from a positive light as you visualize success in its place.

2. *Speak Positively*

There are some negative words that you say so naturally that you do not even realize you are saying them. These are words like I won't, I can't, I shouldn't and so on. When you find yourself saying these words, change them to positive ones to alter the meaning that you are attaching to your situation. Then, use the positive words to state an affirmation. If you find yourself thinking, I can't make 1000 dollars a day, change the words to I can successfully make 1000 dollar each day.

3. Start Now

Every journey begins with one step, as will the journey that you are taking to overcoming wrong affirmations. There is no time like the present to begin thinking positively, and to ensure that this thinking comes through in your behavior.

To avoid wrong affirmations, have enough faith and freedom from doubt to believe that your circumstances can change immediately. Also, let go of the fear that things will not go your way. Using positive affirmations will transform your life, trust in the process and the results.

4. Stay Present

Sometimes negative affirmations take root because we are too busy thinking about something that could happen in the future, rather than focusing on what is happening in the present. Thinking about the future in this way can fill you with anxiety and cause negative emotions, such as fear or anger. Stay in the present, and speak positivity into each moment you encounter.

5. Take Time to Meditate

Dedicate some time on a daily basis to calm your mind with meditation. This will help you become present to your thoughts so that they do not overwhelm you, especially the negative thoughts. With mediation, you are able to stay present and relax, which will help to ease your mind. With peace of mind, it is much easier to make positive affirmations.

6. Be Around Positivity

Making positive affirmations is challenging enough, especially when you start and need to make a conscious

331

effort to believe what you are saying. It can be much easier if you are surrounded by people who are positive, and able to give you feedback which proves to be constructive. Positive people can help you make affirmations that put you back in the right perspective.

7. Take Responsibility

There is no one who is in control of who you are and what you are doing or going through. Sometimes, you may believe that positive affirmations will not work because you are basing their results on what is happening in the lives of other people. To avoid making the wrong affirmations, you need to take full responsibility of your thinking and actions, and understand that by doing so, you can create positive affirmations that will have the effect you desire.

8. Accept Imperfection

As you focus on trusting a positive affirmation, you may find that you make a mistake along the way. Without realizing what you are doing, you then create a negative affirmation to bash yourself for making a mistake. Accept that the process is not perfect and you are bound to get things wrong once in a while. Then pick yourself up, learn from the mistake, and go back to making positive affirmations about your situation.

9. Create a List

If things are not going your way, you may make a negative affirmation to justify all the events that do not seem to be working out as expected. When you notice that you are about to do this, grab a piece of paper and change your thinking by listing down things that you are thankful for. Being grateful puts you in a positive mindset and makes it easier for you to make positive affirmations.

10. Make Use of Quotes

There are so many positive thinking quotes that you can use to change your thinking in an instant. You can have these quotes anywhere, saved on your phone as a screensaver, on the main screen of your computer, or even on little post it notes that you place on your mirror or fridge. Reading these quotes over and over again will help then to resonate within you, and thus, speaking out positive affirmations will be much easier.

Chapter 18. 6 Steps to Create Powerful and Workable Positive Affirmations

To create life-changing affirmations that override negative ideas rooted in your unconscious mind and supply it with an incessant stream of positivity, follow the simple guidelines below.

Step 1: Enlist Your Negative Traits/Qualities/Thoughts

Grab a journal and a pen and enlist all your negative qualities, any negative ideas that make you feel incapable of doing what you want in life and any negativities embedded in your mind including the criticism you have been holding on to or any past failure/setback that has changed your life for the worse. Think back to the time your business failed, when someone said something mean to you, or when your boss said you were inadequate for the job etc.

Remember not to judge yourself for these flaws; just jot them down. While writing any recurring belief (belief you strongly believe in or any idea/suggestion you frequently feed to your mind), observe if you are holding on to that belief in any part of your body.

For instance, when you think of why your first business failed, do you feel any sort of tightness in your neck? When you focus on how unhappy you are with your weight, do you feel a pain in your stomach? By doing this, you become aware of the physical manifestations of negative affirmations; this increases your determination to get rid of them.

334

Step 2: Write a Positive Affirmation Considering the Transformation You Want

Write any affirmation on any positive side of your self-judgment. If you wrote, "I am useless," write a positive affirmation that states, "I am cherished and amazing," or "I am really happy and proud of myself."

At this point, think of the sort of transformation you would like to manifest and then choose any of the previous negative affirmations and make it positive. For instance, if you wrote, "I hate myself because I'm overweight" and you would like to work on carving an attractive, slender physique first, think of how you would like to be and write a positive affirmation based on that.

Step 3: Add Emotions to Your Affirmation

Next, add a few positive emotions to your affirmation to make it emotionally engaging and powerful. If your positive affirmation states, "I am content with myself," change it to "I am very happy that I'm living a content life and this increases my involvement in it." Emotional words increase your involvement in the affirmation and engage your senses. This helps you feel and believe each word of the affirmation as you chant it, which helps it easily imbed in your mind.

Step 4: Keep the Affirmation Focused on the Present

Your subconscious cannot differentiate between what is real and what is imaginary. If you tell it you are successful, happy, confident, or any other positive change you would like to achieve in your life, it will accept this as the reality.

Most times, our positive affirmations fail to work because instead of keeping them present focused, we make them future oriented. Instead of saying "I am confident," you are likely to say "I am going to be confident" or "I am going to put in efforts to increase my confidence levels." These affirmations are not wrong per se, but what makes them ineffective is their focus on the future.

Future oriented affirmations lead your subconscious and unconscious mind into focusing on improving your future, not your present. This means that because your affirmation focuses on the future, you cannot enjoy the desired change in the present.

To turn your desire into the reality now, create present oriented affirmations. Write, "I am confident and happy," or "I am achieving all my goals" instead of "I will be happy" or "I will achieve my goals."

Step 5: Focus on Using Positive Words Only

When building your affirmation, keep it focused on positive words. Instead of saying, "I am not unconfident anymore," say "I am confident." Instead of saying "I am not worthy of meaningless things" say "I am worthy of amazing things." This is very important because words with negative connotation build a weak image in your mind. In fact, your mind omits/overlooks words such as no, never, not, cannot, and then rephrases the affirmation accordingly. If you were to say, "I am not weak," your mind will change it to "I am weak."

After the rephrase, the residual suggestion is neither positive nor will it motivate your mind to think positively. To ensure you do not feed negative ideas to your mind, keep your affirmation purely positive.

Step 6: Keep it Short

After you complete adding positive and emotional words to your affirmation, go through it a few times to revise it and edit out any extra words. The goal is to have a positive, present-oriented, and concise affirmation that delivers the message clearly. Long affirmations take a while to speak and memorize and can be quite boring too, which can make you lose interest in them. On the other hand, concise and to-the-point affirmations are easy to speak and remember and are not so boring. Ensure you keep your suggestion under 15 to 20 words at the most.

Using this systematic procedure, you can create many powerful, actionable, and effective affirmations that can change the course of your life and transform it into a happy, meaningful, content, amazing, and successful life.

There are different ways to practice affirmations and several techniques that enhance their effectiveness.

Chapter 19. Meditation for positive thinking

Meditation should come as no surprise to anyone as the best kind of practice for mental development.

There are many free programs online as well as phone apps that can help you learn to meditate. With practice meditation will become easier and you will be able to block negative thoughts. This will help your affirmations work better and more efficiently.

Meditation is known all over the world for its numerous benefits. For one thing, it is good for your mental health. Researchers have found that those who meditate on a daily basis experience more positive emotions than those who rarely or do not meditate at all.

In fact, a study that involved participants who meditated for three months has revealed that those who continued to meditate even after the study were able to have better mindfulness and social support. They also had an improved sense of purpose and reduced symptoms of illnesses.

Meditation is ideal to be done in the early morning when your mind is still fresh or late in the evening before you to go to sleep. When you meditate, make sure to focus on your breathing. It is crucial to take deep and regular breaths.

Mindfulness meditation is an ideal type of meditation if you want to improve the way you think. This type of meditation is all about focusing on the present moment and not worrying about the past or the future.

When you first begin to practice mindfulness meditation, you may notice yourself having unnecessary thoughts.

Don't worry because this is normal and expected of beginners.

Simply recognize that you are having these thoughts and then let them go. Do not hold on to them. Do not judge them. Just acknowledge their presence. As you continue to practice mindfulness meditation, your mind will be trained and you will find yourself having less of these unwanted thoughts.

Meditation Script

[This text should be read slowly, with plenty of pauses to allow rest and time for the words to sink into the listener; time for them to become sleepy. Significant pauses have been marked within the text.]

There is a common belief that holds most of us back. That our dreams are frivolous.

Do you hold that belief, somewhere inside of you? That your dreams are frivolous. That the things you truly want in life are not noble or important. Perhaps you grew up with messages that dreaming big, or dreaming at all, was a waste of time. Maybe you learnt that success and comfort and security were for other people and not for you. Perhaps you feel ashamed of desiring a different lifestyle; you have a deep sense that it's greedy or selfish to want.

You're not alone.

More people than you can imagine share these feelings with you.

But they're not real. They were passed down to you by generations of people who did not look closely at where their own belief systems had grown from. Passed down through a sense of fear, scarcity and misplaced pride.

And you can be different. You can be where this stops. Because you are doing the work: the fact that you are listening to this recording means that you are doing the work. You are reevaluating your belief systems. You are considering how you got here, and opening up to the possibility that there could be another way of thinking about your life.

That's a powerful thing. So please acknowledge how strong you are for being here; how good it is for you, for the people around you, and for future generations of your family that you are taking the time to learn and grow.

Thank you.

[Pause]

Now...find a comfortable seated position. Either on the floor, sitting on a cushion or two to elevate the hips above the knees; or on a chair with both feet flat to the ground. Make sure that the spine is upright but not too rigid. This doesn't need to feel forceful. You can feel comfortable and relaxed.

Take a few deep breaths in through the nose and out through the nose.

Simply checking in with the body; taking a moment to settle in and get present.

You are here. You are ready. You are doing a wonderful, powerfully positive thing right now. Sit with that.

[Pause]

Because so much of what holds us back is grounded in what we learnt in our early years of life, affirmations are an effective way to rewire our brains. By regularly using affirmations that give your subconscious brain a different perspective, you can shift your natural state from scarcity to abundance.

You can shift to a state in which you are open and willing and grateful to accept success, wealth, love — whatever it is that you dream of.

You can manifest the life of your dreams.

And not only can you do that, but you deserve to do that.

You are worthy of living a life that lights you up. That fulfills you. That taps into your deepest passions and allows you to share your unique gifts freely with the world.

You deserve to do this. And doing this is good for everyone around you and for the wider world — it is not selfish. If everyone lived in alignment with their dreams then the dissatisfaction and anger that causes so much pain in the world would be lessened. Human life would be calmer. We would be able to support and love each other openly.

Take a deep breath in and breathe out through the nose.

[Pause]

I will speak an affirmation once for you to hear. And then we will repeat it together — three times.

We'll do this with three different affirmations in turn. Each one building on the last.

So, starting with the first one:

I am not ashamed or afraid of wanting to achieve my dreams.

[Pause]

Repeat it with me. You can speak it out loud if you feel comfortable to do so. If you don't feel able to say this out loud right now, that's fine — repeat it silently in your mind. What matters is that you focus and connect with the meaning between the words. We'll speak slowly. And after the third repetition there will be a few moments of silence. Absorb that silence — listen closely to it. It's an important pause.

I am not ashamed or afraid of wanting to achieve my dreams.

I am not ashamed or afraid of wanting to achieve my dreams.

I am not ashamed or afraid of wanting to achieve my dreams.

[Pause]

Great. And now, the second affirmation:

My dream life is not unrealistic. It is possible if I allow it to be.

This affirmation is a big one. By using it, we jump straight into one of the biggest limiting thoughts that many people have — that our dreams aren't realistic, and that realistic has to be small and sensible. But this is not true. Realistic does not have to be small. It does not have to fit with the perceived reality that you grew up with. It does not have to appear realistic to your relatives or your friends. It only has to be realistic for you.

And anything can be realistic for you if you welcome it with open arms.

So, three times together.

[Pause]

My dream life is not unrealistic. It is possible if I allow it to be.

My dream life is not unrealistic. It is possible if I allow it to be.

My dream life is not unrealistic. It is possible if I allow it to be.

[Pause]

And then we'll move on to our third and final affirmation. This is about you being capable.

I am capable of acquiring any skill or knowledge that I need in order to achieve my dreams.

Let's speak it three times together. Out loud or silently. And remember to sit and listen closely to the silence after the words, too.

[Pause]

I am capable of acquiring any skill or knowledge that I need in order to achieve my dreams.

I am capable of acquiring any skill or knowledge that I need in order to achieve my dreams.

I am capable of acquiring any skill or knowledge that I need in order to achieve my dreams.

[Pause]

Now notice the breath.

The natural rhythm of the breath.

Your practice is nearly complete. Allow your mind and body to relax; to sink, to settle. This is time to absorb rather than to focus.

And while you relax, sink and settle, I will repeat your affirmations for you. You don't need to concentrate hard this time. Just allow the words to exist in your space. Let them dance around at the edge of your consciousness. Be here with these words.

[Speaker speaks the following affirmations softly and slowly]

You are not ashamed or afraid of wanting to achieve your dreams.

Your dream life is not unrealistic. It is possible if you allow it to be.

You are capable of acquiring any skill or knowledge that you need in order to achieve you dreams.

[Pause]

Open your eyes when you feel ready.

Chapter 20. Negativity Has No Place Here

The world tends to bring negativity to our doorstep. By watching the news, listening to others complain, or simply ruminating on our thoughts, we can get caught up with the negative aspects of life. Being immersed in negativity has both mental and physical effects on our well-being. But how can you avoid the negativity in life?

Focus on who you are. When trying to avoid negativity, you need to decide how you want your life to be. Look for ways to improve but avoid negative self-talk, as this can be detrimental to your self-image.

Declutter. You need to get rid of any clutter in your life, both mental and physical. By decluttering your life and your mind, you free up mental and physical space that is better used in a different way. It's also beneficial to let go of any baggage you may be carrying around.

Appreciate Your Relationships. Make sure you take the time to nurture the relationships that you have and that you value. When you stop to take time to value and reflect on the positive parts of life, you give yourself less time to dwell on the negative aspects of life, and more time to focus on the positive ones.

Record Your Progress. It may be beneficial to consider journaling, and setting goals. Give yourself something to work towards. Keep a journal to record progress and reflect on what you are working towards.

The Effects of Negativity and How to Counteract Them

You know that negativity will cause you harm, but how do you protect yourself from it? Below you will find some tips that will help you to combat the negative influences in your life. Learning to let go of negativity in your life is important to every aspect of your life. Know how to spot negative influences, negative thought processes, and negative patterns in your life.

Sets and enforce limits. When you make your boundaries clear, you are giving others the signal that you will not tolerate something, or that you will not allow the negative energy into your life. By letting others know what your limits are, you are fostering positive relationships.

Allow yourself distance from negativity. If you find situations that are consistently bringing you down and exposing you to negativity, consider making some space between you and that situation. You are not obligated to continue doing something or take part in relationships that bring you mental harm.

Do not react too quickly to the situation, and be mindful of your response. Practice being mindful of how you are reacting to a situation. Reacting too quickly can cause harm in a relationship, and will often bring about a negative aspect of the situation. Make sure that you are keeping your dignity and processing the situation before you respond.

Consider introducing a new topic of discussion. If a conversation is taking a downward turn, change the subject. Give the other person the hint that you do not wish to continue dwelling on the negative topic they have introduced.

Try to be focused on the solutions and not the problems that you encounter. When you dwell on the problems, you only see the negative side of a situation. On the other hand, when you allow yourself to focus on the solutions, you are looking at the situation optimistically.

Allow yourself emotional detachment from other people's opinions of you. Learn to let the opinions of others roll off your back. Don't focus excessively on what other people think of you. Later in this book, we will give you strategies to stop caring what others think of you.

Allow yourself enough time for self-care. When you take care of yourself, you are more likely to look on the bright side. Spend time regularly doing activities that make you feel good.

Understanding Relationships and How to Make the Most of Them

Relationships can be tricky. If you are in a romantic relationship, often it is hard to know how to make the most of it. When you try to understand your partner, you will better understand how they will react and why. With an introverted temperament, you may not read social cues well which can make you struggle in relationships-- both romantic and non-romantic.

Here are some tips to help you make the most out of the relationships that you have in your life. Some tips apply to romantic relationships and partnerships, and others apply to non-romantic relationships and friendships. Either way, you should find new ways to make the best of the relationships that you are in.

Think positive thoughts: Try not to dwell on the negativity that life throws your way. Practicing a positive mindset will benefit you in your relationships. Keep in mind that you don't want someone focusing on the negativity that you bring to a relationship, so strive to be positive. The best place to begin is with your thinking!

Argue in a healthy way. Set ground rules for when you argue. People will disagree regardless of how healthy the relationship is. Having boundaries about what is fair and not fair in an argument is important to retain the relationships even after the argument is over.

Don't fight about money. If you can avoid the money fight, your relationship will benefit. Money is often the biggest cause of stress and arguments in relationships. Keep the lines of communication open and avoid the money arguments. Your relationships will be stronger because of it.

Use words of encouragement. Everyone can benefit from encouragement, but your partner especially can. When you strive to use words that encourage and build up, rather than words that tear down, you are making an investment in the other person.

Have strong friendships away from your relationship. Maintaining who you are outside of the relationship is important. Keep the friendships that you have outside of the relationship. While you are able to have healthy relationships away from each other, you will better be able to focus on your relationship when you are together. Fostering a sense of self is important in any relationship.

Allow enough quality time each week together. Spending quality time together is important. Remember that quality over quantity is important. Quality time includes time where you are focused on each other and you are enjoying yourselves.

Be mindful and don't rush into any situation. This tip is important for romantic relationships. Do not rush to make something permanent. You have time to get to know one another, which is important too. Take your time, and don't rush.

Value each other's opinions and talk to one another. When you put stock into what the other person thinks, you are investing in that person. This is important with the relationships that you would like to preserve. Make sure that you are valuing the opinion of the other person that you care about.

Make sure to have fun and laugh together. Laughter is often the best way to build bonds. Take time to have fun together, and allow for enough time to laugh. When you enjoy each other's company, you can focus on the good parts of the relationship.

Characteristics of a Healthy Relationship

When you look at your relationships, both romantic and non-romantic, it is important to know what is considered a healthy relationship. The common characteristics that both include are:

Respect. Respecting each other in your relationship is important. When you honor the other person, and you care about what that person wants, you are respecting your partner.

Security and Comfort. Security and comfort in a relationship will give you stability and make you feel confident that the relationship is a positive aspect of your life.

Nonviolent. Relationships are nonviolent, and they should never enter a violent phase. If you are in a violent relationship, please seek help and leave the person.

Resolve Conflict. The ability of two people to resolve conflict easily is important in a relationship. How you resolve conflict determines the level of respect in your relationship.

Enjoy Each Other. Enjoying the other person in a relationship is important. You should enjoy spending time together and listening to the other person talk. If you don't, or that person doesn't seem to have that same level of enjoyment for you, the relationship is probably not healthy.

Support One Another. Supporting one another makes a relationship stable. You may not always agree, but offering your support to the ideas and goals of the other person is important.

Interested in the Other Person's Life. Take an interest in the other person's life and know what they want. When you pay attention to their ideas, their goals, and their aspirations you look at the person as a whole and you show love.

Privacy and Confidence. When you have confidence that what you tell a person is going to remain private, you are building up a healthy relationship.

Trust. You must be able to trust the person that you are in a relationship with. If you cannot the relationship is not healthy.

Clear And Open Communication. Clear and open lines of communication are important in a relationship. You must be able to talk to each other and not fear being misunderstood.

Encourage Friendships. When you encourage other friendships outside of your relationship, you are giving the other person freedom to be who they are and enjoy others will have the same interests and goals is them.

Honesty. Honesty is important in a relationship, whether a romantic relationship or non-romantic relationship. When you are able to be honest with the other person, you know that you are valued and that you are safe.

How to Focus on the Good Parts of Life and Relationships

Life is full of positive relationships and interactions. When you allow yourself to focus on the good, and leave the bad behind, you will gain more from both life and the relationships you are nurturing.

Emotional Connections are Important. In order to focus on the good parts of a relationship, it's important to maintain a strong emotional connection. By doing this, you need to be mindful of how you are responding to the other person's emotions. You need to avoid criticism and rejection of their emotions and by doing this you will become closer.

Positive Environment. Strive to keep things positive. By trying to keep the environment of the relationship positive, you are fostering a relationship that will keep you engaged emotionally. In order to do this, you should strive to use small acts of appreciation, and make it a goal to do this on a regular basis. If you're looking for a place to begin, compliments are always a good start.

Empathy is Important. You need to listen to what your mind is telling you and not always rely on your heart. In order to do this, you need to practice empathy which allows you to control your feelings and stress. Make sure you are keeping in view the positive aspects of your partner, and remember that you love them. You need to forget about being right and make it a goal to understand the view of your partner. Also, make it a practice to remember the positive areas and traits of your partner, and try to overlook the negative parts and traits. Keep in mind some negative traits are dangerous, and you should never tolerate violence or abuse.

Happy Life with Happy Relationships. For a happy life have happy relationships. The stronger your relationship the better able you are to cope with the curveballs that life is going to throw your way. When you have a strong connection to people that love and value you, you have a solid foundation to stand upon when a bad situation happens in life. This connection is something that we need to foster because it is important to who we are at our core.

Conflict is Inevitable. Disagreement is just fine. Do not allow yourself to avoid conflict just because you are scared to disagree. In order to have a healthy relationship, you need to feel safe and be allowed to disagree. On the other hand, you need to foster an environment where your partner feels safe to disagree as well.

Maintain Your Sense of Self. In a healthy relationship, it's important that you have interests outside of the relationship itself. By keeping your own identity, and preserving connections to your family and your friends, you were setting the foundation for a healthy relationship. It is perfectly OK to have interests that do not include your partner. Make sure that you are still able to do things alone, and you do not rely solely on your partner for interaction.

Communicate. Communication must remain open and honest in order for a relationship to be healthy. This is the key to any relationship, not just romantic ones. When you know that you can be open and honest with the other person, you can feel safe to let them know what your desires and your needs are. This is important within a relationship so that there is satisfaction on both sides.

Actively Listen. You need to listen and engage in what the other person is saying. Make sure that you are responding appropriately. Make the main goal of listening to the other person is to gain perspective. Don't listen just to hear the words, but rather, listen to understand what the other person is trying to say. Actively listen for points that you have in common. Forget about listening for the purpose of changing another person's mind; that is not effective. As you are listening make sure to pay attention to the tones they are using, and the rising and the falling of the other person's voice. Paying attention to nonverbal cues is important as well.

Compromising is Key. Make a point to find out what is important to the other person in the relationship. As you are doing this, you are building a solid foundation for compromising. Keep in mind that as you are doing this, the other person needs to be doing the same thing. In a relationship, resentment is formed when there's one person who is giving and the other one is just taking. To avoid this, remember to compromise.

You don't need to win in a relationship. As mentioned before a compromise is the most important thing and should be the goal of any relationship. You need to make sure that in the process, you are being respectful and valuing the views of the other person. As you are doing this make sure that when any conflict arises that the fighting is fair. You need to keep in mind

353

that you respect the other person and stay on the issues that you are trying to resolve. If you pick your battles things will go better. It makes no sense to argue about something that cannot be resolved.

Avoid Attacking the Other Person. When you have a grievance, strive to not attack the other person either verbally or nonverbally. Use phrases that focus on you and not on the behavior of the other person. Phrases such as "I don't like it when" or "I am sad when you" are effective. It's also best to stay away from any past arguments or grievances that you've had your partner. If something has not been resolved, avoid bringing it up. Also, avoid blaming and keep the topic about the conflict that you are having at the moment.

Forgive. Make sure that you are able and that you are willing to forgive. If you find that you cannot forgive, you need to leave arguing. The same goes for if the conflict will not ever be able to be resolved. Forgiving is key when having an argument because, without it, there will never be an end to the conflict.

Call a Time Out. If you find that the level of the argument is rising, suggest a break to release stress and to calm down. Even when you're in the heat of the moment, be mindful of what you are saying so that you don't say or do something that you may regret later. An important factor to remember while you are having a conflict with your partner is that you love that person.

Know When to Stop. You need to know when to let go. Understand that not all arguments can be resolved so it's important to understand when to stop and move on. If something will not be resolved, you need to be able to give up and walk away.

Pay Attention to Body Language. Nonverbal cues, such as eye contact, tone of voice, posture, and physical mannerisms oftentimes say more than any word can. Because of this, you need to pay attention to the body language that the other person is displaying. Respond appropriately, but also make sure that your words match your body language. You need to promote an environment where positive interactions are the norm. Make the interactions that you have dependent on the love and the happiness that you wish to share with you the person.

Relationships can be tricky and hard to understand. When you know what to expect, how to react, and what is healthy, you are better prepared to handle the different aspects associated with relationships. Hopefully, the tips listed above will prepare you, and help you, when you are dealing with people that you love.

In addition, hopefully, you are learning how to keep negativity out of your life. The importance of avoiding a pessimistic outlook on life will keep you happy, healthy, and able to cope with the different situations you will encounter in life.

Chapter 21. Living The Life

Now that you already have an idea about how you are going to pursue the happiness that you want. It is now time to learn a new lesson in order to maintain the happiness that you will be able to have. You have to stop taking things for granted and be sure that you will be able to treasure the things that you have and the love that has been given to you.

Here are some of the things you can do to stop taking things for granted.

Be content with what you have

Every person has their own share of blessings that comes from the higher being, but if you are at the bottom of the food chain, it is only natural to ask for more, for a better life, for a better tomorrow. The problem is that most people are not contented with what they have and try to pursue happiness and success even if they have to step on other people. It is not right to disregard other people just because you have a goal you have to achieve, and they are not part of it. You have to love the things you have and be contented with them.

Pay it forward

Learn how to share the blessings you've received to others even if it is a small one. For example, if you happen to be blessed with good food and an abundance of them, then give food to those who need them. You should know that the blessings you received are meant to be shared with other people and not just keep for your own sake. You have to pay the things you received forward to the people who might need them. Donate to charity; spend some time with your family and friends to make them happy.

Appreciate the little things

People love it when you take note of the little things they do for you. They are sensitive creatures that love being praised and being appreciated. While most people do not have the manners to appreciate the things other people do for them, you have to keep in your mind that the people around you are all fighting a battle on their own so you cannot blame them for the things they never really dead.

What you do onto others will come back to you

Have you ever heard of the quote from the bible that says, 'Do not do to others what you do not want others to do to you.' So be generous and give people the things you can provide for them and yet set a limit in doing so. Help those in need so that when you are the one in need, they will help you as well. What it really wants to say is that you have to believe in Karma and realize that what goes around comes around.

See the good in everything and everyone

It is normal for people to tend to focus on the bad instead of the good. Our minds tend to cling to the negative without giving much attention to the positive. It is so easy for people to spot the negative. Thus, seeing the good in the bad is a skill. Veer away from the norm. Go teach yourself to stop focusing on the negative. Don't look for weaknesses, but look for areas of improvement. Don't look for threats, but look for challenges. Don't look at failures, but see the motivation to try again and do better. See the point? There is always something good in everything. Be thankful for all the "bad" things in your life because they are blessings masked as adversities/crisis that you are supposed to unmask and see and experience the beautiful changes they bring into your life.

This goes to people as well. See the good in everyone no matter how hard it is because you have no idea what they have been through, or what they are going through that made them the way they are now. Drop the judgment, and understand where the other person is coming from. There are reasons why people are the way they are.

Seeing the good in everything and everyone might not be easy, but the happiness you'll get out of it is worth it, not to mention that it takes maturity to be able to learn this beautiful skill. If each of us know how to see the good in everything and everyone, imagine how better off this world could be.

Stop worrying about what others might think

You have only one life to live, so don't spend it worrying about what others might think. Immature people will criticize you anyway, so just do the things that make you happy. Never ever let people's perception of you be much more important than your happiness. The only person who is allowed to judge you is yourself. Why worry about what others might think? You don't need them to like you anyway. Be so focused on living your life that you have no time to think about whether or not others think you are doing it right. If you depend your happiness on people's judgment of you, I assure you, you will live miserably for the rest of your life. The sense of gratitude comes the moment you stop worrying.

Take risks

Go out there and expose yourself to the world no matter how scary it may seem. Taking risks is part of life. Do something you have never done before. Do something that really scares you. Staying in your comfort zone gives you convenience, but going out of your comfort zone gives you a sense of fulfillment and accomplishment that will lead to happiness. You don't get say thank you to missed opportunities, you just regret them. Save yourself from the regret and say thank you for the experience.

Make mistakes

There is nothing wrong with being wrong. What is wrong is always being right. Imagine your life without the mistakes you have made, do you think you'll be the person you are now? Do you think you'll be where you are now? The wrong decisions you've been beating yourself for are the ones that actually lead you to the right place. Don't be so scared to commit mistakes. If you don't commit mistakes, how will you be thankful for the things you thought you have done right? How will you be thankful for what you have now? Mistakes will make you realize that there is always something to be thankful for.

Be the light to people's darkness

People find meaning and purpose. This is natural. You have one and only purpose in this life, and that is to be a blessing to people. Make your existence beneficial for others. Even if you are going through the darkest days, even if there is too much on your plate, even if the world gives you all the reasons to hate your life, always choose to be the strong one and find ways on how to help others despite your personal difficulties. Be the candle that can light people's darkness. By being a blessing to others, you will see how blessed you are in life. Being a rock for others even if you yourself feel like falling apart is a measure of true strength, and that strength is definitely something to be thankful for.

Always give yourself some alone time

Being surrounded by people is healthy especially if these people are those who are very positive, motivated and happy in life, but make it a point to give yourself some silence. Give yourself some time to meditate. Your me time are the times you can stop, sit back, relax and see how far who have come now, and see how beautiful your life is despite all the challenges you are facing. At the end of a rough day, give yourself the time to regroup even for at least 10 minutes. Your alone time is your time to put yourself together. Your alone time is the time you get to appreciate who you are and what you are now. After spending time with yourself, you'll find yourself grateful for where you are, what you are, and what you have now.

Life won't give you rainbows and butterflies, you have to create them, and going through the storm is part of the process. It's easy to be thankful for the good things, but it is the "bad" things we should really be thankful for because they bring out the best in you, they bring out the strength you never thought you have. If you maintain a sense of gratitude despite all adversities, you'll find yourself genuinely happy and contented with your life.

To be able to forgive others and yourself

You can't claim to have forgiven a person when you still hold grudges. Your ability to forgive is a true strength that you should be very proud of. Forgiveness entails understanding where the other person is coming from. When you forgive, you are choosing to be the better person. Forgiveness is also a sign of maturity. Moreover, forgiving others means forgiving yourself. Forgive people because you deserve that peace in your heart.

Forgive yourself for forgiving others. Sometimes, forgiveness takes time, and that is okay. You don't forgive in an instant, and that is normal. Don't pressure yourself because that will make forgiving much harder. Give yourself some time. For others, it might take a really long time to forgive, but what's important is the willingness to forgive. Just forgive others even if it is much easier not to.

To shed baggage

When you hold a grudge against someone, there is that feeling of heaviness in your heart. The heavy heart will stop you from being happy. Stop carrying that heavy baggage. You just have to let it go. Release the bitterness. You'll just make your life difficult if you keep on carrying the baggage. Be strong enough to leave all the baggage behind and move forward. I assure you, you'll be surprised at how happy you are after letting go of all the baggage in your life.

To avoid burning bridges

It is so easy to burn bridges when you are really mad at someone. Sometimes, burning bridges is the first thing you'll think of when you hate the person at that moment. Do not allow this to happen. Do not let your emotions eat you up and cause you to burn bridges. If you think burning bridges will make you feel good, think again. It might make you feel good temporarily while all the emotions are there. In the long run, you'll regret burning bridges. Don't let something temporary cause you to cut something or someone out forever. If you're mad, just get mad, but don't burn bridges. You'll never know when you'll need to pass that bridge again.

To avoid making your world smaller

When you are at war with someone or when things aren't so good between you and someone or some people, it feels like you are living in a much smaller world. At some point in your life, you have felt this way, right? Did you feel good about it? Exactly. The answer is no. Nobody gets to feel good when he or she makes his or her world smaller. Those who think it is okay to make their worlds smaller are missing so much out on life. Those who feel good about making their worlds smaller are just faking it. Believe me, the world is already small, so why make it smaller? There will be a time when you'll meet the same person you hate again. There will be a time when you'll see your ex again. See, in this life, things happen repeatedly, and it's a small world after all. Do not let something or someone have that much power over you that you will resort to making your world smaller.

To avoid disappointments

Most of the time, you tend to hold a grudge against someone when that someone means so much to you. That is because you felt betrayed because that person or that something mattered to you. After everything you've done for the person, disappointment is what you'll get. It sucks, doesn't it? Now, avoid getting disappointed by not holding a grudge. See, if you are holding a grudge against someone, and that someone has wronged you, or you felt wronged by the person again, you'll feel disappointed again over that person until everything that he or she does seem to disappoint you. It is as if every little thing the person does disappoints you. It will now be a cycle of disappointments even if there is nothing to be disappointed about. Save yourself from the disappointment. Do not hold grudges.

To totally detach yourself from the hurt

Holding a grudge over someone is planting the hurt he or she has done to you. It's okay to feel the pain, savor it if you want, but eventually, detach yourself from that pain. If you keep on holding a grudge, you'll keep on remembering the pain. Detach yourself from the hurt to free yourself from the pain, but don't forget the lesson pain has taught you. Just detach yourself from the pain, the feeling, not from the person. Detaching yourself from the pain is different from detaching yourself from the person who has caused the pain. Most of the time, people get this wrong because they detach themselves from the person, not from the pain causing them to be bitter despite cutting ties with the person. Don't cut ties with the person, cut ties with the pain itself. Forget about the pain, not the person.

Holding grudges won't make you happy. It makes you the loser since you are the one who's bitter and unforgiving. Holding a grudge will make you feel bad not only for other people but yourself as well. Do yourself a huge favor, stop holding grudges.

Remove the negativity in your life

The first thing to do to cut that baggage you are carrying is to cut it completely. Remove it; erase it or whatever you want to do with it as long as it disappears. Negativity is awful because it is contagious, it passes from one person to another, and it can affect your mindset as well as it spreads throughout your body. Here are some ways you can get rid of the negativity in your life.

Throw your negative thoughts away

Most people often do not realize that it is natural for them to think of negative thoughts. What you have to do is be aware of these thoughts so you can throw them out of your mind and give some space for the positive thoughts to come in. Sometimes, these negative thoughts overpower us, and we give in without a fight. Examples of this are pride and envy. The best thing to do is be aware of it, and just completely stop thinking about them. It may not be easy at first, but once you give it your best, you will overcome it.

Ask yourself what you want

This is an important way to get rid of your negativity. Ask yourself whether you want to be happy or not. If you want to be happy, you can start by doing things. In the case that you do not want it, try to think more clearly. Once you have taken the time, you can ask yourself again until you come up with an answer that will satisfy you.

Look for people who are positive

One of the best ways to remove the negativity is to surround oneself with positive things. Friends who are positive influence their friends to be positive as well go find this type of people. Be around positive people and it will surely rub off on you, the longer you hang around them.

PART 2: GUIDED MEDITATIONS FOR ANXIETY

MANAGE YOUR EMOTIONS, FIND THE STRESS SOLUTION, STOP WORRYING AND OVERTHINKING

Guided meditations for anxiety: introduction

Anxiety is a subjective, complicated emotion. Anxiety is brought by many causes and expressed by a wide range of symptoms. These symptoms may encompass behavioral, cognitive, and emotional components. This is the reason why you can ask a group of individuals about their experience and understanding of anxiety, and get various explanations and definitions which are different from what it means to them to be anxious to them.

People differ in how frequently, and with which intensity, they experience anxiety. The duration over which they have anxiety also differs from one person to another. Most people consider anxiety to be normal, and they have learned to adapt to it when it occurs. An ordinary degree of anxiety is part of our daily human experience. Unfortunately, other individuals experience anxiety to such a heightened level that it leads to great distress. This level of anxiety can impair a person's wellbeing and normal functioning. It can affect several vital areas of a person's life, such as their occupation, studies, and relationships. When anxiety comes to that level where it begins to be distressing and interferes with a person's wellbeing and normal functioning of an individual, then we start to speak of an anxiety disorder.

Anxiety can make life feel like a nightmare. You always fear the worst, so you are constantly negative. You are sometimes paralyzed by fear, which limits how much you do with your life. Your life is restricted more and more as you become more and more fearful. Sometimes, it can be hard or even impossible to talk to other people or to get in your car and drive when you fear the worst all of the time.

The worst part of anxiety is that other people in your life don't understand it. Therefore, they get frustrated with you. They don't understand why you can't just loosen up and have fun. They don't get why you have meltdowns in the middle of grocery stores or why you voice strange and even bizarre fears. "You're so negative," is one of the criticisms that you may experience. Your loved ones may also wonder why they are not enough to calm you down. "I'm here, so you should feel fine," is something that you might hear from your loved ones.

Don't let the negativity of other people bring you down. You suffer from actual mental illness. There is nothing wrong with your personality and you are not stupid just because you can't automatically shut off your symptoms like a faucet. What you suffer is terrible, and no one can take that away from you. Stop listening to critical people and instead start taking care of yourself.

When your life is affected by anxiety, it is time for a change. You may feel that you are resigned to this difficult life forever, but that is not so. There are numerous coping techniques and even cures for what you feel. This book is one of the best first steps that you can take for yourself. This book will show you how to take control of your thoughts when they run wild and put an end to the crippling fears that rule your existence.

For the past ten years of my life, I have dealt with anxiety. I received the formal diagnosis of General Anxiety Disorder when I was eighteen, but I suspect that I suffered from this disorder starting at a much earlier age. I know how it is to be ruled by fear and to have difficulty enjoying life like other people. I also know how it is to "ruin" relationships because of mental illness.

While it has taken me a long while to get control over this disorder, I have learned not to let it rule me. Also, I have learned to stop blaming myself. This is a mental disorder that I suffer, not something that is my choice.

While anxiety is not your fault or your choice, it is also not your slave master. You can gain control over it and prevent it from manifesting and ruining your life. You can stop anxiety in its tracks and live life the way that you choose. You just have to learn how, and this book will show you. Overcoming anxiety is an intense mental and personal process that you should dedicate some time to accomplishing. The rewards will be rich.

I will show you some of the things that I have learned over the years about anxiety so that you can understand your disorder better. I will also show you the many tricks and tips I have learned over the years. From meditation to mindfulness as a skill to loving yourself, I will teach you how to think better to avoid the patterns of thinking that lead to anxiety. Finally, I will share a great supplement with you that will make your anxiety disappear. Called Premium Anxiety Formula, this supplement beats medication because it has no side effects and is not habit-forming or expensive. Plus, it works! By the end of this book, you will have the skills to cope and even cure your anxiety.

Keep in mind that these things take work. You cannot just overcome something crippling like anxiety overnight. However, you really can minimize the effects of anxiety on your life very easily and quickly. Almost immediately you will start to notice results if you employ the methods in this book. Still, some of these things take time. Be patient with yourself and with these techniques. Don't give up just because you do not see immediate results. Eventually, you will become the master of your own mind and heal your anxiety. Until then, expect some work and a few setbacks. It is all part of the normal healing process! Just like learning to ride a bike, you are learning a new skill of healing anxiety. So take your time.

Living life with anxiety and depression can be a true nightmare. But you don't have to live in the nightmare forever. I will show you how to successfully climb out of the hole that you may be trapped in now so that you can live life to the fullest and finally heal yourself. I will show you how to begin healing, while also showing you how to cope with your symptoms in the meantime.

Chapter 22. Anxiety

What is Anxiety?

Anxiety is your body's response to the feeling of fear or uncertainty about what is to come. Some of the symptoms synonymous with fear include:

- Rapid breathing
- Racing heart
- A "burst" of energy
- Butterflies in your stomach

Everyone feels anxious at times; whether it's your first day in school, giving a speech, or going for a job interview, this feeling is quite a regular thing. Anxiety can be a way for our body to keep us safe from harm. For example, imagine you're taking a walk through the forest, and you're dragging your feet because you're tired; however, you see something that looks like a bear or a snake at the corner of your eyes. You will suddenly forget that you're tired and feel a burst of energy that helps you get away from that location.

If you feel anxious about an assignment that is due, anxiety will motivate you and can help you get it done faster than you earlier thoughts. However, when you start feeling anxious about something unusual, then it can be very unhealthy. Unhealthy anxiety is what is known as an anxiety disorder. Any anxiety that impacts on your daily life is a disorder. Rather than have anxiety as a response to danger, the person with a disorder begins to feel anxious in situations that are perfectly normal, like taking a means of public transport or meeting new people.

The Negative Effects of Anxiety

Anxiety increases your heart rate and breathing in the short term; it directs blood flow to your brain where it's needed, and this physical response helps you to face an unwanted situation. However, if it gets too intense, it can make you feel nauseous and lightheaded. If anxiety becomes excessive and persistent, it can have a devastating effect on both your mental and physical health.

You can have an anxiety disorder at any point in your life. The symptoms of anxiety can stay hidden for a while, as such; don't wait till you get the sign before you embrace a lifestyle change, start immediately.

Anxiety disorder will affect your:

- **Central Nervous System**
  If you've had long-term anxiety and a series of panic attacks, it will make your brain release stress hormones more regularly than it should. This can increase the occurrence of some symptoms, such as dizziness, headaches, and depression. Some hormones and chemicals in your body are designed to help you cope with anxiety when you feel anxious your brain floods your nervous system with these chemicals and hormones. Examples of these chemicals are cortisol and adrenaline.

- **Excretory and Digestive systems**
  This might seem too extreme, but it's true. Anxiety has a way of affecting your excretory and digestive systems. Some of the symptoms you'll notice are diarrhea, stomachaches, nausea, and some other digestive issues. You can also experience loss of appetite occasionally.

Some connection has been noticed to exist between the development of irritable bowel syndrome (IBS) after a bowel infection and anxiety. IBS can lead to constipation, vomiting, or diarrhea.

- **Immune System**

  Anxiety triggers your flight or fight stress response, which causes a flow of hormones and chemicals like adrenaline into your body system. This influx of chemicals will increase your breathing and pulse rate so your brain can get more oxygen. This flow of chemicals and hormones prepares you to react well to an intense situation. It can make your immune system function better for a short while. Your body should come back to normal when you are in a calm environment. However, if you regularly feel anxious or the intense situation lasts for a long time, your body never gets the sign to go back to its original state. If your body does not return to its original state, it can weaken your immune system, thus leaving you vulnerable to all types of infections. Your regular vaccines may also not work well if you have an anxiety disorder.

- **Respiratory System**

  Anxiety can make you breathe rapidly and shallowly. If you have been diagnosed with chronic obstructive pulmonary disease (COPD), anxiety can land you in the hospital due to anxiety-related complications. Anxiety can also make symptoms of asthma worse.

A Summary of Causes and Treatments

Most people feel anxious at some point in their life, but there can be certain factors or triggers that cause other people to feel it more severely than normal. These can include someone's genetics, their environment, how their brain is wired, and what life experiences they've had. If a person associates something with fear, it is likely they will develop anxiety surrounding that thing. Although it is typical for people to have some sort of trigger for their anxiety, this is not true for all cases. Some people have very generalized anxiety about nothing in particular; they are simply always worried or dreading being out in the world.

For some people, one type of anxiety can cause them to develop another type of anxiety. For example, someone who has anxiety about suffering harm or getting sick might develop a germ-related obsessive-compulsive disorder as a way to ensure they will never get sick. Or, people with a social anxiety disorder might eventually develop agoraphobia if they never force themselves to interact with others.

Risk factors for different types of anxiety disorders typically coexist in people who suffer from them, which demonstrates that no single experience is likely to cause someone to develop a disorder. Scientists have found that nature and nurture are strongly linked when it comes to the likelihood that someone will develop severe anxiety. Genetically, research has shown that people have about a 30 to 67 percent chance of inheriting anxiety from their parents (Carter, n.d.). Although someone's DNA might be a factor in them developing anxiety, it cannot account for all of the reasons that have developed it.

Environmental factors should also be taken into consideration when trying to find the root cause of anxiety. Parenting style can be a large factor in whether or not a person will develop anxiety. If parents are controlling of their children or if they model anxious behaviors, the child might grow up thinking these are normal behaviors they should model. This can lead to feeling anxious based on learned behavior. Other factors, such as continual stress, abuse, or loss of a loved one, can also elicit a severe anxious reaction because a person may not know how to handle the situation they find themselves in.

In addition to the environment, a person's health can often cause anxiety as well. If someone is diagnosed or living with a chronic medical condition or a severe illness, it can cause an anxious reaction. One possibility is if the illness is affecting the person's hormones, which can cause stress, or if their feelings of not having control are worsened by a diagnosis they cannot fix.

Some people might not realize that the choices they make daily could be contributing to their anxiety. Things such as excessive caffeine, tobacco use, and not exercising enough can all cause anxiety. Caffeine and other stimulants can increase a person's heart rate and simulate anxiety symptoms. Not exercising can lower a person's level of happy hormones and make their muscles tense or sore, which can also contribute to stress. A person's personality can also determine how severe their anxiety might be. Shy people who tend to stay away from conversations and interaction might develop more severe social anxiety because they are not exposed to those situations often.

When experiencing anxiety, it can seem like there is no way out, but there are actually quite a few different ways a person can work to ease their worries, ranging from clinical to holistic approaches. What type of treatments will work depends on the person, and often, how severe their struggle is.

A few clinical ways to treat anxiety include counseling, psychotherapy, and medication. These are not the only ways a person can be medically treated, but they tend to be the most conventional routes for treating mental illness. Counseling is a type of therapy where the person is able to talk to a licensed practitioner and receive feedback and advice about their situation and how to handle their emotions. Most counselors have a master's degree in the psychology field and are licensed through their state. This type of therapy is usually considered a short-term solution for people who are struggling but not debilitated by their anxiety.

Psychotherapy is typically a more long-term solution for people whose lives are impacted by their anxiety. This type of therapy can focus on a broader range of issues and triggers, such as a person's anxious patterns or behaviors and how to fix them. Cognitive-behavioral therapy is often used in this type of therapy to work with the person to adjust their thoughts and behaviors.

Some people find relief once prescribed medication to help them manage their anxiety. This route is usually reserved for people who are struggling the most and having trouble calming themselves on their own. There are various types of medications, such as SSRIs (selective serotonin reuptake inhibitors) and SNRIs (serotonin-norepinephrine reuptake inhibitors) that alter brain chemicals to reduce anxiety or worry.

Making changes to their lifestyle and habits can also help people with anxiety relieve some of their symptoms. This is a more natural approach to managing anxiety and can be successful for people who are dedicated to making positive life changes. Small things such as diet adjustments and increasing activity levels can reduce anxious feelings. Establishing a consistent sleep schedule is also important to help someone ensure they are getting enough rest each night. Stress fatigues the body, and it may need more time to fully recuperate at night if it was taxed during the day. Making sure the body has a routine can also make someone feel safe and know what to expect from their day.

Meditation can also be a good way for people to calm their minds and ease anxiety. Taking time during the day to be still and quiet might help someone stop the constant worry they feel during the day and relax for a moment. Once they start training their body to relax, it is more likely that they can keep it up during the day. Finally, avoiding stimulants such as caffeine, sugar, and tobacco, and depressants such as alcohol can greatly improve a person's chances of overcoming their anxiety. These substances contribute to the brain's hyperactivity and can often increase feelings of anxiety.

Getting Rid of Anxiety with Meditation

Meditation instructs us to be progressively aware of the present and less in our minds. We have a propensity for enabling contemplations to enter our psyche and tail them. Occasionally, these are charming considerations, yet commonly these can be stresses, unpleasant musings, on edge emotions, and anxiety.

Frequently, we enable ourselves to pursue these contemplations and even become these considerations. Even though nothing might happen to us physically at that exact second, regardless, we may feel uncertain or on edge about the future because of our reasoning.

Meditation for anxiety is an unmistakable, guided encounter that enables us to work on winding up progressively present, just as furnish a system to manage musings and the truth that is our occupied and dynamic personality. This training is otherwise called care, which once more, prepares our cerebrum to be available by concentrating ceaselessly from intuition and into things that ground us into the present, for example, breathing and physical sensations.

How Anxiety is Reduced with Meditation

Guided meditation for nervousness causes us to watch our contemplations and feelings without decisions. The basic thing the vast majority do when an idea enters their brain is to tail it, judge it, harp on it, and become lost in it. Rather, a standard meditation practice trains us to be available.

This enables us to control the manner in which we see and respond to our nervousness, rather than enabling our uneasiness to control us.

This is supported by studies as well. In fact, Wake Forest Medical Center conducted several of these focusing on brain scans where areas were both deactivated and activated by patients who suffered from anxiety while practicing mindfulness meditation.

It also showed that those volunteers who had no experience with meditation before actually reported relief from anxiety, had their ventromedial prefrontal cortex and anterior cingulate cortex activated. These areas are where both worrying and emotion stem from. Each volunteer had a minimum of 4 sessions that lasted 20 minutes each.

Contemplation for anxiety likewise gives individuals a strategy, instrument to adapt, and arrangement to anxiety and even fits of anxiety as they occur. Frequently, when a fit of anxiety or a wave of anxiety comes, we do not have a clue how to manage it. More often than not, managing it can mean worrying about it, which just serves to intensify the emotions and circumstances. With guided reflection, we have an apparatus that we can go to and use to all the more viably manage anxiety.

Studies have additionally demonstrated that anxiety sufferers who go to guided reflection have revealed expanded sentiments of control, an expanded feeling of general prosperity, just as an expansion in by and large hopefulness. These sentiments go far in alleviating the recurrence and power of anxiety.

Chapter 23. What Is Meditation?

Definitions of meditation vary, but the best one I have seen is: A ritual that allows us to get a good perspective on our lives. Even though it has that effect, meditation is not about becoming a better person per se. When you meditate, you should not be trying to eliminate harmful emotions or bad thoughts. The key is learning how to observe them in an objective manner to get a better understanding (and ultimately, control) of them. Meditation as an activity is a skill that you can only practice but never quite perfect. That is why some people struggle at it while others find it rather easy to do.

Even more important for this book, meditation is the best and most effective way of attaining wellness in all three areas of your life. When you meditate, you attain mindfulness, grounding your mind in the present and eliminating stress. At the same time, your body finds peace during the time of meditation. But it is the specific practices of meditation, like Kundalini Yoga, that really boost our physical wellbeing. Finally, meditating allows us to reconnect with the universe and activate the superconscious mind. The peace that you find from meditating is caused by the fact that by so doing you create the perfect conduit to achieve complete wellness in mind, body, and spirit.

We will discuss meditation in greater depth. We will look at the exact ways through which it boosts out wellbeing in the three key areas of being and energizes us to continue pursuing greatness in everything that we do. We will also look at the exact meditation techniques through which we can enhance our connection to the universe and boost our ability to lead a happy and successful life. But to understand meditation, we have to start from the very beginning and evaluate its origins. Only after understanding the source will we evaluate the exact impact of meditation over our lives and the exact ways to do it.

Why We Meditate

You see, the reason that we meditate is not just because it helps us to improve our concentration span or to end procrastination. These are just the outcomes of meditating. We meditate because it is the only way to connect the physical, intellectual, and spiritual elements of our being. We are made up of the mind, the body, and the spirit.

But it is also important to note that the mind is what links the body to the spirit. This is exactly why we meditate. You see, we have the conscious, subconscious, and superconscious minds that correlate with body, mind, and spirit respectively. We meditate to establish a link between all three parts of the brain.

The Conscious

The conscious mind helps us to interpret the world around us. Consciousness is the way we interpret the things we hear, see, touch, smell, and taste. When you manage to activate all these senses (or as many of them as you are able to), then you will be able to achieve a level of mindfulness that allows you to immerse yourself in the present moment. We recognize the conscious mind a lot more than the other levels of the mind because we interact with it a lot more, but it covers the smallest area compared to the other two. Nevertheless, activating your consciousness in everything that you do while you do it will make you a lot more productive. It will give you the chance to live every moment of your life rather than going through the motions without quite appreciating life.

This is one of the most prominent Buddhist lessons on living a wholesome life. The guiding concept is that you should actually be eating while you eat and washing utensils while you wash utensils. And in a world that has been invaded by technology and multitasking, this lesson is even more crucial. It calls for honest self-examination and a willingness to change and live more by overcoming the desire to always be doing as much as possible at the same time.

The Subconscious

The subconscious goes a little deeper than the conscious and touches on our memories and previous life experiences. The subconscious informs our behaviors and reactions to various events by ensuring that all the things we do follow a very specific pattern. This pattern is made of preformed habits, thoughts, and desires. The subconscious has a very interesting relationship with the conscious mind. On the one hand, the conscious mind commands the subconscious reactions that we have to different events. Therefore, if you are confronted by a problem that has previously brought failure into your life, your first reaction will be brought about by your subconscious mind. You will react to that event based on your previous experience with it.

On the other hand, the subconscious mind directs our conscious sensing. This is why you tend to be biased toward certain things or why you love to wear a certain kind of perfume or use a specific type of soap. Your mind has built associations between the things you experience and your feelings. It commands your conscious mind to do certain things to produce a specific kind of effect. Of course, the interaction between the conscious and the unconscious minds is a lot more complicated when you are talking about behaviors that affect success, but the template is the same.

If you want to create real change in your life, you will have to start by working with the subconscious mind to find out why you have experienced failure in your life before. You can then build up a new set of habits and associations in your mind meant specifically to drive you toward success. Meditation is one of the most effective ways to let go of harmful subconscious notions and do some subliminal self-conditioning to attain the highest possible levels of success.

The Superconscious

At the highest level of mindfulness, where most people do not even appreciate its power, is a part of our mind called the superconscious. The superconscious links directly to the god power of the universe—the providence, the infinite power, and the omniscience. You can only activate the superconscious mind for short periods because it is only through meditation that you can do it.

However, when you do activate the superconscious, you will be in a position to reap all the goodness of the universe. Even more notably, it is only through the superconscious that you can discover your life's purpose. This then becomes the driving force of your life and enables you to dedicate your life to something greater than yourself. Being able to reach this level of awareness is one of the key goals of practicing meditation the Buddha way. The connection that you generate between the three levels of consciousness by unlocking the unconscious is basically what nirvana is all about. At this level, you will have the opportunity to harness the power of the universe to manifest great success and prosperity in every area of your life. One important thing to note is that you can only reach this level of awareness through meditation. This is what makes meditation such a critical ingredient in your pursuit of success.

Other Reasons Why We Meditate

Other than the scientific reason for meditation, linking the conscious, subconscious, and superconscious, we meditate to reap the rewards of this practice over our lives.

Meditation Eliminates Stress

Professionals in the most stressful careers can benefit from the stress-relieving benefits of meditation. From teachers to doctors and Wall Street Bankers, meditation has been found to help overcome stress, bring down the levels of depression, and help people overcome burnout (Wanderlust, 2016).

Other than stress, meditation is also the best way to fight anxiety. You see, anxiety has the effect of taking people from the present moment and transporting them into worries about the future. Meditation boosts your brain and helps you to overcome anxiety caused by stressful life events and generalized anxiety disorders.

It Increases Your Level of Happiness

Because meditation helps you to manage your stress in a healthy manner, it gives you a chance to focus on improving your career and relationships. You will even be in a better position to pursue other interests to take the level of your happiness even higher.

Meditation Relaxes You

When you are going through a tough spot, any opportunity to take a break and rewind comes as a godsend. However, the ambitious mind is not designed for relaxation. Even before you are done pursuing your current goal, you will already have a full to-do list of other things that you would like to accomplish. The opportunity to relax with meditation comes in handy because it keeps you grounded and impervious to the small triggers that often unravel the best-made plans.

It Helps Boost Cerebral Activity

Successful people in business, sports, and other areas have been found to have highly integrated brains. These brains improve their functionality and boost their chances of success. Meditation is one of the most effective ways through which you can work to attain this integrated brain functionality and reach success in your chosen field.

Chapter 24. Getting Started

Most people who report having quit meditation also expressed complaints that stem from the lack of understanding of some of these concepts. I, therefore, advise you to read it carefully before proceeding.

We will look into some of the basic ways to start the practice of meditation. We will look at some of the known forms of meditation that would serve as a good starting point, systematically. These are breathing, counting and mindfulness meditation. Remember, if you feel like it might be tricky doing it on your own, you can always seek the assistance of guided meditations and group settings.

The great meditators of the past discovered a connection between external realities and our body and mind. They discovered that we can live a life of higher consciousness by being able to observe what we feel within while still paying attention to without. They discovered that our thoughts and emotions could be our slaves contrary to what is the reality.

To notice how your emotions, shift, observe your breath. When we relax, our breathing is regulated and deep while fast when we experience excitement. With this in mind, the Buddhists discovered that as our breathing can alter our state of mind the same way our state of mind shifts our breathing. In return, this means that if we learn to breathe correctly, we have the power to do away with many unpleasant feelings that torment us on a daily basis.

The negative emotions that we experience coupled with the negative effects they bring about to deal with a lot of damage to our personal and emotional growth. By learning to do away with these self-inflicted vices, we

385

allow ourselves to grow in greater proportions in comparison to people who do not heed this advice. With a calm and clear mind, we make better decisions and play a good fit as a functioning member of society. Before getting into the actual first practice, it would be nice to learn the correct method of breathing.

The natural way our body is supposed to breathe is the abdominal breathing method. At first, it may appear unnatural but this is indeed the natural way for our bodies to breathe. From conception up until a point after birth, this is how our bodies breathe. However, as our age progress, we diverge from this mode of breathing and start breathing while expanding the chest. This newly adopted method only causes the mind to be in a state of anxiety. One should carry out abdominal breathing in this method:

- o Assuming you are in a comfortable sitting position, keep an upright posture with your feet apart and touching the ground.
- o Place your hands (with the thumbs touching) against the lower section of your belly and let them form a rainbow arc.
- o Keeping your chin tucked, press your tongue behind the upper row of teeth. Keep the eyes open and do not stare into any objects.
- o Gently, inhale. As you exhale, push out the lower belly and feel the air rush out. Do not completely fill your belly with air; having it three quarters filled is sufficient.
- o The exhaling should be equally gentle. It occurs through the nose. Push in your belly to symbolize squeezing out the air. Each step should last you at most 4 seconds each for uniformity.

As aforementioned, it may seem strange to breathe in coordination with the belly for beginners. This gets better and starts to feel more natural with more practice. Furthermore, it is the natural way to breathe.

Beginner Breathing

First, find a good sitting position that will not interfere with the process. You can use the meditation pose or sit on a chair with your hands resting on the sides and a straightened back. Do not get too comfortable though- you might 'meditate' until the next morning.

Minimize any form of distraction that can take your away attention from the meditation process. Some of these things may be a mobile phone, flashing lights, kids looking for your attention, your pet or even the weather. Find out if you should keep warm or wear loose fitted clothes before you start meditating. You may wish to close your eyes or even focus on a specific spot or object in your surroundings.

Once you are seated and comfortable with your eyes closed (or open), relax your muscles and start observing your breath. Do not try to change anything about it. The body knows the amount of air it requires. Just observe your nostrils as air flows naturally through them-in and out. The air may be cool, warm, or itchy. Every feeling is the right feeling- just observe without any judgment.

Stray thoughts may come in droves but do not hate yourself or form any resentment towards them. Just observe how your mind has the tendency of wandering and try to bring back your thoughts to breathe observation. Keep breathing and keep going deeper. Notice how the sounds around you keep drowning the deeper you take your attention into your breathing.

If stray thoughts keep recurring, notice the pattern of these thoughts. Notice what they are about, what they mostly consist of and if they are from the past or present. Bring your attention back to your breathing and continue observing your breath. At first, it may even be difficult to observe two breaths before the mind wanders. This is totally fine as it is part of the journey. Keep noticing without judgment.

Bodily distractions often come into play when meditating. Some common ones are itching, discomfort or even pain. Sometimes, different sets of emotions may arise such as sorrow or joy but they are impermanent-whatever they are. This should not stop you from the process. Simply observe what they are without judgment and accept whatever stories come up. Then, slowly guide yourself back to observing your breathing.

When your time runs out, bring back your attention to your body and to your surroundings. Notice how relaxed your mind is and how your breath remains the same as you open your eyes. Repeat this daily and cultivate the practice before increasing your time. You are bound to see results.

Mindful Walking Meditation

This technique comes in handy for people who are always on the move or cannot get themselves to sit and meditate. In fact, its efficiency stems from the fact that you do not need to add another routine to your daily activities to make it work. All you have to do is walk mindfully. You can always walk mindfully as you carry on with your normal routine. This practice helps to cultivate a lot of awareness as one observes within while facing the distractions of life.

It would be advisable to choose an appropriate place where you are likely to get fewer distractions as well as have good walking space. Begin with a stationary, upright position. Feel the weight of your body on your feet. You have the freedom to place your hands behind, either resting on your sides or even clasped around your chest- whatever feels comfortable. As you do this, remain relaxed and observe whatever sensations you feel objective.

Start walking using short slow steps and pay attention to the feelings that arise and pass on your feet. These feelings can vary from pain, pressure, heat or even heaviness. There is no right or wrong feeling to experience. All you have to do is observe them as they arise and pass. In this practice, the feelings one encounters as they walk are the anchor unlike in breathing meditation.

Keep walking and pay close attention to the sensations experienced on your feet as you make every step. As your foot rises and as it falls back to the ground, what do you feel? After making nonjudgmental observations, keep walking towards the chosen destination while keeping a natural and relaxed posture. When you get to the end of the walk, stand for a couple of seconds, and observe what your body feels. Before turning, center your attention back to your feet and start walking slowly again.

If the initial pace is chosen does not seem to suit the experience, feel free to switch it up a bit to the level of your comfort. You might find that walking fast works better for you! Notice how impermanent the walk is; how you keep going back and forth in the same path. You may also notice how impermanent the sensations that occur as you walk are. Just simply observe and keep practicing.

In comparison to beginner breathing, the mind is bound to wander even when doing mindful walking. This is totally fine. Noticing that your mind has wandered is half the journey. You, however, need to refocus your attention back to the next step gradually. If you notice your mind spent twenty minutes wandering, that is still fine. The fact that you noticed and refocused yourself is the most important part. Oh, and keep your eyes open!

Counting Meditation

Counting meditation is exactly as it sounds. You just need to be relaxed with your eyes closed and count up to the desired number. Ridiculous? I think not! Do you remember when we talked about the use of anchors? In this case, the numbers are your anchor. Anytime the mind decides to drift away, slowly bring back your attention to where you left off and continue counting. A practice like this can really do wonders for your attention span. Remember to observe with no judgment.

If the real intention is present when performing this practice, you will notice the intensity of the thought patterns subsides. Your thoughts will go in tandem with the counting. The more you learn to bring back your mind to focus, the more your mind detaches itself from its habitual patterns. Self-awareness develops.

These are just some of the basic meditation techniques that serve as great starters for a new meditator. If you grasp either one of these first, transitioning to the rest of the techniques taught in this book will be easy as one, two, and three.

Chapter 25. How To Calm The Body

Exercise is a highly recommended stress reliever for many reasons. Physical activity has many benefits in addition to reducing stress, and these benefits alone (increased health, longevity, and happiness) make exercise a worthwhile habit. And as a stress management technique, it is more effective than others. The combined benefits of these two facts make physical exercise a lifestyle that is worth following.

Do physical activity

The definition of physical activity in this context has not been limited only to exercise. Physical activity is any activity that engages your physique. Mostly it will lead to perspiration. When an individual engages in physical activity, he or she is obliged to concentrate fully on that particular activity. Exercising is a very renowned way to counter depression. Regular exercise has time and again been used as an anti-depressant. When one is exercising, endorphins are boosted. These are chemicals that enable an individual to feel good.

The statistics of how many people deal with stress is always on the upward. When one experiences stress, it has a lasting effect in their lives since it cuts across what an individual is engaging in at a particular time. To eradicate stress completely is an uphill task, and one would rather manage it. Exercising is one of the best methods to manage stress. Many medical practitioners advise that individuals should engage in exercises in a bid to manage stress levels.

The advantages that come with a person engaging in exercises have far been established to be a countermeasure against diseases and as a method of enhancing the body's physical state. Research has it that exercising helps a great deal when decreasing fatigue and enhancing the body's consciousness of the environment. Stress invades the whole of your body, affecting both the body and mind. When this happens, the act of your mind feeling well will be pegged on the act of the body feeling well too. When one is in the act of exercising, the brain produces endorphins that act naturally as pain relievers. They also improve the instances upon which an individual falls asleep. When the body is able to rest, this means that its amounts of anxiety have dropped by a large margin. Production of endorphins can also be triggered by the following practices. They include but are not limited to meditation and breathing deeply. Participation in exercise regularly has proven an overall tension reliever.

Doing relaxation exercises

Another method of reducing stress levels is through the use of some relaxation techniques. A relaxation technique is any procedure that is of aid to an individual when trying to calm down the levels of anxiety. Stress is effectively conquered when the body itself is responding naturally to the stress levels in the body. Relaxation can be often confused with laying on a couch after a hard day. This relaxation is best done in the form of self-meditation, although its effects are not fulfilling on the impact of stress. Most relaxation techniques are done at the convenience of your home with only an app.

The following types of exercise are highly recommended for stress reduction because they have specific properties that are effective in reducing stress in short and long-term stress management:

Yoga

The gentle stretching and balance of yoga may be what people think when they practice, but there are several other aspects of yoga that help reduce stress and to have a healthy life. Yoga entails the same type of diaphragmatic breathing; this is used with meditation. In fact, a few yoga styles include meditation as part of their practice (in fact, most types of yoga can take you to some degree of meditation).

Yoga also includes balance, coordination, stretching, and styles are the exercise of power. All support health and stress reduction. Yoga can be practiced in many ways. Some yoga styles feel like a gentle massage from the inside, while others sweat and hurt you the next day, so there is a yoga school that can work for most people, even for those who have some physical limitations, to be attractive.

Walking

Walking is one of the easiest medications to relieve stress that is excellent because of the benefits this technique offers. The human body was designed to travel long distances, and this activity generally did not cause as much wear as it did. Walking is an exercise that can be easily separated by the speed you use, the weights you carry, the music you listen to, and the location and the company you choose.

This type of exercise can also be easily divided into 10 minutes of sessions, and classes are not needed, and no special equipment is needed beyond a good pair of shoes. (This is an advantage since studies have shown that three 10-minute workouts provide the same benefits as a 30-minute session: great news for those who, due to their busy schedule, need to practice in parts! To find the More smalls!)

Martial Arts

There are many forms of martial arts, and although each one may have little focus, ideology, or set of techniques, they all have benefits to relieve stress. These practices tend to pack both aerobic and strength training, as well as the confidence that comes from physical and self-defense skills.

Generally practiced in groups, martial arts can also offer some of the benefits of social support, as classmates encourage each other and maintain a sense of group interaction. Many martial arts styles provide philosophical views that promote stress management and peaceful life, which you can choose or not accept. However, some styles, especially those with high levels of physical combat, have a higher risk of injury, so martial arts are not for everyone, or at least not all styles work for everyone. If you try several different martial arts programs and talk to your doctor before following the style, you have a better chance of finding a new habit that keeps you fit for decades.

These three examples are not the only types of exercise. They simply show some benefits and are usable by most people. There are many other forms of workout that can be very powerful, such as Pilates, running, weight training, swimming, dancing, and prepared sports.

Everyone brings their stress management benefits to the table, so discover and practice the form of exercise that appeals to you the most.

Mindfulness Body Scan Meditation

This technique requires a more formal atmosphere than the breathing technique as it is best experienced when you are lying down or sitting in a really comfortable posture.

While lying down may seem like a fabulous way, initially, it might not be a good idea in the long-run because novices tend to fall asleep in this position. Also, while a good 30-minute duration is needed for effective results, you may make the best use with whatever little time you get.

Sit down on a cushion or a chair or lie down comfortably on the floor. Avoid lying on a mattress if you find it difficult to stay awake. Close your eyes because it makes it easy to focus. Now, pay attention to your breath. Slowly move your attention to the places where your body is in contact with your chair or floor. Investigate each of your body mentally.

The different sensations you experience could be tingling, pressure, tightness, temperature, or anything else. Sometimes, you may not feel any sensation too. Notice the absence of sensations also. Your body becomes an anchor for your mind to hold on so that it doesn't wander away.

Again, be aware when your mind wanders, and gently get it back to where it was before it moved off. When you are done, open your eyes, and mindfully get your focus back on the outside environment.

Another crucial aspect of the body scan mindfulness technique is to release the tension in the various parts of your body as you scan it. When you focus on a particular section of the body, say your shoulders, you suddenly realize that you are holding them too rigid and creating tension in that area. By focusing on that part, tension is automatically released from there.

These are formal ways of body scans and breathing mindfulness meditation techniques. You can do these mindfulness activities even while sitting in your chair in your office. Take a 5-minute break and do a body scan or focus on your breath even as you sit at your desk. You don't even have to get up from your seat. Also, you could do it during your daily commute or while waiting for someone or standing in line for something or anywhere else. Mindfulness meditation does not need anything else but your mind, which is always with you.

Mindfulness Meditation through Mantra Chanting

A mantra is a phrase, word, or syllable that is repeated during the meditation session. Mantras can be repeated in mind, whispered, or chanted aloud. Mantra meditation involves two elements, including the mantra that is being chanted and mindfulness meditation using the mantra as the anchor. Mantra chanting keeps the mind focused and facilitates mindfulness meditation. People also use the mantra as a form of positive affirmations.

Identify the best mantra for your needs. You can choose your mantra based on the reason for the mantra chanting. Are you looking at getting back your health? Are you seeking peace? Do you desire for something to happen in your life? Are you looking for a deep spiritual awakening?

Sit comfortably with your back straight but not rigidly erect. Focus on your breathing first, which will help you get into the mindfulness meditation state. Ensure your intention for the mantra chanting and meditation is clearly imbibed in your mind. Now, start chanting the mantra. Don't expect miracles when you start your chant. Simply repeat the mantra slowly, deliberately, and in a relaxed manner. In this mindfulness meditation technique, mantras are the anchors that help your mind to focus.

There are no 'best' mantras for mindfulness meditation. You can choose anything from the scriptures of your personal religion, or you can choose positive and empowering affirmations such as:

- o I am happy and content at this moment.
- o All my treasures are inside of me.
- o My heart is my best guide.
- o It's always now.
- o I am complete, and I don't need anything outside of me to make me whole.
- o Nothing is permanent.
- o This too shall pass.

Chapter 26. Breathing Exercises Throughout the Day

Breathing is a fundamental principle of our lives. You must breathe in and out to live. Many times, people suffer from breathing-related problems, which later on affect them. Some have lost their dear lives because of having difficulties in breathing. Others are suffering because they are unable to breathe well. Therefore, it is essential to note the exact significance of breath.

The first important of breathing is that it reduces anxiety. Breathing also helps in the elimination of insomnia. It has the power to manage your day to day cravings, and also it can control and manage your anger response. Breathing brings your whole body into more excellent balance as it can initiate calmness within you. You will realize your entire being becomes normal again after a proper process of breathing and level of stress will be no more. For those having a high level of emotional frustrations can also apply breathing techniques all through the day so that they might get well too. Nothing is as sweet and pleasant as having an excellent relaxed body.

Breathing also aids in other functions within your bodies, such as muscle relaxation, digestion, and even peristalsis processes. The movement of fluids within your body is made possible by the help of breathing. Breathing helps in the transportation of your body elements such as nutrients and oxygen. It also aids in the removal of waste products. It is better to note that breathing has got that most considerable impact on your respiration as it can donate the required oxygen for respiration. You can acquire the exact energy needed for normal body functions. You will feel strong because power has been formed in your body tissue. Your muscles will be stable since the energy to undertake all your body functions are there. Therefore, you will realize that breathing is a continuous and dynamic process that has no end. Throughout the day, you will understand that breath is an incurring process. We are going to look at several breathing ways that can help eliminate and reduce any form of anxiety within you.

The first breathing technique that you will realize is part and parcel of your whole day is reducing stress through breathing. Before doing this breathing process, try as much as possible to adopt a good sitting position. The position should be comfortable and relaxing. You can also place your tongue behind your front upper teeth and do the following:

- o Start by making sure your lungs are empty. You can do this by allowing the air inside to escape through your nose and mouth. You can facilitate this process by doing some enlargement of your shoulder and chest and contracting your stomach so that you increase the exhale process.
- o Now you can breathe in through your nose. It should be tranquil and silent. Remember, it is supposed to take only 4 seconds.
- o The next step is to hold your breath, let's say for about 7 seconds. Don't rush here as your breath should just come naturally.
- o Then go ahead by breathing out. You have to force all air out through your mouth. You can purse your lips too and making some sounds of your preference. This should take at least 8 seconds.
- o Repeat this process four times.

Therefore, this breathing technique to delete stress in life is seen as a formidable way to control anxiety. Many researchers, such as Dr. Weil, have recommended these techniques to many patients of anxiety they have healed. According to him, you need to do it in four cycles so that you start realizing its benefits. He went ahead by illustrating that, the moment you do this, feeling of lightheaded encroaches. This will help you to feel relaxed and calm. A relaxed mind and feeling of calmness clear off the stress in your mind. Therefore, your level of anxiety will reduce. You will start having a perfect life without stress and anxiety. Remember, this process takes time. It is now recommended that you perform it in a sitting position that's not only affordable but also comfortable. This type of breathing is the famous 4-7-8 breathing.

The next breathing technique that you can efficiently perform is belly breathing. Belly breathing is not difficult to implement. It is among the most straightforward breathing techniques that can eventually help you to release stress. The following steps are deemed appropriate for your breathing.

- o Look for a sitting posture or lie flat in any way as far as it is comfortable.
- o Place your hands on both your belly and chest, respectively. Remember to put one and just below the rib cage.
- o Now you can start breathing. Take an intense breath through your nose and let your hand be pushed out of its position by the belly. The other hand should not move even an inch.
- o The next step is to breathe out very loud and produce that whistling sound with your pursed lips. You can feel that palm on your belly moves in as it pushes out the air.
- o You are allowed to repeat this process more than ten times and make sure to take your time with every single breathing you are undertaking.

- Remember to make a note on your feelings at the end of the whole process.

Therefore, belly breathing is a type of breathing that will help you to reduce tension within your stomach tissues. Your chest tissues and even your ribs will feel relaxed. In the end, the anxiety within your body decreases, and your calmness comes back to normal.

We also have roll breathing that you can eventually use to delete some sorts of anxiety, stress, depression, and even unpleasant feeling within you. Roll breathing has several important in your body. Roll breathing enlarges your lungs and, as a result, makes you be able to pay a close watch on your breathing. The rhyming and rhythm of your breath become your full focus. You can undertake this breathing anytime and anywhere. However, as a learner, you should use your back on the ground with your legs bent. Then start by doing the following:

- Place your two hands on your belly and chest, respectively. Take a note on the movement of your hands as you concentrate on your breathing process. Continue breathing in and out.
- Focus on filling the lower lungs so that your belly moves up when you are inhaling while your chest does not move an inch. It is better to note that breathing in should be through your nose while breathing out must be through your mouth. You are allowed to repeat this process even ten times so that you can realize better results.
- After filling and emptying your lungs, you can now perform the other step of filling your upper chest. You can manage this by first inhaling in your lower lungs then increasing the tempo so that it reaches the chest. Here, you should breathe regularly but slowly for quite sometimes. During this process,

note the position of your two hands. One placed at the belly will slightly fall as the stomach contract. The one put on your chest will rise as more air is breathed in your chest.

- o It is now your time to exhale. Go ahead by exhaling slowly through your mouth. You should make that whooshing sound when your hands start falling, respectively. Always, your left hand will have to fall first, followed by your right hand. Still, on this, notice the way tension leaves your body as your mind becomes relaxed and calmed.
- o Repeat the whole process of breathing in and out for at least 3 to 5 minutes. In this case, make sure you are observing the movement of your chest and belly. Take note of the rolling wave's motion.
- o Your feeling matters a lot in the whole process. Take a more exceptional look at how you feel in the entire rolling breathing.

Your body regains its full free state, and you will feel more relaxed. You can, therefore, practice this rolling breathing process daily and make sure this goes for several weeks. By doing so, you will be able to perform this kind of breathing exercise everywhere. Also, you can eventually achieve this instantly on most occasions. It will help you regain your relaxation and calmness back. At the end of rolling breathing, your anxiety will be at bay. However, this process is not for everyone since some may feel dizzy during the exercise. You can reduce the breathing speed and accelerate slowly. You can then get up slowly after feeling relaxed, calmed, and lightheaded.

Another breathing technique is morning breathing. When you wake up, your body is still exhausted and tired. You feel that your muscles are still weak and wholly tensed. You will realize that your stiffness has got an impact on your day to day activities. The best breathing exercise to follow here is the morning breathing process. It can clear any clogged breathing passages. You can use this method throughout the day to remove the back tension that may be a nagging and a worrying issue to you. The following steps will eventually help you to perform this task with much ease and less effort.

- o Stand still and then try to bend forward. You should slightly bend your knees, and your hands should closely dangle on the floor or close to it.
- o Start inhaling and slowly exhaling, followed by a deep breath as you return into a standing position. You can roll upward slowly and making sure that your head comes last from the ground.
- o Take your time and hold your breath, whether for five seconds or even for 10 seconds. You should do this in your standing position.
- o Start exhaling. That is, breathing out slowly while trying to make a return to your initial position. You can bend forward a little bit.
- o Take note of your feelings at the end of the exercise.

The most important thing about this breathing exercise is that it has the power to instill in you more energy, thus enabling you to carry on with every task of the day. You will be relaxed and calm. The level of anxiousness will reduce. In the end, you will feel more lightheaded and entirely energetic.

The next breathing exercise throughout the day can also involve skull shining breath. The skull shining breath is also known as kapalabhati in another language where the term initially originated. It is a dominant type of breathing that enables you to acquire a relaxed and calm mind and brain. It always boasts of the right way of killing the anxiety in you by eliminating the tension, especially

403

in your skull. Remember, it is good to note that the pressure of the head can negatively influence your whole day, and the impact can remain with you for long.

Skull shining breath is not difficult to undertake, and this will give you that morale of even performing it throughout the day. You can start by having long breathing in then follow it with a quick and extremely powerful breathing out. Exhaling should originate from your belly, especially the lower part.

However, after getting familiarized with the whole contraction process, you can now start on inhaling and exhaling at a faster rate. Increase your pace here and make sure all the breathing process takes place through the nose. In this process, do not involve your mouth at the initial stages. You can go on with the process repeatedly until you start feeling very much relaxed.

You can now take note of your feelings at the end of the breathing exercise. Remember, this breathing process can eventually prevent muscle tension too. It also helps in releasing abdominal pain. Your worries, stress, anxiety, and even clogged breathing sites will be well.

Breathe Deep

Throughout any day, there are bound to be things that cause your stress levels to rise slightly. There are also going to be thoughts that pop into your head and cause you to feel anxious. Our mind can be our own worst enemy, but the good news is we can take control. There are many ways that we can help ease our fears, and deep breathing is one of them!

These techniques are extremely easy to do and can be done anywhere, even at your desk or on the bus to work! If you find it hard to concentrate, you can also purchase a guided relaxation tape, or download a stress-relieving app, as these will guide you through breathing exercises until you get the hang of doing them yourself.

Try this:

- o Close your eyes and breathe in through your nose for a count of five, hold it for five, and then exhale through your mouth for five, in a slow and controlled manner. Repeat that for as long as you need to gain control.
- o Once you're feeling a little calmer or in control, picture the thing that is causing you stress or anxiety as an item or a color. For instance, it might be a black ball, or it might be a gray cloud. It doesn't matter what it is; it simply needs to symbolize the thing that is negatively affecting your day.
- o Now, visualize yourself forcefully pushing that item far away from you, and visualize it disappearing into the distance.
- o Finish off with the same breathing technique you started with, before gently coming back into the room.

This is a method you can use for any type of stress or anxiety that is bothering you, and it's a great way to get rid of an issue that is upsetting you at any stage during the day.

Another essential breathing technique is ensuring that we are taking deep, full breaths. When we are even the slightest bit stressed, we start breathing shallowly. These shallow, short breaths do not give us enough oxygen and can even lead to full-blown panic attacks. To stop poor breathing, place your hand an inch or two above your stomach. Now, slowly breathe in through your nose until your stomach touches your hand. Go with our usual 5 counts inhales, and hold for a few seconds before slowly exhaling out through your mouth.

When our breathing is shallow, we only fill up the top portion of our lungs with air. Placing your hand above your stomach ensures that you are breathing deeply enough where your entire lungs are filled!

Deep breathing is the foundation of many calming strategies. It can be done on its own or with other methods like meditation, tai chi yoga, etc. Deep breathing is easy because we need to breathe to remain alive, but strongly and efficiently for mental relaxation and stress reduction. Deep breathing focuses on breathing the stomach thoroughly and clean singly. It is easy to learn that you can do it anywhere, and it regulates your stress levels. Sit down with your back straight, inhale through the nose as the belly grows. Inhale as much clean air as possible into the lungs. It makes it possible to get more oxygen into the blood. Exhale the mouth as the belly drops to force as much air as possible out and close the abdominal tract. If you find it difficult to do this sitting, first try to lie down. You could put your hands on your chest and stomach to see if it's wrong.

Chapter 27. Meditation for Anxiety

Throughout this book, we have taken the time to understand anxiety, its triggers, signs, and some of the types of anxiety disorders. It has become clear that everyone faces anxiety at one point in their lives while others seem to have it constantly haunting them. It also became clear how the word does not get the recognition it deserves.

We are going to look into different meditation techniques which are used to deal with anxiety and panic disorders. If you are suffering from either, this is the book for you. Who knows, it might save you the frequent trips to the doctor to get anxiety pills.

Anxiety and Stress Relief

The goal of anxiety and stress relief meditation is to learn how to let go of whatever is weighing you down and realize the peace and calmness the mind can experience. It serves the purpose of helping someone understand the position they are now in. The past and the future are impermanent. By letting these thoughts cloud our judgment and state of mind, we accept the troubles they drag along with them.

When it comes to anxiety and stress relief, it is highly advisable to separate yourself from everyone else. You need time to restore yourself to your most productive element because you might rub off some of the bad energy onto others. If need be, hide in a properly ventilated closet-as long as you are comfortable.

Close your eyes and try to relax your body. This is important to prepare it to get into a state of well-being.

Focus your attention on yourself. This is your time; forget all the other things that cloud your mind. You want to be at peace and resonate peace and this is your time to manifest its existence. Start by inhaling and exhaling slowly through the nose and mouth in that order. Observe your body and the buildup of tension accumulated from the anxiety and stress.

You can imagine a stream of river passing and washing away all the buildup of anxiety and stress. Let it all go; let it all wash away. You can imagine anything. You can also decide to fold your stress and anxiety in a leaf and let it go in whichever direction the wind decides. Every time you exhale, envision all the worries go away. Your mind is your palace of imagination. You can do anything in the space you have created for yourself now.

Slowly, go back and observe your breathing again. Keep inhaling through your nose and exhaling through the mouth. You can decide to let it happen naturally or give it intervals of three seconds. Your space your choice. If your mind keeps wandering, you can perform a couple of deep breaths to bring back your focus to your breathing.

Now, imagine you are all alone at the beach and you have worn your favorite pair of swimsuits. You want to take a dip because you are aware of the calming effect water has on you. Picture yourself running towards the water and splashing your way in. To your surprise, when you take a dip, you start to glow and feel so nice. The more you dip yourself into the water, the more your worries wash away leaving you with a nice aura and a sense of peace. Keep imagining this before going back to observe your breathing.

Notice if there is any change in your breathing. Does it feel more natural and relaxed? Do you feel better? If not, start with the breathing again. Center yourself and your thoughts. Do not let your source of stress or anxiety

408

plague you in this space. Remember, this is your personal space. This is your time. Nobody can take away your time. You can use any relevant scenario as a visual tool to let go of the stress and anxiety that had manifested itself. It does not have to be exactly what is above. If it works for you, that is all that matters. Keep transitioning from your breathing to visual scenarios until the time you desire. Even after feeling better, you might decide to continue doing it for a while just because you can. There is certainly no harm in that.

Apart from the above method, mindfulness meditation, some audio guided meditations and Vipassana meditation serve as good alternatives to try. The practice of meditation does not restrict you from trying out something different if the one you are accustomed to doing does not show results. Any technique that is good for you is the best.

Self-Healing for On-The-Spot Anxiety

Anxiety can clock in at any time it feels like. Let us compare it to that manager who decides to walk into the office, yet nobody expected them to show up because it was their day off. From minor misunderstandings to large problems, anxiety always comes packed differently to every individual. Luckily, several methods that deal with anxiety immediately occur exist. These methods are:

Mindful Breathing

Take some time out for yourself for just five minutes. If you cannot, just pay attention to yourself wherever you are and start to breathe deeply while assuming an upright posture. Notice how the lower section of your bells expands as you breathe in through your nose and contracts as you breathe out through your mouth. Deep breathing is associated with lowering the heart rate, which in turn reduced blood pressure.

Focus on the Present

As soon as you feel the anxiety starting to kick in, in whatever situation you are, just start to focus on what is happening presently. If you are walking, focus on how your feet hit the ground and how the wind is blowing against your face or hair. If you are eating, focus on how your fingers feel holding that spoon. What kind of sensations do you feel around your mouth as you eat? Pay attention to these details and slowly witness yourself starting to feel less tense.

Scan Your Body

This technique combines bodily awareness and breathing. It helps individuals experience the connection between the body and the mind. Start by observing your breathing. Inhale and exhale through your nose. The purpose is to clear all the stories in your head and concentrate on yourself. After a few minutes, focus your attention on a specific group of muscles and release any tension you feel. Move to the next muscle and so the same. Keep doing this until you have covered the whole body. You can do it in whatever order you like.

Use Guided Imagery

Due to the availability of the internet, it is easy to find apps or audios online that can help you create guided images. However, this technique might not be so efficient for people who have a problem constructing mental images. If you have the ability to construct mental images with ease, make sure that the imageries are relatable to you. Otherwise, you might not understand what is going on-which beats the whole point. Guided imageries are there to help someone reinstate the positivity in themselves. If you find it difficult to visualize such images in your mind, you can stare at one imagine for a few seconds, and then close your eyes with the idea of retaining the image in your mind. As you practice this technique, you will find it to be easier and easier to achieve mental imagery.

Start Counting

In school, it was a common thing to hear teachers or parents say, "If you feel angry or you want to say something out of bitterness, just count to ten first." It is funny how this holds true. Counting is one of the many easy ways to deal with your anxiety anywhere it occurs. You do not have to count to ten; you can even do it to one hundred if it feels right. Challenge yourself and count backward as well. This way, you can really get your mind into it.

Sometimes the anxiety goes away quickly, while other times it does not. Whatever the case, ensure you try to keep calm and collected. Counting distracts you from the cause of anxiety and keeps your mind busy. This will eventually return you to a state of calm.

Interrupt Your Thoughts

From my experience with anxiety, your thoughts can so powerful to the extent of making you actually feel like your fears are going to manifest themselves. The thought itself then again doubles your anxiety and the cycle just keeps going. Then again, you realize that the majority of these things never get to happen and that you were so anxious for no good reason.

Interrupting your thoughts as they come can bring you back to a sense of calm. You can do this by starting to think about a person you love- a person who brings peace into your life. If you like a certain music album, skip to your favorite songs and jam along. Remember to always return your focus to yourself and observe how you feel after a few minutes. Observe how none of these feelings is permanent.

With these few tips, you are ready to break your anxiety cycle.

Panic Attacks

A panic attack is an unexpected feeling of intense fear that leads to other serious physical responses where no actual risk or obvious cause is present. They may occur at any time, even when you are asleep. Sometimes they have no trigger. A panic attack gives you breathing difficulties, makes your heart pound and it gives you a feeling that you are going crazy or are about to die. It is not a pretty experience just from what it sounds like. Other symptoms that occur may include sweating, shaking, fever, nausea, your legs may 'turn to jelly' and feeling a disconnection from yourself.

Many people only get to experience less than five panic attacks in their lifetime. The problem usually then goes

412

away after the stressful episode has ended. Some people have very constantly recurring panic attacks and they happen to stay in constant fear with the danger of having another panic attack-these people suffer from a condition called panic disorder.

It is difficult to pinpoint what exactly causes feelings of panic and the onset of attacks, but they tend to be common in families. Major life events such as marriage, graduation and retirement and the death of someone you love also show a bond with panic attacks and panic disorders. Some medical conditions can also be cause panic attacks such as hyperthyroidism and low blood sugar. The use of stimulants in the likes of caffeine and cocaine can also trigger panic attacks and disorders. If you suffer from panic disorders, it would be advisable to refrain from such.

In the event that you have had a panic attack and it has passed, it would be nice to give your body what it needs. You might feel fatigued, hungry, or even thirsty. Make sure you give yourself some good treatment after it happens. It is advisable to inform someone that you can confide in about the situation. It is not a bad thing to ask for help.

Below are breathing techniques that reverse the symptoms of panic disorders.

Diaphragm Meditation for Panic Attacks

When we encounter a situation of distress, the pattern and rate of our breathing become different. On a normal day, we always breathe slowly using our lower lungs. However, in situations of distress, our breathing shifts to be shallow and rapid while situated in the upper lungs. In the event that it happens when resting, it can cause

413

hyperventilation. This also explains some of the symptoms experienced during panic. Luckily, by knowing how to change your breathing, you can start to reverse the symptoms of your panic attack.

The body has a natural calming response called the parasympathetic response that triggers by changing how you breathe. It is very powerful and is the complete opposite of the emergency response (the feelings that kick in during an attack). When the calming response comes into play, all the primary changes brought about by the emergency response start to shift.

The two meditation techniques recommended to help with this disorder are natural breathing technique and the calming counting technique. The natural breathing technique is pretty much the same thing as the abdominal breathing technique. If you can practice breathing like this on a daily basis, it will only prove beneficial.

The Natural Breathing Technique (Abdominal Breathing Method)

Gently inhale a normal amount of air through your nostrils making sure it fills your lower lungs. You can decide to place your hands beneath your lower belly to supervise this or you can do whatever seems comfortable. Make sure to exhale easily while focusing on the movements of your lower belly. Feel it expand as air gets in and go down when you exhale. Carry this practice with a relaxed mindset not forgetting to fill your lower lungs with air. Try your best to actually "feel" the oxygen rushing into your body and making its way through your blood. You will feel how every tissue in your body imbibes the fresh oxygen you have just inhaled.

Calming Counts

Assume a comfortable sitting posture and take a deep breath. As you are exhaling, slowly whisper to yourself to relax. Keep your eyes closed to avoid losing focus. Now, start taking natural breaths while counting down from a desired number. Make sure to only count after a successful exhale. As you keep breathing, throw your attention to any areas of tension. Imagine the tension getting loose and shriveling, leaving you feeling calm and refreshed.

When you arrive at the end of your countdown, open your eyes, and notice any difference in what you are feeling. If it has worked but not as efficiently as desired, give it a longer try making sure your willpower is set to let go of the panic. Eventually, you will notice yourself get better.

Studies have shown that these meditation techniques, if practiced even when one is not anxious, are bound to yield the same results. If you can, dedicate a little time every morning and evening to practice the technique that works best for you.

Two things should be highly observed when practicing these techniques: focusing on changing negative thoughts and not thinking of anything else while meditating. This is because our thoughts directly influence our breathing and changing your negative thoughts can help lessen the symptoms quickly. Concentrate most of your effort into not thinking about anything else. Do not even think about your next breath; it should happen naturally.

Chapter 28. Guided Meditation for Anxiety

Find a comfortable place to sit. Either on a chair or on the ground.

Adjust your posture accordingly and sit upright with your spine straight, neck tall and shoulders relaxed.

When you are ready, gently close your eyes.

Allow yourself to settle in the here and now.

(10 seconds)

Become aware of your surroundings. Notice any sounds around you. They may be loud or subtle. Maybe there is a sound of the clock ticking. Or, the humming noise of your air conditioning. Or, noise from the streets. Maybe you can hear the chirping of the birds outside. Or, it is completely silent. Just notice whatever sounds or silence in your environment.

(20 seconds)

Now, pay attention to your thoughts and notice what thoughts are popping up in your mind

(5 seconds)

What are you thinking about?

Are you thinking of your problems or your plans for the day?

Just become aware of the thoughts in your mind and let them go.

(10 seconds)

Now, bring your attention to your breathing.

Take a deep breath in through your nose and feel it fill your body.

(5 seconds)

Exhale completely and let the air leave your body.

(5 seconds)

Keep breathing deeply.

(30 seconds)

When you notice your mind wandering, just focus on your breathing and bring your attention back to my voice.

(30 seconds)

Feel the sensation in your nose as the air touches it.

(15 seconds)

Become aware of the air as it fills your lungs till they are fully inflated.

(5 seconds)

Then, gently release your breath and feel as your lungs become deflated. Feel the air leave your body through the nose.

(5 Seconds)

Now, return to your normal breathing rhythm. Let your breathing assume its own natural rhythm and just observe each inhale and exhale.

(30 seconds)

Remain alert and aware. If your mind wanders, bring your attention back to your breathing.

(30 seconds)

Now, notice the parts of your body that are in contact with the ground. Fell the support of the surface beneath you.

(10 seconds)

Direct your focus to your toes. Wiggle all your ten toes and feel them relaxing.

(10 seconds)

Make circles with your feet and let your ankles relax.

(10 seconds)

Notice your calf muscles and knees. Tighten the muscles around them and let go.

(10 seconds)

Bring your attention to your thighs, squeeze them together and release allowing them to relax.

(10 seconds)

Take your attention to your buttocks and feel them pressing down the surface beneath you. Relax them and let go of any tension around them.

(10 seconds)

Focus on your pelvic area and relax it.

(10 seconds)

Move your attention to your back. Do you feel any tension?

Tighten the muscles in your back and release them. Feel them relax as the tension around your back dissolves away.

(10 seconds)

Gently, take a deep breath through your nose and feel the air fill your entire body and then exhale completely releasing it.

(10 seconds)

Take a deep breath in and fill your belly completely allowing it to expand as much as possible and then exhale letting it fall and completely relax.

(10 seconds)

Round your shoulders and upper back and squeeze your chest muscles and then release and assume an upright position allowing the chest to open au.

(10 seconds)

Now, bring your attention to the shoulders. Squeeze them up towards your ears and then release them down letting go any tension as you feel them relax.

(10 seconds)

Stretch out your hands in front of you and make tight fists and then release spreading your fingers wide.

(10 seconds)

Rets your hands on your lap.

Drop your chin towards your collar bone and let the back of your neck stretch and release and tension.

(10 seconds)

Lift your chin as up as possible and allow the front of your neck to stretch and release tension.

(10 seconds)

Clench your jaw, close your eyes and tighten your facial muscles. Breath in deeply and hold your breath in for 7,6,5,4,3,2,1 and exhale gently as you allow your jaw and facial muscles to relax and then open your eyes.

(10 seconds)

Sit in the awareness of your entire body. It is relaxed and alert.

(30 seconds)

Bring back your attention to your breathing.

Inhale deeply and silently repeat the mantra 'I am inhaling.'

Exhale slowly as you silently say to yourself, 'I am exhaling.'

Keep breathing and reciting the mantras "I am inhaling", "I am exhaling".

(30 seconds)

When you notice your mind wandering, gently bring you attention back to your breathing and repeat the mantra.

I am inhaling.

I am exhaling

(30 seconds)

Gently direct your awareness to your body.

Feel the surface you are sitting on.

(5 seconds)

Notice the temperature on your skin.

(5 seconds)

Listen to the sounds around you.

(5 seconds)

Listen to your breathing.

(5 seconds)

Notice the sensations in your body.

(5 seconds)

Gently wiggle your fingers and your toes.

When you feel ready, open your eyes.

You are now ready to go on with your plans for the rest of the day.

Chapter 29. Guided Body Scan Meditation for Anxiety

Welcome to this body scan meditation. Think of the next 30 minutes as an opportunity to dwell in your body and to be in the present moment as it is.

(5 seconds)

Begin by finding a comfortable place to sit with your back straight but not stiff. If you are seated on a chair, allow your feet to rest on the ground. If you are seated on the ground, you may either cross your legs or straighten them. You could also do this meditation lying down with your feet extended in front of you and your hands resting beside your body. Adjust your body accordingly until you settle into a comfortable pose.

(10 seconds)

Gently close your eyes.

Become aware of the thoughts in your mind.

(10 seconds)

Our aim in this meditation is to release all the tension in your body and mind, so as to help you release stress and anxiety and to become calm and peaceful.

We will begin our scan from the top of our head to our toes. We will listen to our bodies and notice all the sensations then release all the tension and pains.

I will mention a part of your body; take your attention to that part of the body and scan it to detect any stress or tension around it. You will then visualize a yellow beam of energy shining on that part of the body as it washes away the pain, tightness or tension.

(5 seconds)

Now, bring your awareness to the top of your head and observe the sensations on this part of the body.. Do you feel any tension? What sensations can you detect on this part of your body? Take a breath and send the energy light to it. See the light dissolve all the tension on the top of your head.

(20 seconds)

Bring your attention to your forehead. Is there tightness or any other noticeable sensation on this part of your body? Focus the yellow beam of energy to your forehead and let it melt away all the tension in this area.

(20 seconds)

Move your attention to your eyes. Scan them and check if they have any tension lodged in them. Do you feel any tightness behind your eyelids? Send the yellow beam of energy to the area around your eyes and feel as it dissolves the stress in your eyes.

(20 seconds)

Slowly move your awareness to your cheekbones and the cheeks. Observe whether there is any tension around them. Inhale and direct the yellow beam of energy on both cheeks allowing them to release tension and to relax.

(20 seconds)

Bring your awareness to your ears. Scan them for any tension and send the beam of energy to wash any tension that could be on your ears away.

(20 seconds)

Notice your mouth and jaw. Sense any tension around it. Shine the beam of energy on your mouth and jaw to clear away all that tension.

(20 seconds)

Become aware of your chin. Scan it for any tension. Now, shine the healing wave of energy to clear all the tension lodged in your chin. Feel as your chin relaxes.

(20 seconds)

Feel the back of your head. Slowly, scan it to detect any tension hidden in this area. Inhale deeply and let the yellow beam of energy consume all the tension held at the back of your head. As you exhale, allow your head to relax completely.

(20 seconds)

Take your awareness to your shoulders. Scan them for any tension. Now, send the energizing beam of energy to your shoulders and let it wash all the tension in that area.

(20 seconds)

Notice your chest. Notice how it rises and fall as you breathe in and out. Feel your heartbeat behind the chest. Scan every inch of your chest and check for tension lodged there. Focus the beam of energy to your chest. Let it clear all the tension, little by little until the entire chest area is fully relaxed.

(30 seconds)

Move your awareness to your back. Notice all the parts of your back from the upper back to the lower back, the spine and the entire torso. Scan the entire back for any tension, pain or tightness.

(5 seconds)

Shine the yellow beam of energy on your back. From the upper part of the back, to the middle part of the back and down to the lower back. Let this energizing light melt away any tension you are holding on to on your back.

(30 seconds)

Now, take your awareness to your stomach and the belly area. Visualize all the organs held within your rib cage and belly area. Your stomach, intestines, reproductive system, kidneys, liver, bladder, and all other organs. Scan your belly, ribcage and the organs beneath for tension or tightness.

(10 seconds)

Now, shine the beam of light to your stomach, rib cage and the organs beneath and let all the tension held on this area of the body dissolve.

(30 seconds)

Move your attention to your left arm.

Become aware of every part of your left arm; the biceps, triceps, forearm, palm and fingers.

(10 seconds)

Send the energy to your left arm to clear all the tension. Feel as the muscles in the whole of your left arm relax.

(10 seconds)

Now, move your awareness to your right arm. Notice all the parts of your right arm; biceps, triceps, forearm, palm and fingers. Scan for any tension in your arm.

(10 seconds)

Inhale and shine the beam of energy on your right arm and let all the tension in your right arm melt away. Feel as the right up relaxes.

(10 seconds)

Gently bring your awareness to your pelvis. Notice your buttocks, hips and groin area. Scan them for any tension, pain or tightness. Visualize the yellow beam of light shine upon your pelvis as it washes away all the tension leaving the buttocks, hips and groin completely relaxed.

(30 seconds)

Notice your left and right thighs. The thighs have the largest muscles in your body. As such, they can hold a lot of tightness and tension.

Bring your attention on the upper part of your right thigh and move your attention from the upper right thigh bit by bit up to the right knee as you scan for tension on the inner right thigh, top of the right thigh, back side of the right thigh and the outer edge of the right thigh. Now, visualize the relaxing beam of energy wash away tension from the upper part of the right thigh to knee.

(30 seconds)

Now, bring your attention on the upper part of your left thigh and move your attention from the upper left thigh bit by bit up to the left knee as you scan for tension on the inner left thigh, top of the left thigh, back side of the left thigh and the outer edge of the left thigh. Now, visualize the relaxing beam of energy wash away tension from the upper part of the left thigh to knee.

(30 seconds)

Become aware of the lower part of the legs. Notice your knees and the knee caps. Scan them for any tension and envision the yellow light dissolving all the tension that is on this part of your body.

(10 seconds)

Now, bring your attention to your left and right shins and calves.

(5 seconds)

Become aware of both of your ankles.

(5 seconds)

Scan your lower legs from the knees to your ankles for any pain or tension.

(10 seconds)

Inhale and shine the beam of energy beam on both of your legs from the knees to the ankles. As you exhale, feel your lower legs relax.

(15 seconds)

Gently move your awareness to your feet. Become aware of the bottom and the top part of your feet. Observe your feet and check for any tightness around them. Ease the tension there with the beam of light and feel as your feet relax.

(10 seconds)

Now envision the yellow beam of light shining on your entire body. It moves slowly from head to toes a sit washes away any remaining tension on your body.

(30 seconds)

It then moves from your toes to your head, bit by bit as it energizes every cell on your body.

(30 seconds)

Your body is now fully relaxed. You feel calm, peaceful, centered and grounded. Rest in this alert awareness of your body and in total relaxation for a moment.

(180 seconds)

Begin to deepen your breath. Gently wiggle your fingers and toes and when you are ready slowly open your eyes.

Chapter 30. Benefits of meditation

Meditation Helps to Reduce Stress

The modern-day lifestyle that we lead is hectic and inadvertently leads to stress and anxiety on some level. Stress has become one of the most common problems that people suffer from these days. You may think that you can put it off or might have resigned yourself to the fact that it is a part of your life. However, stress can lead to a myriad of health problems like high blood pressure, an increase in the risk of cardiovascular disorders, and insomnia, just to name a few. The stress chemical in the body is called cortisol. Your body can usually regulate the levels of cortisol within it, but the more your stress levels, the higher the amount of cortisol secreted. This can cause issues like panic attacks. Cortisol secretion needs to be regulated. All of these issues can, however, be dealt with using the help of meditation. It will help in reducing your stress levels and help you deal with anxiety-inducing issues in a productive manner. Overall, by practicing meditation, you will notice a decline in your stress and anxiety levels.

Meditation Helps Keep Emotions Under Control

Humans are emotional creatures. However, it can be hard for us to control our emotions at times, and this can have dangerous consequences. This is especially true in the present world that we live in. The increased amount of pressure and anxiety you experience can cause a build-up of many negative feelings. If you let emotions like anger build-up, it will only harm you. Not just you, but also those around you. Meditation will help you maintain your calm and stay composed even in the face of adversity. When you are able to stay calm, then it is easier to rationalize your thoughts. Apart from this, it will also help you make better decisions. You must not let your emotions control you, and meditation will help you get a handle on your emotions.

Meditation Increases Serotonin Secretion

You might have heard of serotonin, the "happy hormone." The human body secretes various hormones that have a huge impact on how you think and feel. These chemicals in your body will affect how happy, sad, or angry you are. Serotonin is a chemical that helps people stay happy. Studies show that regular meditation helps in increasing serotonin secretion. This chemical has a positive effect on your mind and body. Low levels of serotonin are observed in people suffering from depression and other mental health issues. So, meditation is one of the most effective means of tackling depression.

Meditation Improves the Ability to Focus

Having the ability to focus better is something everyone aims for in life. However, most people have trouble with this. Being able to focus can help you in so many ways. If you are a student, it will help you study better. If you have specific goals in life, you will be able to focus on those goals and work accordingly. Lack of focus can make you lose track of what you do and lead an undisciplined life. Research shows that those who practice meditation tend to have a better ability to focus on their tasks and perform better than those who don't practice meditation. Different meditation techniques will help you hone your ability to focus and enhance your cognitive skills.

Meditation Increases Creativity

It is also said that meditation can get your creative juices flowing. When you meditate and reduce your stress levels, your brain is allowed to function better, and you can be more creative. This creative ability is often negatively impacted by high-stress levels. Meditation will help you embrace the good and the bad in your life without harming your happiness or health.

Meditation Increases Empathy and the Ability to Connect

You need to learn how to empathize and connect with others if you want better relationships. Meditation will help you learn compassion and thus act compassionately towards people. People who meditate tend to have an increased capacity for kindness and understanding towards others. You will be able to think of things from others' perspectives and react to situations in a better way. Meditation can enhance this empathetic ability and improve your social interactions.

Meditation Helps Improve Relationships

Do you feel like your relationships with your loved ones could use some extra help? Meditation can help you with this. Meditation helps increase your empathy, and this will help you immensely. It helps to increase your awareness so that you can pick up on cues from those around you. This will help you understand how they are feeling in certain situations. By getting a read on the situation, it will be easier for you to react and respond in the right way. Apart from this, it also helps reduce any chances of misunderstandings cropping up. Once your emotions are stabilized, the chances of letting any negativity through will decrease.

Meditation Enhances Memory

Do you feel like you have become forgetful? There could be many reasons behind this, stress being the main culprit. Regardless of what the cause is, meditation can help improve your memory, if practiced regularly. You will be able to focus on things and become more conscious of your surroundings and your own self. You will also be able to retain information for longer and thus be less forgetful. Meditation can be a great memory-enhancing tool regardless of what you do or what your age is.

Meditation Improves Immunity

Another benefit of meditation is that it is a holistic way of boosting your body's immune system. If you feel like you get sick too often or just want to be healthier, you should try meditation. Various meditation techniques like yoga are known to help in strengthening the immune system. By meditating regularly, you will notice a positive change in your overall immunity.

Meditation Helps You Overcome Addictions

Addictions are a serious affliction that can be really hard to contend with. It requires a lot of self-control and discipline to let go of any type of addiction. This could be smoking, alcoholism, or just about any unhealthy habit that has a negative impact on your health and well-being. It's not just the addictions that affect your physical health. There are other addictions like watching too much pornography, using excessive social media, binge eating, etc. These change your body and mind in many negative ways. There are certain meditation techniques, like Vipassana meditation, which is often used to help addicts overcome powerful addictions. Just meditating will not solve all your problems, but it is a great tool to help you move forward and leave your addictions behind. So, if you or anyone you know suffers from an addiction, trying meditation is a good place to start.

Meditation Benefits Cardiovascular Health

It is actually common sense that meditation is good for the heart. If you observe how regular meditation helps you when you need to relax and how it decreases your tendency to be anxious, at that point, is there any good reason why it shouldn't also help reduce the risk of cardiovascular issues, similar to hypertension?

For a considerable length of time, many assumed that to be the case, yet a couple of specialists appeared to be intrigued enough to research and document the physical outcomes on the heart after meditating. The leading researcher to explore this connection was Herbert Benson from Harvard. His important book, distributed in the mid-1970s, The Relaxation Response, raised a lot of discussions inside intellectual circles. Through medical testing, he showed that changes occurred in the body.

At first, other colleagues were skeptical of his discoveries. Nobody had ever genuinely thought that there could be medical advantages related to this meditative training. In any case, his testing withstood the thorough investigation conducted by others. In the last two decades, mainstream researchers picked up progressively genuine enthusiasm for the subject. The research started, yet more explicitly, the American Heart Association Journal published an article that reported the ability of meditation to bring down an individual's risk factors that are associated with all types of cardiovascular illness.

The American Journal of Hypertension recently also published positive on the medical advantages of meditation. In this research, it was found that a gathering of meditating people viably brought down their blood pressure, contrasted with a second group that didn't meditate. The decrease in blood pressure for these individuals was so apparent, truth be told, that the meditators had the option to reduce their utilization of antihypertensive drugs by about 25 percent. Stress is related to something beyond coronary illness.

Stress can cause disruption in a lot of physiological functions. At the end of the day, when you're worried all the time, it manifests in the form of any number of medical issues. One of the systems you may have noticed this in is through gastrointestinal dysfunctions. It's not "all in your head," it's been extensively recorded that changes in physiology and hormones happen in your body in relation to stress. These cause various stomach issues, as a response to a distressing condition - either acute or chronic.

A few people also experience sleep disorders due to stress. In some of these cases, sleep issues are linked with irritable bowel syndrome. Fortunately, these physical changes can be reduced and eased through consistent meditation practice.

Meditation Aids Weight Loss

It's hard to be your best when you're troubled with weight issues. Sadly, numerous people who are overweight do not have a good self-image and lack a sense of self-worth. Without that, they may believe that their ideal life is far out of their grasp. Meditation can do something amazing here, in two different ways. To begin with, it's not unusual to start eating when you're stressed out.

If you are someone who does this, you realize that what you go after first is generally something salty, sugary or greasy. It's not about your absence of self-restraint - blame the hormonal changes related to too much stress instead. Your body craves this kind of unhealthy food when it is under distress.

A lot of research demonstrates that the physical impact of stress on your body can be greatly diminished through meditation. It starts by diminishing the body's cortisol level, which can then mitigate those obstinate yearnings for food. Maybe meditating doesn't offer that equivalent comfort that you get from the bag of chips, candy, or fries (or even all three). Yet, it can help curb those cravings in any case. This is a part of the process that will allow people to pick up a superior mental self-image, which, then, empowers them to concentrate on seeking the life that they need to lead. Stress is very slippery. It penetrates your entire being. Maybe, however, its most notable impending impacts are on the person's immunity. Consider it. How often have you caught a cold or even the flu following an unpleasant event?

Meditation can definitely help you with this also. People under pressure are known to have decreased amounts of basic white blood cells, which are essential for battling foreign attacking microscopic organisms and infections, which can cause cold, influenza, and other illnesses. Meditation is undoubtedly now seen as a great way to insightfully deal with the stress in your life.

Meditation Helps Manage Headaches

A headache is one of the most common signs that your body is experiencing too much stress. What's more, it's difficult to concentrate on what is important to you when a headache is floating over the majority of your thoughts.

It's hard to think, and at the same time, it's hard to use sound judgment, and it's tough to enjoy yourself. Maybe it doesn't come as anything unexpected that meditation is the ideal method to loosen up those muscles and suppress that pain.

In addition to the fact that it works for most people, its positive effects are likewise scientifically confirmed. Even for a brief timeframe, going within yourself as meditation allows you to make changes in your brain waves to another higher state. This is a dimension of awareness that is known to help advance the process of healing. The takeaway here is that through meditation, you can adjust your brain waves. Researchers were once convinced that an individual's brain waves are unchangeable. They trusted that we are brought into the world with specific patterns, and these couldn't be modified, despite our ability to switch between different dimensions of cognizance.

Today, however, it's broadly acknowledged that your brain waves can be changed—and meditation is one way in which this can be accomplished. The most recent studies have taken a look at people who have been meditating for over fifteen years. Long-term meditation changes the functioning of the brain, which permits the individuals who meditate to achieve a more elevated amount of mindfulness than the individuals who don't. In any case, nothing is preventing you right now from disposing of that migraine through a ten-or fifteen-minute session of meditation, so why not try it?

As you can see, meditation has a lot of benefits for those who practice it regularly. There are actually more ways in which it helps than just the ones mentioned above. If you genuinely want to experience the benefits of meditation, you need to get started.

How Can I Establish A Good Meditation Practice?

One effective way to consistently practice meditation is to create and plan out a practice that you can follow, according to your needs, your daily schedule, routines, and timing.

The thing about meditation is that you need to be mindful of everything that you experience in your session. With mindful meditation, there is a goal and a purpose. It is to help you be conscious and mindful of everything you do.

Benefits Of Establishing A Meditation Practice

A foundation of your meditation session is important because, in many ways, when you set the stones to your practice, your brain will start moving toward making this practice happen. For example, if you decide to buy a new meditation mat, your mind will be reminded (or you will remember) that you purchased the mat, and you want to know the feeling of sitting on the mat and practicing.

Without a firm foundation, you will not be consistent

It won't be long before whatever you're doing eventually crumbles and falls because there's nothing supporting it. That's just one way of describing how important it is to develop a sound meditation practice right from the very beginning of the process.

It helps you create a habit

But although meditation is something that is beneficial for everyone, not everyone is currently putting it into practice. Some people are not practicing meditation at all. Why? Because it isn't a habit. A lot of us lead very busy lives, so sometimes our plates seem too full to take on anything else. There will always be a reason not to start something, which is why it is entirely up to you to make time for it.

The purpose of establishing a meditation practice is because you want to make meditation a habit, a part of your daily life, and something that you are willing to do every day without even thinking twice or resisting it because you are pressed for time.

It makes your practice ingrained, almost second-nature activity in your life

Meditating will become much like how brushing your teeth or showering, preparing something to eat, and even going on a daily commute to work. Those habits are so deeply ingrained in you that you do them without any effort or a lot of thought put into it.

That is what establishing a meditation practice aims to do for you right now, and it is something you need to establish as a foundation to make your practice consistent.

Chapter 31. Mindfulness Meditation

When we experience stress and anxiety, it is often simply worrying over the past or fears that we are having about the future. The best way to overcome these constant fears is to be mindful in the present moment to keep your thoughts grounded in reality. In this meditation, we are going to help you stay mindful so that you can focus on what matters the most—healing.

You cannot heal if your thoughts and emotions are glued to some time period that is out of your control. You cannot change the past, so guilt and remorse are only going to keep you stuck in a different dimension. No matter how prepared we can be for the future, there is still a level of unpredictability that we will never be able to conquer. In this meditation, you are going to learn exactly what it means to stay in the present moment to start the healing process.

Meditation for Self-Healing Mindfulness

For this meditation, you will want to be in a completely comfortable place. It is preferred that you do this meditation when you are able to fall asleep afterwards, but that's also not entirely necessary. Doing this outside where you can take a nap with nature would also be an excellent way to fully feel the beneficial effects of this meditation.

This is going to be a visualization exercise that will help take your mind to a calm and relaxed place. You will remove any thoughts that are keeping you glued to some time period which you cannot change. In order to really

438

feel the benefit of this meditation, focus on your breathing and keep a clear mind.

Anytime that a thought starts to travel into your mind, gently push it away. You do not have to force them out of your mind. You do not have to block out negative thoughts and punish yourself for having them. Simply let them drift in and out like a car passing you by. There is no need to latch onto these thoughts and you don't need to shove them to a corner of your brain. Let them come into your mind and push them out as soon as they do.

Focus on your breathing once again. Breathe in through your nose for five and out through your mouth for five. Breathe in for one, two, three, four, and five, and out for five, four, three, two, and one.

Keep every part of your body relaxed and let your eyes gently close. No need to hold them closed tightly to the point that you are straining yourself. Let your eyelids gently stay shut. We are going to count down from twenty. When we reach one, you will be into the meditation. Let your mind become completely black and continue to feel the air come in and out of your body.

Breathe in for five and out for five.

Your mind is completely blank. You do not see anything at all. The only thing your mind is focused on now is feeling the air continue to cycle throughout your body.

In your mind, you start to see a small bright dot. The dot continues to grow bigger and bigger until you discover that you are engulfed in sunlight.

You look around and discover that you are surrounded by lush, green trees. Each thing that you see around you is a reminder that you are a part of nature. All of these various aspects are part of a living ecosystem in which

439

you are also operating at this moment. Breathe in the fresh air and feel as it fills your body.

As you look in front of you, you see that there is a little trail between some of the trees. You take a step forward and begin to walk around. You can feel as the dirt and the leaves crunch beneath your feet. It is a beautiful fall day, and the orange and yellow changing of the trees is filling you with a sense of warmth. There's a light breeze but nothing that is keeping you too chilled in this moment. You can see bits of the sky above you. Bright blue is beaming through the break of the leaves. You continue to walk forward and see in front of you that there is a very large path. Now, many individuals have already walked down this path themselves before. You are not concerned with what has happened over the past or the potentials of the future. You are completely grounded in the present moment, and only focused on this at the time being. Breathe in this good energy and breathe out anything that has been keeping you trapped in a place which you do not have control. Everything that you have experienced leading up to this moment has brought you to be the exact person that you are. Even if you are not happy with who this person is at the present moment, there will be one day where everything makes sense. You will be able to look back on your past and know that each struggle was just another step towards making you the individual that you are. Not everything has been easy for you up until this point, but it has been a learning experience that teaches you something greater about yourself. Breathe in now as you begin to accept the things that have happened in your past. Breathe out as you are letting go of any of the emotions that you have experienced. You continue to walk towards more and more trees, and you think about how nature is so incredible. You are a part of all of these living things.

440

No matter what these trees and flowers and other little plants might experience, they continue to live on. There is nobody tending to them.

These plants don't have a gardener who comes and makes sure that they are free from any diseases or root rot. Nobody is watering them and nurturing them. They're able to take care of themselves on their own because they are a part of a larger system. Bugs help to keep them pollinated and plants around them will also aid in the way that they grow. Animals might come and feast on them, and they soak up as much sun and rain as they possibly can.

This is a reminder of the powerful ability that all living things have to carry on, no matter what the circumstances might be. Your body will always be there and provide you with the nourishment and fulfillment that is needed to make sure that you are as healthy as possible. No matter what you give to your body, whether it is something healthy, or a type of junk food, you will be able to take the most important and beneficial aspects of this using your body. Everything that exists inside of you is something that happens on its own. You don't have to tell your body how to process and break down food. It naturally does this all. All of this is a reminder that you are a part of a greater living organism. This earth is flowing around so freely and gently, as it should be. You continue to walk forward, and you notice that there is a little pond. You walk up to it and see that there are some little fish swimming around in the bottom. These fish could be a source of food.

These fish could be somebody else's family. These fish are their own living organisms, and they are simply existing. They swim against the current, and they look for food on the top of the surface. No matter what they might experience, their main focus will always be on continuing to live. It is a powerful reminder that when you feel lost, you can always rest assured that your intention and purpose is to simply carry on living, breathing.

Breathe in as you notice the site and breathe out as you let go of any sort of thoughts that are keeping you glued somewhere else. It is okay to think and plan for the future. And we all have moments where we reflect on the past. The issue comes when you obsess over these things. If you are only thinking in different time periods, other than what is occurring now, then you will not be able to give your full energy to the things that are currently surrounding you. Breathe in the excitement over staying mindful and productive in this moment. Breathe out any desire to stay stuck in a different time period.

You look down and notice the fish. You could grab any one of them that you wanted. This pond isn't that large and not that deep. You would probably be able to pick one up as long as you gave it a few tries.

This is something within your power, and you have a choice. You choose not to and instead let these fish continue swimming on. There's no point in taking one of these fish from the pond. Sure, you might be able to use it for food later, but you don't need that. You simply continue to watch as these fish float around. You don't scare them away and you don't try to move them. They're simply there. This is how we need to start to treat our thoughts. Our thoughts can sometimes just be like fish swimming around in a fishbowl. The thoughts will always be there. They won't go away. The thing is, you don't have to feed these fish. You don't have to pick them up. You don't have to move them around. You don't have

442

to kill them. You don't have to do anything. You can simply let them continue to swim around and around. Your thoughts do not have to be given attention. These thoughts can come into your mind, but you don't have to be afraid and push them out so negatively. Instead, you can simply focus on yourself and create a positive and healthy mindset. When you have negative thoughts, remember that they can simply swim away like fish. Breathe in and out, in and out.

You sit next to the pond and close your eyes once again. You dip your toes down into the cool water. Even though it is a fall day, it is not freezing just yet and instead the water gives you a reminder of the last little bit of summer that's left. Breathe in and out, in and out. You close your eyes and lay back against a thick layer of leaves on the ground. You feel completely comfortable, at peace and at ease. Breathe in and out, in and out.
You close your eyes, and everything starts to fade away once again. All is becoming black and there are no thoughts left that are travelling through your mind.

This is a safe and relaxing place that you can travel back to anytime that it is needed. You are completely at ease and peace is seeping out of every last one of your pores. You have no thoughts that are keeping you stuck in a negative place now. You cannot heal unless you are relaxed and free from the fears that have been holding you back for so long. Breathe in for one, two, three, four, and five, and out for five, four, three, two, and one.

Continue to feel yourself relax. You are sinking deeper and deeper and further and further into the couch. There isn't a single thing that is keeping you held back in this moment. You are entirely relaxed and at ease. We are going to count down from twenty once again.

Chapter 32. How to Meditate

Meditation is a great - and logically demonstrated - habit for a solid body and mind. Be that as it may, a few people battle with the time, consistency, center, and system required to get meditation right.

What great many people don't know is, you don't really need to take a seat and close your eyes for a considerable length of time a day - in light of the fact that there are other far less demanding approaches to get your psyche into a thoughtful state, and appreciate the advantages of this ancient practice.

For example:

1. While you walk your dog

As you're strolling Jack, instead of meditating a large number of things you're stalling on, take a stab at giving careful attention to your environment.

Recognize the sounds, the general population, the climate. What do you smell? What would you be able to see? What would you be able to hear out yonder? How does your body feel?

By taking a careful walk, you're discharging endorphins, which enable you to build your joy level, and even diminish stress and live longer.

2. While you make coffee or tea

- Begin your morning with more profound concentration, lucidity, and peace by rehearsing this simple reflective custom.

As you make your tea or coffee, concentrate your attention on your developments.

- Close your eyes and notice the tea, take a taste, enjoy it. Furthermore, as you experience the ritual custom, be deliberately mindful of your breath.
- You can likewise apply this while you cook your most loved supper or heat.

3. While you do the dishes

- Doing dishes or clearing your floor doesn't need to be an errand. Actually, this is the ideal time for you to associate with yourself and feel grounded.
- Concentrate on your breath and your body's sensations.
- On the off chance that you see your mind wandering, take yourself back to mindfulness by thinking about the general population and things throughout your life that fill you with delight and appreciation.

4. While you shower

- Have you at any point asked why your best thoughts tend to come while you're showering?
- "The shower is where we can develop mindfulness. When we get tranquil, when we get still, when we rest, you could state, in mindfulness, our natural drive to see associations that we didn't see the prior minute is unobstructed."
- On the off chance that you need to take it somewhat further, as you shower, you can even envision accomplishing your objectives and the feeling that will wash over you as you do.

5. While you tune in to your main tune

- Practicing mindfulness or meditation can be as straightforward as tuning in to your main song - insofar as you're totally centered around your breathing and the feeling that the song brings out in you.

445

6. While you ride the transport or sit in your auto

   o Sit serenely. Take long and full breaths. Recognize the warm sun stroking your face. Welcome the delightful city lights or scenes. Also, let your mind take you all alone trip.

As you now know, the benefits of meditation can be conveyed into the most ordinary exercises - helping you acknowledge life all the more, inhabit a slower pace, embrace new propensities, and be more joyful.

Practical Advice on meditation

To what extent Should I Meditate?

In the event that you are new to meditation, I suggest beginning gradually. Begin with only 5 minutes every day. Bit by bit increment the time more than half a month. When I began reflecting, five minutes felt like an unfathomable length of time. I now practice for 30 minutes every day, and here and there, I am astonished at how rapidly it passes!

Where Should I Meditate?

Locate a comfortable spot where you can sit. You can sit on the floor (utilizing a pad or pad for help if necessary) or sit upright in a seat, with your feet laying on the floor.

A few people suggest that you shouldn't rest on your back; however, I figure you ought to think in whatever stance works for you (unless resting influences you to fall asleep!)

You can meditate anyplace, yet I like having an extraordinary place in my home for my training. You can take in more about making a meditation space in your home here.

446

What Do I Do?

The least demanding meditation strategy is to count the breath. I forget about each in-breath and breath with a similar number. So my mind concentrates on "One" (in-breath), "One" (out-breath), "Two" (in-breath), "Two" (out-breath), et cetera. When I hit 10 (which seldom occurs before my mind has wandered!), I begin once again at one. On the off chance that you don't care for counting, you can essentially rehash to yourself "in, out... . in, out... "

At the point when your mind wanders, which it WILL DO (that's what the mind does!) tenderly guide your attention back to your breath. On the off chance that you have to begin once again counting in light of the fact that you don't recollect the latest relevant point of interest, that is fine! The key is to not reprimand or judge yourself for giving your attention a chance to wander. Actually ...

Seeing that your psyche has wandered is the general purpose of meditation, you are winding up more mindful of the activities of your mind!

Indeed, even the moderately basic guideline to "take after the breath" can sound somewhat obscure or confounding. A supportive method is to bring your attention where you most notice the vibe of the breath — in the chest and lungs? The nose? The stomach? That is your stay. Each time your mind wanders, return to the physical vibes of relaxing.

At the point when thought emerges, it's anything but difficult to get diverted and tail them and draw in them and explain them and investigate them... An accommodating practice is just to name the contemplations: "stressing," "arranging," "recollecting." Don't stress over making sense of the exact mark for the kind of thought you're having. Simply "considering" will do, as well!

What's more, if the thoughts don't leave? It's still alright.

I adore that depiction of the training.
How Do I Fit This Into My Day?

The critical thing is to make it a propensity. After numerous long stretches of a reliable practice, it will end up being a vital piece of your day, such as practicing or brushing your teeth!

Changing your habits over some stretch of time really makes new neural systems in your mind, and the training will turn out to be a piece of your day by day schedule.

Knocks along the Road

In any case, Nothing's Happening!

Meditation is about non-judgmental mindfulness. We have not to bring desires into our practice. You may encounter a snapshot of significant understanding amid a meditation session. Or, then again, you may be truly exhausted. You may feel fretful and disturbed. Or, on the other hand, you may feel quiet and relaxed.

Meditation is tied in with grasping whatever is right now. The advantages of meditation — more noteworthy mindfulness and discretion, increased calm and empathy — will rise after some time. In any case, every individual session will be totally unique.

So, in case you're exhausted, simply take note of, "This is the thing that fatigue feels like." If you're content, take note of, "This is the thing that satisfaction feels like."

- Meditating for 10 minutes daily is limitlessly superior to meditating for 70 minutes once per week. Attempt to meditate oftentimes (consistently if conceivable), regardless of the possibility that that just means sitting for a couple of minutes.
- Start little. In the event that you endeavor to meditate for 30 minutes right from the beginning, I can practically ensure that you will get disappointed and disheartened. I prescribe beginning with five minutes, and just increase that time when you're comfortable. Regardless of the possibility that you sit for five minutes, and you find that your mind wanders the entire time, you will, in any case, get unfathomable advantages from meditation.
- Pick a gentle alarm. On the off chance that your clock is uproarious and jolting, reckoning the caution will occupy your attention amid meditation.
- Meditate in a peaceful place. Having fewer distractions around you will normally enable you to meditate better, and will make your meditation significantly more profitable.
- It's most straightforward to lose your attention amid your out-breath. Your in-breath is exceptionally articulated and simple to focus on, and the vast majority's mind wanders on their out-breaths (me included). These merits remembering.
- Be simple on yourself when your mind wanders. It's anything but difficult to wind up plainly disappointed with yourself when your mind wanders, yet don't. Your meditations will be substantially more gainful when you delicately bring your mind back.

449

Chapter 33. How to Practice Mindfulness Meditation

Unlike other types of meditation, being mindful doesn't require a large time commitment or a space that is quiet and calm for a specific period of time. While these things will certainly help you get into the required mindset at first, eventually, you will find that you can get your mindfulness on while at the gym, doing chores, or even commuting to and from work. Regardless of where you do it, the basics of mindfulness meditation are always the same.

Stick with a specific time

As with any new habit, it is crucial that you create a routine around your mindfulness meditation practices for the best results. Generally speaking, you can expect it to take about 30 days for a new habit to really stick, which means that you will need to commit to going hard for just four weeks before you can expect to start seeing the best results.

Unfortunately, due to its few requirements and low impact nature, it is often quite easy to push off your set mindfulness meditation time for a later than never comes, especially if they are already very busy as it stands. If you find yourself always coming up with an excuse to get out of meditating at the moment, you may find the following piece of advice particularly useful. "Practice mindfulness meditation for fifteen minutes every day unless, of course, you are extremely busy, in which case you should practice for thirty minutes instead." Don't let the outside world intrude on your potential for inner peace, find a time each day that works for you and stick with it no matter what; in a month's time, you will be glad you did.

Find a quiet place

In order to reach a state of mindfulness, you are going to want to find someplace comfortable, and quiet to sit, though not so quiet and comfortable that you are tempted to fall asleep. Then, all you need to do is breathe deeply, in and out.

Breathe

Start by doing your best to calm your mind by taking a few deep breaths and then announce your intentions aloud to make them more tangible. From there, take several more deep breaths and focus on the sensations that your senses are providing you as you do so. Consider how your lungs feel as they expand and the smells this action brings to your attention. If you are sitting, consider the feel of the chair on your skin, the temperature of the room, and the movement of any wind across your skin. Let the sensations flow from one to another, working their way down your body completely.

Continue breathing deeply, but keep your eyes and ears alert and providing you with more information than you previously thought possible. Focus on this information to the exclusion of everything else. You will likely find it difficult to shut out the constant flow of information that is running through your mind relating to things you need to do, regrets over past actions and plans that must be made, but this is completely normal. If you find your focus drifting away from the moment, take note of the mistake and move on. There is nothing to be gained from beating yourself up over it, and you will only take yourself out of the moment even more.

Visualize

Once you have reached a relaxed state, to remove the excess thoughts that are likely running through your head, all you need to do is picture them as a stream of bubbles that are rushing by in front of your eyes. Simply take a step back and let the thoughts flow past you without interacting with them. If one of them catches your attention and draws you into more complex thought, simply disengage and let it go. Don't focus on the fact that you were thinking about it, because that will just draw you out of the moment, simply remain in that state for as long as possible. Eventually, this will help with negative thoughts you experience in the real world as well.

In fact, with enough time and practice, you will likely find that you are able to maintain a mild meditative state even when you are otherwise focused on the world around you. This is known as a state of mindfulness, and it should be the end goal of everyone who is new to the meditative practice. Being mindful means always being connected to a calming and soothing mental state as well as one that is full of joy and peace, which benefits not just yourself but everyone around you.

Ignore those pesky judgments

Mindfulness is not necessarily quieting the mind or finding an eternal state of calmness. The goal here is simple. You want to pay attention to the moment you are in without judging it. When you judge a thought or something you may have done in the past, you likely, tend to dwell on it. That isn't living in the moment and is not conducive to mindful meditation. While this is easier said than done, it is a crucial step to mindful meditation. With practice, it will be easy to achieve. Be mindful of the moment, of your senses and your surroundings.

Take notice of the times you are passing judgment while practicing mindfulness. Make a note of them and move on. It is easy for your mind to get lost in thought. Mindfulness meditation is the art of bringing yourself back to the moment, over and over, as many times as it takes. Don't get discouraged. In the beginning, you will find your mind wanders a lot. Reel it back in and keep moving forward. Even if your mind does happen to wander, and it will, don't be hard on yourself. It happens. Acknowledge whatever thoughts pop up, put them to the side, and get back on track.

Keep it up

When you first start practicing mindfulness meditation, it is very important that you do so under the understanding that you aren't going to see any results from your hard work at first and rather need to commit to the process fully before you can start receiving any rewards. Specifically, you will need to keep in mind that it is natural for your mind to wander freely for a time before you are able to guide it to where it needs to be. To better understand the mindset that you should be striving for, you might find it useful to consider the moment of complete blankness the mind experiences once it has heard a question, but before it can generate an answer.

Tips For Meditation

We will share some more suggestions and tips to allow you to continue with your meditation practice. These are not aimed at making you an expert but just to assist you on the journey. It is not necessary to try all of these tips at the same time. You can try one or two at a time to see if they help you. There will be some that work better than others. Find what's right for you.

Begin Your Practice with 2-Minute Sessions

It may sound like it's pointless to meditate for just two minutes, but trust us when we say it's anything but. It's simple to do this and is the easiest way for a beginner to learn to practice meditation. Just dedicate two minutes of each day to meditation. Continue this for a week. It's easier to follow through with these two minutes than pressuring yourself to sit still for half an hour. Once you get used to these two minutes, you can add more minutes the next week and so on. You will soon see that you easily meditate at least 15 minutes daily after a couple of weeks, and that will be more than enough time for most. So don't worry and don't make excuses about not having time. Everyone has two minutes to meditate.

Practice Your Meditation Every Morning

A lot of people say that they will meditate every day in the beginning, but most of them fail to follow through with this claim. Don't assume that you will always remember or be inclined to do it. Commit yourself to meditate every single morning after you wake up. After you wash up, just set aside a few minutes for this, and you will see how much better your day goes. Early mornings are considered the best time to meditate.

Don't Worry About the Process and Focus on Beginning the Practice

When people start meditating or think about starting it, they often waste a lot of time and energy on worrying about how they should go about it. They waste time in looking up too many methods, finding the perfect mat to sit on, learning chants, etc. All of these are a part of the practice but not the essence of it. You need not spend so much time on this and should try to go with the flow. Just

454

find a comfortable place to sit where you won't be disturbed or distracted by anything. Sitting right on the ground is completely fine, and so is sitting on a chair. To begin with, focus less on all this and more on spending two whole minutes just meditating. The stress of these trivial things will hinder your meditation. So try to get more used to meditating itself and worry about all this later.

Pay Attention to How You Feel

Once you begin meditating, you need to try being more attuned to your personal feelings. Pay attention to how you feel and how this practice is affecting your body. Tune in to the thoughts that pass through your mind. Don't focus on them but notice them as they flow past. Be accepting of all the feelings and thoughts that you experience during meditation. Nothing is wrong or right, so don't judge yourself for any of it.

Count as You Breathe

Breathing is an important aspect of meditation. Find the right place to meditate and then close your eyes as you sit comfortably. Start concentrating solely on your breathing. Focus on your breath as you inhale and exhale. Notice how you take in air through your nose and into your lungs. Pay attention as it leaves your body. When you take in a breath, count one. Count two when you breathe out. Continue the counting as you keep breathing and focus on this alone. It will help you focus more.

It Is Okay for Your Thoughts to Wander

The human mind tends to wander a lot, and you need to be more accepting of it as you meditate. You don't have to assume that you are not allowed to think anything when you meditate. This can be impossible to avoid, at least at first. When you meditate, try not to think but be accepting when thoughts come in. When you notice your concentrating wandering off from your meditation to your thoughts, push back your mind slowly. It can be disappointing, and you might feel like you are doing it wrong, but it is all right. Just slowly come back when your mind wanders away.

Be More Accepting

Like we already said, it is natural for thoughts to appear as you meditate. Don't be defensive, and try to push them away all the time. Instead, be more accepting and allow them to come and pass. Take note of these thoughts, and you can focus on them later. But as you meditate, allow them to come and go naturally. Your thoughts are a part of you, and you need to accept and forgive yourself for everything that you are.

Don't Stress About the Method of Meditation

You might be worried that you are meditating the wrong way at first. A lot of people get stressed about this and think it will be ineffective if they don't practice the right method or do it the right way. The truth is, there is no perfect method of meditation. You can try the various methods we have mentioned and use them as guidelines, but ultimately, you need to do what feels best for you.

Your Mind Doesn't Have to be Empty While Meditating

Some people think that meditation means getting rid of all thoughts and clearing the mind completely. However, this is not true and can be almost impossible for most people. It can be possible to clear your mind out sometimes, but for the most part, it's not what is essential for meditation. It's normal to have thoughts,

456

and you don't have to force yourself to push them all out. Just be more accepting of them and let them pass without focusing on them. Work more on your concentration, and you will see that it gets easier to reduce distracting thoughts over time.

Take Some Time to Accept Your Thoughts and Feelings

Having thoughts while meditating is totally normal. When a thought passes through your mind, it is okay to take a moment and pay attention to it. In the beginning, we recommend to just let the thoughts pass and focus more on breathing. But over time, you can try noticing more of your thoughts too. You should avoid focusing on anything negative and try to bring in more positive thoughts. When you notice your thoughts, you will be able to learn more about yourself. But only allow yourself a moment for this before continuing with your meditation.

Learn a Little More About Yourself Every Day

Meditation is not just about improving your focus or being better able to concentrate. It is about helping your mind develop too. When you become more accepting of your thoughts and feelings, you will learn a lot about yourself. Don't push yourself too hard to think or feel a certain way. Be accepting and learn about yourself. No one can know you better than yourself.

Be Your Own Friend

You need to try learning more about yourself, but this should not be done with a mindset of self-analysis and judgment. Instead, be kinder to yourself. Think of it like learning more about someone you like. Accept who you are and be your friend. Don't be cruel and judgmental towards yourself.

Pay Attention to Your Body

After you get better at counting breaths and meditating, you can try something else. Now you should try focusing on your body. Do this with one body part at a time. As you meditate, focus on a specific body part and try to pay attention to how it feels. Start with the lowest point in your body and move on until every part of your body has been acknowledged. This will allow you to pay attention to your body and learn more about it. You will be able to notice if something feels wrong too.

Be Truly Determined

You cannot say you will meditate regularly and then fail to follow through. It is important to dedicate yourself to this practice. Don't take it lightly. Make sure you stick to this resolution for at least a few weeks. Motivate yourself to follow through with it every day. It will soon become a habit, but not if you lack determination right from the beginning.

Meditate, Regardless of Where You Are

It doesn't matter if you're on a trip or have to work overtime on some days. Don't skip your meditation practice. You might reduce the amount of time you can dedicate to it, but you should still meditate. You don't necessarily need that meditation corner in your home for this. It can be done while sitting in a car or even while you sit in your office chair.

Use Guided Meditations

It may seem hard to meditate when you first begin. Guided meditations can be instrumental in this case. Use these audio or video files to help you get started. They are very simple and accommodating regardless of whether you are a beginner or have practiced for some time.

Have Someone to Be Accountable To

If you keep by yourself your resolution to meditate, you are less likely to follow through with it. It will be easy to give up because there is no one to berate you over it. This is why you need to have someone that will hold you accountable. It could be a friend or family member. Just keep checking in with them, and they will help you stay on track. You can also find someone to practice it regularly. This could be someone you live with, work with, or even someone who will go to lessons with you. Finding a network of people who are interested in meditation will help in reinforcing your new good habit. These people can help support you through your journey. You can find online forums or communities of people who practice meditation too.

Chapter 34. Dealing with Stress

Stress, however unpleasant, is a normal reaction that occurs in our body and is sometimes beneficial. It is the body's response to changes that are occurring and require adjustment or response. These responses can be physical, mental, or emotional. As a normal part of life, stress can be triggered by everyday things around us such as our environment, our thoughts, and our body. These stressors can either be positive such as getting married or negative such as getting fired from job. The more stressors you experience, the more load you are likely to feel on your nervous system. Simply put, stress can be defined as the feeling we get when we're overwhelmed and struggling to cope with demands. Even so, anything that poses a threat or challenge, real or perceived, causes stress.

Stress acts as an indicator of danger and is thus beneficial for our survival. This is where the 'fight or flight' response comes to play. Stress flushes our body systems with hormones to help us confront or evade danger by telling us when and how to react to danger. This is the fight or flight mechanism and is the reason stress can be defined as the body's natural defense against danger. This mechanism always fuels a physical reaction –that is to either get away from the situation or stay and fight the stressor. Following the flush of hormones, our bodies tend to produce larger quantities of chemicals and hormones such as adrenaline, cortisol, and noradrenaline that in turn cause a specific response in the body such as increased heart rate, alertness, sweating and muscle preparedness all which will aid the final response of fight or flight.

Stress is helpful and can be a motivator; in this context it is referred to as eustress –that is positive stress that keeps us productive and on the go. In many cases, it helps save our lives by helping us react in a way to stop or prevent danger, for example, jerking off the road when you see a car coming your way. In other cases, it serves as a motivator, for instance, helping you focus on a project that's due or keeping you on guard during a presentation or speech. We all experience and go through stress differently but like everything else, too much of it is dangerous and can lead to health problems.

Effects of Chronic Stress

Our nervous systems are not good at distinguishing between physical and emotional threats. For instance, your body cannot distinguish between the stressed caused by an exam or a robber in front of you. In either case, your body is likely to give off the same reaction. The more your stress systems are activated the easier you can be triggered and the harder it is to get out of a state of constant stress. This is referred to as chronic stress and is the most harmful form of stress- it goes on for long periods and occurs when one never sees the end to a stressor and stops finding solutions.

This is even more common in today's demanding society. This leads us to get used to it and become unnoticeable as it makes up part of our personalities. Nowadays, our bodies are in a constant heightened state of stress, which more often than not leads to serious health problems. Stress disrupts almost all of one's body systems and can rewire the brain causing one to be vulnerable to anxiety, depression, other mental illnesses and in other cases, it can cause heart attacks, strokes, violent actions, and suicide.

While stress is usually a short-term experience of your body's reaction to a trigger, anxiety is a sustained mental disorder that is triggered by prolonged periods of stress. Anxiety does not usually fade away once the stressor is

461

evaded, on the contrary, it stays for long and can cause impairment and damage to areas of functioning such as societal involvement and one's occupational responsibilities.

Signs and Symptoms of Chronic Stress

It is important to understand and be aware of the common signs of stress overload as you may get used to indulging in stressful situations and not pay much attention to the damage it's causing to your health and wellbeing.

Emotional Signs and Symptoms

Feeling overwhelmed

Agitation and anxiety

Anger, mood swings and feeling irritable

Isolation and loneliness

Irritability

Forgetfulness

Anger

Restlessness

Insecurity
Fatigue

Sadness and depression

Rise of mental or emotional health problems

Cognitive Signs and Symptoms

Racing thoughts

Poor judgment

Memory problems

Anxious thoughts

Constant worrying

Pessimism and negativity

Concentration problems

Behavioral Signs and Symptoms

Insomnia

Oversleeping

Relationship problems

Frequent crying

Eating more or less than usual

Cravings

Sudden anger outbursts

Substance abuse to relax

Procrastination and laziness

Neglecting responsibilities

Nervous habits such as shaking one's leg or nail-biting

Withdrawal from society

Physical Signs and Symptoms

Nausea or dizziness

Loss of sex drive

Increased heart rate

Chest pains

Aches and pains

Nervous twitches

Stomach upset

Various diseases

Fainting

Frequent flu and/or colds

Constipation or Diarrhea

Anger Management

Anger describes an unpleasant emotion characterized by strong feelings of antagonism and displeasure that ranges from mild irritability or annoyance to intense fury or rage. Our triggers for anger differ from person to person, however, we are exposed to these triggers often. Anger is a normal human emotion that when recognized and appropriate action is taken to deal with it can bear positive outcomes. In this case, it may even become a motivator inspiring one to advocate for social change or stand up for certain injustices. Anger notifies us when we need to take action and rectify something while giving us the motivation, strength, and energy to act. However, when anger is unresolved or left unchecked it can lead to inappropriate and/or aggressive behavior. In this case, it may be referred to as a 'negative' emotion.

Over the past few years especially in the industrial and the now post-industrial era, there has been a significant and continuous rise in stress and anger. This shows that stress has a role in influencing anger. If one is more prone to anger then a lot of stress is likely to trigger feelings of anger. When stress becomes too much and ceases to be a motivator, it may cause us to feel irritable or just angry to the core. When this happens, one is usually overwhelmed with tons of stressors and typically one feels like they lack the resources to deal with stress effectively and has an outburst of anger. This type of stress is referred to as distress. If stressors are understood and steps are taken to maintain equilibrium and deal with the stress, then one can limit distress thereby controlling and limiting one's anger.

Techniques for Anger Relaxation and Management

Techniques for anger relaxation are frequently used in anger management therapy to help us understand our anger and act in ways that are positive to alleviate the negative aspects of anger rather than suppress feelings of anger. These techniques work most effectively when practiced frequently. Some of the techniques are as follows:

Controlled Deep Breathing

When we get angry, several subtle physical changes occur and notify us of these feelings. One of the most noticeable is the change in breathing. When one is angry or upset, their breathing becomes shallow and quick. Noticing this is one of the first steps of this technique. Once one noticed the change in breath, one can make a deliberate effort to deepen and slow their breathing –this will help in maintaining control. These breaths ought to come from your belly rather than your chest. The breaths should be twice as long when coming out as when coming in, for instance, one may breathe in slowly as they count to four and breathe out even slower as they count to eight.

This slow, deep, and deliberate breathing will help relax your breath and return into a normal, relaxed state. Since all things present in the body are interconnected, controlling, and relaxing one's breath should in turn control and relax muscle tensions that are caused by anger thereby reducing feelings of anger significantly.

Progressive Muscle Relaxation

One of the other noticeable physical changes related to anger is muscle tension. This tension can manifest in different parts of one's body and can collectively clump in specific areas such as the neck and shoulders. This tension can even remain long after the anger is gone. Progressive muscle relaxation involves deliberately tensing and tightening your muscles both stressed and unstressed for a slow count of ten then relaxing or releasing these tightened muscles. When practicing this, be sure to release muscles immediately you feel pain. This technique requires you to work progressively from one muscle group to another (for example from head to toe) until you have taken each muscle through a cycle of tension and release. With diligent practice, one may notice their ability to do this cycle of the full body in a few minutes. This technique of tightening and releasing muscles can prove more relaxing than relaxation itself.

Visualizing Yourself to Calmness

Visualization refers to the mental formation or representation of an object, image, situation or set of information. Visualization techniques can also be employed to help with the management of anger. Our brains constantly visualize in the process of simulating future scenarios. This visualization happens so effortlessly that we barely notice it in the same way we barely notice our breathing. When we become aware of our visualization, we can use it as a tool to reduce or reverse anger. Visualization to help with anger is done by imagining a place or scenario that makes you feel calm or relaxed and focusing on details (sometimes with the aid of audio material such as music) such as smells, sounds and how good it feels to be in that space. This is usually done when one is sited comfortably and quietly with their eyes closed.

Visualization has four key benefits that improve how we deal with anger. Firstly, it rewires and programs one's brain to help them realize the strategies, tools, and resources they can use to achieve peace and harmony away from anger. Secondly, it builds our intrinsic motivation to take actions necessary to change the habit pattern of the mind, which is reacting to anger. Thirdly, it sparks one's creative subconscious, which helps us with the sublimation of these negative feelings into more socially acceptable forms of expression such as dance, poetry, music among others. This sublimation helps us express rather than suppress these feelings of anger. Lastly, visualization aids in the law of attraction thereby drawing you closer to circumstances, resources, tools, and people who can help you achieve your goals of anger management.

Various meditation techniques are also used in anger management and relaxation. Mindfulness meditation and Vipassana meditation both encourage us to accept the anger when it manifests itself and observe it as it is without reacting to it or engaging with it. This usually causes us to be fueled and consumed by it causing it to become problematic. In retrospect, when we just simply observe anger as an emotion, neither good nor bad, we learn to work with anger, as it is however or whenever it arises skillfully without it spiraling out of control. When we engage in guided meditation we learn how to relax and gain relief from stress and stressors that may end up causing anger and allow us to process these feelings healthily. This technique can be used with children too especially those with heavy temper tantrums. Peaceful and guided meditations help children, adults, and teens improve self-esteem, relieve anxiety, and stress, and feel generally refreshed in mind, body, and spirit and develop positive mental attitudes in their daily activities.

Grief Management

Grief can be defined as the heightened sense or feeling of pain we feel when we experience loss. This pain is severe as the loss is a reflection of something or someone we love and one may feel engulfed and overwhelmed by it. Grief can follow the loss of someone such as the death of a loved one or the destruction of a relationship to the loss of a pet or even something like the loss of your home. Grief is complex and has no specific rules or set timing. Grief can have symptoms similar to depression such as insomnia, sadness, and loss of interest in self-care. Grief is different from depression as it doesn't impair self-worth. However, grief is not experienced by everyone in the same way. In some cases, it may be accompanied by feelings of guilt or confusion. Prolonged grief can last up to months if not dealt with and can result in isolation as well as chronic loneliness. Nevertheless, its symptoms tend to lessen over time but can be triggered by anniversaries or thoughts about the loss at whatever time.

It has been proposed by professionals in psychology that grief has five stages. These are denial, anger, bargaining, depression, and acceptance. Denial is the first stage of grief and is characterized by the world feeling overwhelming and meaningless. We tend to feel

468

numb and as though life makes absolutely no sense and we wonder how we can go on. In the case of the loss of a loved one, for instance, one may be thinking they cannot live without the deceased and wondering what the point to life without them is. The next stage of grief, which is essential for the healing process, is anger. In the same case, one may be asking questions like "Why did they have to die so soon?" or "Where is God in all of this?"

As one progresses on the path of grief, they get to the next stage of bargaining where one feels like they would do and sacrifice anything and everything for their loved one to be spared their demise. In this case one may begin praying and making promissory offerings to their particular God or Goddess saying things like "I promise to be a better child to my parent if you bring them back," or "I promise to do better for the community if I wake up from this and it's just a dream." During this stage, one is engulfed in 'what-ifs' and 'if only's'. After bargaining, we tend to go deeper into the grief as we bring our attention to the present and face the feelings of emptiness and sadness caused by our loss. This stage usually and feels everlasting, however, it is important to understand that it is an appropriate response to great loss and it will not last forever. This is not a clinical depression or a sign of mental illness.

The last stage of acceptance is usually mixed up with the idea that we should be okay with the loss. However, in reality, most people are never okay with the loss they experience. We usually just learn how to live with it accepting the reality as it is and not as we would like it to be. We accept the new reality as the permanent reality and making it the norm, which we have to adjust to and learn to live with.

Without a doubt, grief is related to and can cause or be caused by stress. Change is one of the reasons stress and grief are intertwined when you lose something, you have to reboot and rearrange things about your life that were connected to the loss, which can potentially act as a stressor. Another reason for this relationship is the pressure from yourself and sometimes society to get over your loss, move on and become 'normal' again. Interpersonal stressors such as hurt feelings, conflict and feelings of alienation and isolation from family and friends following the loss of someone can also be related to this relationship between grief and stress. Internal conflict and an overload of emotions which one usually feel unequipped to handle is another reason for this relationship. Lastly, frustrations that come from not getting what you want are another connecting factor to this relationship. When one experiences grief and loss, they tend to want back what they have lost or wanted a change in circumstances, but our wishes are not what we have in reality causing frustration and stress.

How to Meditate for Grief and Loss

Meditation for grief is one of the most effective ways to deal with grief and loss by helping us get rid of the symptoms of depression and anxiety, pain as well as mend our relationships with others and bring us closure through introspection and reorientation. Breathing meditation and relaxing meditation techniques are good to restore a state of calmness in the mind and body as well as help alleviate certain pains. Guided meditations help us reduce the suffering that comes together with grief. According to teachers of these guided meditations such as Shinzen Young, suffering is a result of pain and resistance. With this understanding, one realizes that they should not resist the loss that has already happened and that they should accept it as part of the experiences in their lives. In as much as pain could be harder to eradicate as it is the mark and relic of love, this understanding reduces suffering significantly and gives us a boost to work patiently and mindfully with ourselves as we reengage with life after whatever loss you have gone through. Mindfulness meditations as well as Vipassana meditation work in this same manner aiming to eradicate the suffering that is accompanied by grief.

Chapter 35. Stress and Workplace Awareness Meditation

When working somewhere, one is usually in a different environment with people from all walks of life and pressures from authority figures and oneself. These objects and situations can potentially be acute stressors and trigger; therefore, the stress in the workplace is normal. However, when stress becomes extreme and overwhelming, it can interfere with your productivity, relationships with colleagues, performance, mental and physical health and also spill out to other aspects of your life such as your relationships with friends and family.

While one cannot control the entire workplace environment, there is no need to feel defeated when faced with a difficult situation that triggers stress. When faced with stressors, some steps can be taken to improve your coping skills, relationships in and out of work, productivity, job satisfaction and overall well-being no matter what your individual goals, work demands, and ambitions may be.

Meditation is among the best practices to come out of stressful situations especially at work almost immediately. It works by helping us to regulate our emotions and retuning the brain to be more resilient to stressors. Practicing meditation in the workplace increases our productivity and motivation by turning stress into success. Most people may think of meditation as another task on their to-do list with the demands of a quiet and calm place; however, it is important to understand and take meditation as being able to be in the midst of trouble, noise, and hard work while maintaining calmness and equanimity in your heart. The two most recommended forms of meditation to manage stress in the workplace are transcendental meditation and mindfulness meditation.

Transcendental meditation has a great deal of research backing its ability to help relieve stress at the workplace and reduce cortisol and anxiety. Continuous and diligent practice of transcendental meditation shows to notably improve productivity and work satisfaction so much that business owners and large companies such as General Motors, Sony, Toyota, and IBM are beginning to invest in meditation programs and making them available for their employees to double their output and wellbeing. This form of meditation shows to improve emotional intelligence, which in turn advances the relationships you have with your colleagues and helps you effectively deal with and express your own emotions.

Mindfulness meditation as a way to deal with workplace stress is more commonly practiced due to the rise in popularity of the practice over the last few years. This technique aims to improve our clarity in our worldly perceptions, which consequently helps us make better decisions. Moreover, being less agitated results in greater inner strength and more stable emotions leading us to be happier and have more fulfilling lives. To reap these benefits, it is important to start meditating especially at the beginning of your day or before you begin working. This can be even easier if you start a meditation group at work with some colleagues and practice mindfulness meditation together before you begin working. It is important to also practice mindful breathing where you randomly take 3-5 mindful breaths and go back to doing what you were doing.

In addition to this, it is also essential to take advantage of the time you use walking as an opportunity to meditate and practice mindful walking. Here one observes their walking with deep awareness and if not in a hurry, it would not hurt to slow down and let your mind follow. Another essential practice tied to mindfulness meditation in the workplace is deep listening. In this case, one listens wholesomely with the intent of understanding as opposed to replying. Normally when we listen with the intent to reply we are usually thinking about our next statement and how to interject our particular opinion rather than taking time to pay attention to and understand fully what the other party has to say. This practice will improve workplace relationships and reduce the frictions and arguments that cause stress at work. Lastly, the practice of mindful speech will also help reduce stress by improving our overall interactions and relationships. When speaking mindfully, one takes the time to think about what they are about to say and visualize and understand the impact it will have on the recipient of the message whether positive or negative. In this case, it is important to consider how our statements will be interpreted and try our best to convey information that will elicit positive consequences and responses.

Abdominal Breathing for Impulse Control

Occasional impulsive behavior is a normal part of life. We experience and engage in impulsivity from time to time whether it is by eating a slice of pizza when on a diet or buying something we do not need. For a person without impulse control however, it is difficult to resist sudden urges, which more often than not seem forceful. For such individuals, it seems like activities that would be deemed normal if done less frequently or less intensely are out of their control. Many are the occasions that these impulsive behaviors violate other people's rights and cause conflict with whatever societal values and norms put in place by one's culture or society. These impulses tend to occur frequently and rapidly without the consideration of the consequences it may breed.

A problem with impulse control is usually noted by a constant repetition of the behavior despite negative consequences, experiencing strong cravings and urges to engage in the problematic behavior, incapability to have power over problem behaviors and engaging in problem behavior to feel pleasure or relieve pressure. Some other symptoms of impulse control are obsessive thoughts, inability to delay instant gratification, lack of patience and severe tension and/or anxiety experienced before engaging in the impulsive behavior. Impulse control can be a key feature or symptom in some mental illnesses such as bulimia and paraphilia; however, some types of impulse control disorders stand as disorders by themselves. Some of the most common forms of impulse control disorders are:

- o Pyromania – this is the inability to control the urge to set fires. A person with pyromania usually reports feelings for pleasure following their behavior or relief from anxiety or emotional blockage.

- o Kleptomania – this refers to the uncontrollable urge to steal something and is different from stealing for a necessity such as water or food. In this case, people steal things that are meaningless and unnecessary.

- o Trichotillomania – This is a disorder that is usually characterized by a strong urge to pull out one's hair. Even when this act is painful, the urge surpasses any concern for pain.

- o Intermittent explosive disorder – this refers to the inability to control anger outbursts to even the smallest of triggers whereby the rage can spill out of control and turn into physical acts of violence.

- o Pathological gambling – also referred to as compulsive gambling it was once considered an impulse control disorder but recent research shows that it is more of a process addiction. Here one is unable to resist the urge to gamble. The thought of gambling becomes too overpowering causing one to feel like engaging in gambling is the only relief they can get.

- o Unspecified impulse-control disorder – in this case, one shows the general signs and symptoms of an impulse-control disorder however, the impulse observed does not fall into any pre-recognized criteria.

One of the most recommended techniques to control one's impulses is abdominal breathing. This technique is similar to mindful breathing in that one deliberately slows down and deepens their breath. When practicing this, you need to inhale slowly through your nose then exhale even slower through your mouth while making a hissing sound almost like a balloon losing air trying to make the hiss last as long as possible. This technique involves controlling your breath to calm you down and reduce your cravings and urges.

Chapter 36. Meditative Guide For Positive Consciousness

As one of the simplest forms of meditation, positive consciousness works almost exclusively on the rebuilding of conscious mind maps. For whatever reason, at some point in your life, your self-esteem, your self-confidence, and your courage to move forward have all been tampered with.

By focusing on positive consciousness, you can attempt to see all these self-inflicted wounds. No longer are your thoughts at the mercy of other people's perceptions of you. In contrast, you will now become whoever it is that you need to be in order to meet your own demands and aspirations. As you seek a suitable position to begin this meditation, stretch out your body to first rid it of any wasteful energy that has been left over from the day before.

As you seat yourself, stretch out your back until you feel a sharp pull, and at this point, lower your neck to be level with the floor. Outstretch your arms upon the tops of your knees and lift your palms upward and leave them facing toward you.

You are now ready to start your meditative guide.

As you slowly close your eyes, fix within your mind's eye a point from which you are meant to gather all consciousness. Remember that your consciousness has suffered in recent days and, as such, is in need of healing. By promoting positive consciousness, not only are you rebuilding this broken stream of good will, but you are fortifying it so that it will be protected from any future harm.

477

Breathe in carefully to the count of five.

Hold to the count of four and then slowly release.

You are resilient.

You are calm.

You are undisturbed.

You are gifted.

Exhale deeply, purging yourself of all the negative stress and energy that has been building in your body, and instead, open your mind's eye and with it, you should be able to see and feel the energies around you.

You are seeking within yourself a way in which you can let go and be at peace.

The cool darkness behind your eyes is inviting you to feel calm and at peace. The bright lights at the periphery of your mind are showing you the endless possibilities that you have at your disposal.

I am capable.

I am smart.

I am efficient.

I am worthy.

I am talented.

I am resourceful.

I am bright.

I am attentive.

As you remind yourself of these things, open your mind once again to see the various energies that are flowing through your being. With your mind, start to follow each

478

individual channel of energy until you can see how they flow beautifully into each other.

This time, as you repeat each positive affirmation, weave it through one of the strands of energy so that it will flow perfectly though your mind from now on and forever after.

I am capable.

I am smart.

I am efficient.

I am worthy.

I am talented.

I am resourceful.

I am bright.

I am attentive.

Each of these thoughts is now an inviolable part of your consciousness. As your energy begins to build in your center, allow it to move upward to your mind and, as you raise your neck, lift your face forward to accept the new revolutionary truths that have become a part of your reality.

You are powerful.

You are significant.

You are respected.

You are loved.

Repeat the last four phrases in your mind once again.

I am powerful.

I am significant.

I am respected.

I am loved.

Breathe in.

Release.

Breathe in.

Release.

Breathe in.

Release.

As you prepare yourself to open your eyes, you are embodying a positively minded individual.

Chapter 37. Daily Meditation Affirmation Routines

Morning Affirmations Meditation

Are you looking to start off your day on the right side of the bed? If you want to wake up energetic and ready for any day ahead of you, I highly suggest starting your day off with a morning meditation, topped off with some positive affirmations to get you in a positive mindset.

Of course, you can listen to this meditation at any time of the day, but it is a perfect start to your morning and will only take a small amount of time to energize you and get you started!

As we start this meditation, I now invite you to go ahead and take some deep breaths. With each breath you take, allow the airflow to begin to energize you. Inhale deep into your lungs and exhale everything out.

Breathe in...and exhale. Allow for your breaths to be slow, deep, and calm. Each breath you take brings in the air that your body needs to help get you started. Allow your breaths to fill you with energy and let go of any fatigue you may be feeling at this moment. For the next few moments, this is all I want you to focus on. Just concentrate on your breath. It does not matter what tasks you have for the rest of the day. All you need to think about is breathing in, breathing out, and getting your energy set up for the day.

[Pause]

You are going to be ready for this day ahead of you. Breathe in positive energy and allow all positive thoughts to enter your mind. With your next few exhales, let any negative feelings go. If you feel any tension built up in your body, let that go too. You do not have the time nor the energy to waste on negativity. There is only energy and positivity right now. Breathe and remind yourself to be positive.

[Pause]

Now, I want you to squeeze your hands into fists gently. As you do this, feel as the muscles strengthen in your arms and your shoulders. Feel now as the strength and energy begin to flow through your veins. You are powerful, and you can accomplish anything you want to. You are capable of accomplishing anything that you need to get done today. You can do anything you put your mind to. Now, relax your fists, and allow your muscles to relax.

[Pause]

As your body begins to awaken, feel how warm and energetic you are starting to feel. If you would like, try to open and close your hands a few times. I want you to become mindful of how wonderful your body feels as it wakes up, ready to tackle anything that comes at you today. Allow yourself to become excited for the day, ready for anything that can happen today; there are so many possibilities. Feel now as this positive energy waves through your body and allow your mind and soul to become alive.

[Pause]

If you are feeling up to it, I now invite you to enjoy a gentle stretch to get your muscles going. Go ahead and place your fingertips together and gently stretch your arms above your head. Reach for the ceiling and feel the soft pull down your shoulders and into your sides. If you want, gently lean from side to side and feel as your muscles begin to warm up. When you are ready, bring your arms back down and bring your awareness to your toes. Take a deep breath and allow the energy to surge through you.

[Pause]

Next, I want you to start to wiggle your feet a little. As you flex your feet, feel as the muscles in your legs enjoy a gentle stretch. Go ahead and spend some time waking your legs up. They are well rested from the night before and are ready to be put to work! Now, hold your feet still and enjoy the sensation of energy tingling through your toes, into your ankles, and up your legs. Take another deep breath in and allow for these sensations to wash over your whole body. The more you move, the more energetic you begin to feel.

[Pause]

Now that your body is awake and feeling energetic, it is time to open your mind to positive thoughts to carry you through the day. In the next few moments, we will go over some self-esteem affirmations to boost your confidence and get you excited for the day ahead of you. If, at any point in your day, you feel your stress and anxiety start to take over, I invite you to take a few moments to breathe and repeat the following affirmations to yourself.

As I say the following affirmations, I invite you to continue to focus on your breathing and stretch; however, you feel fit. If you still feel tense in some areas, go ahead and stretch these areas out. This is your time; use it to your advantage. If you start your day off on a positive note, it can get better from there, even if you hit a couple of rocky patches. Feel free to repeat after me or simply listen to the following; it is completely up to you.

I am capable of achieving anything that I work hard for.

[Pause]

When times get tough, I have the ability to work through them.

[Pause]

I deserve to be happy.

[Pause]

I am a strong individual, and I am in charge of my life, even when I cannot control the circumstances.

[Pause]

I am worthwhile, even when people make me feel like I am not.

[Pause]

I accept myself for who I am.

[Pause]

I am proud of all of my hard work and accomplishments.

[Pause]

I deserve happiness because I work hard for it.

[Pause]

I have many wonderful qualities.

[Pause]

I love myself.

[Pause]

I am grateful for my life.

[Pause]

I am grateful for all of this energy I am feeling.

[Pause]

I am ready to tackle this day and anything that comes my way.

[Pause]

I will handle everything with as much grace as possible.

[Pause]

In tough times, I will remember to breathe and remain calm.

[Pause]

I am in control of my thoughts and my body.

[Pause]

I choose to be calm and peaceful throughout the day.

[Pause]

I am ready to get started with this day and will remember to be at peace.

[Pause]

Fantastic. As we draw this meditation to a close, take a few more moments to breathe on your own time and focus your thoughts and intentions for the day. When things become overwhelming, remember to find your breath, and you can work through just about anything. At the end of the day, it all comes down to your mindset, and by starting with this meditation, you are ready to overcome anything with positivity. Now, breathe and get ready to start your day.

[Pause]

[Meditation Time: 40 Minutes]

Breathing Awareness Meditation

Before we begin this meditation, I now invite you to find a position that is comfortable for you. As you settle in, take a few moments to make sure all distractions such as your cellphone and laptop are closed. For the next few minutes, I would like you to just focus on yourself. As you meditate, there is nothing else that matters. If you are feeling anxious right now, that is perfectly okay. We all go through these feelings. What matters right now is that you do something about it.

[Pause]

As you settle into position, go ahead and take a nice, deep breath in. If you would like, allow for your eyes to begin to flutter closed. If you are not comfortable with this, simply keep them open and start to soften your gaze. When you are comfortable, all I would like you to do is find your breath. With each breath you take, simply become mindful of how it feels to breathe in fully and exhale everything out. When we feel anxious, we often forget the very basic concept of breathing. Our thoughts begin to move quickly, and our breathing patterns begin to match. Perhaps you are mindful of this, but most likely, you had no idea because you were so focused on being anxious, and that is okay! Just breathe and tune your focus in on yourself.

[Pause]

Right now, all you need to focus on is the air entering through your nostrils. It does not matter why you feel anxious, and it does not matter what tasks need to be completed once this meditation is finished. Allow for all of the thoughts in your head to exit and focus only on your breath.

[Pause]

On your next breath, I want you to become mindful of how the air travels into your lungs and allow for your belly to expand fully. As you breathe out, feel how your belly gets smaller, and the air moves peacefully back out through your mouth or nose. You may notice that you inhale, feels different from your exhale. Breathe in and feel the comfort of the cool air as it enters your body and how warm it feels as it leaves.

[Pause]

If you ever become distracted during your practice, that is perfectly okay. We all get distracted sometimes. If you find yourself getting distracted by noise or thoughts, allow these to pass without judgment and bring your focus back in yourself. There is no need to change anything right now. All you are doing is relaxing and breathing. Simply bring your attention back to your breath and continue a few more moments to breathe on your own.

[Pause]

If you would like, you can count with me as you continue to find your breath. On your next breath, I invite you to hold the breath for a few beats. Allow for the air in your lungs to nourish your body and your thoughts. I want each breath to relax you and clear your mind of all worry. When you are ready, we can begin.

Breathe in softly...and hold for one...two...three...and slowly release. Excellent.

Let's do that two more times together.

Breathe in softly...and hold for one...two...three...and release.

[Pause]

Breathe in...and hold for one...two...three...and slowly release.

[Pause]
Wonderful. At this point, you are probably already feeling much better. Go ahead and take a few more breaths on your own time.

[Pause]

During times of anxiety, I want this to be the first practice that pops into your mind. While breathing is a simple task, it can be highly effective. We all experience anxiety in different ways. If you start to become overwhelmed with tasks or emotions, take a step back and find your breath. With each breath you take, gently remind yourself that these feelings will pass, and as long as you are breathing, you are going to be okay. When you are ready, we can continue to the next meditation to keep working through overcoming your anxiety.

The 3 Minutes Breathing Space

This simple exercise is utilized in MBCT programs and Cognitive Behavior Therapies. It helps people get unstuck and move forward with their lives, even after embarrassing breakdowns.

While performing this mindfulness practice, refrain from evaluating and choosing your thoughts. Instead, you have to become aware of them and your breathing. The previous exercises made you concentrate on one part of your body.

Contrastingly, the 3 minutes breathing space will make you expand your senses. As a beginner, you will only be required to focus on your breathing. But you have to be mindful of the effect of respiration on various areas of your body. Feel the sensations it creates and its effects on your body as a whole.

Does that sound too complicated? Well, don't fret because it is very easy to practice. It only involves 3 simple steps.

a) Firstly, look for a comfortable area wherein you can't be disturbed by anyone. And if possible, turn off your cellphone and laptop. There must be no distractions. Next, notice the thoughts inside your head, and don't change the things you're observing.

b) The second step involves focusing on your breathing. Sit in a covered flat surface and sit up straight. Once you are settled, concentrate on your intake and expelling of air. Be aware of the rise and fall of your chest and abdomen. Feel the air as it enters and escapes your nostrils. What do you smell? Do you hear your breathing?

c) Third, you have to expand your senses. You should still focus on your breathing, but all the while, you must be aware of the other sensations your body is feeling. Other noise or disturbances are unnecessary. Are your legs cramping? Do you feel hot or cold? Be aware and focus on those sensations as well.

The goal of this exercise is to establish awareness for body sensations and to emphasize shifting of attention and to move on from one focus to another. Accordingly, you should only linger for a minute in each step. The 3MBS exercise prepares you for other mindfulness practices, and it encourages "moving of attention."

The exercise can help you get unstuck from automatic routines. It also provides you space wherein you can get a breather from stress or taxing tasks.

Mindfulness on the Bus or Train

If you utilize public transportation, you can take the time spent getting where you are going to practice mindfulness meditation as effectively as if you were sequestered peacefully in your own home. There is one caveat; however, in order to practice mindfulness meditation effectively, it is important that you feel comfortable in the space in which you find yourself. If you find yourself in a situation where something requires your full attention, you will likely be unable to reach your full mindfulness meditation potential.

While listening to music while practicing mindfulness meditation in public is not recommended, you may find it helpful to wear headphones as this is a clear signal to those around you that you do not wish to be disturbed. Furthermore, you may find it helpful to set some type of timer because when you get into the zone while being mindful, it can be easy to lose track of time.

With the preliminaries out of the way, the first thing that you are going to want to do is to plant your feet firmly a comfortable distance apart from one another, whether you are standing or sitting. If standing, take care that you are in a place where you can easily keep your balance. With your feet firmly planted, slowly stretch out your body so that you assume the proper posture for your current surroundings. Take a moment to feel your body move with the rhythm of the train/bus and consider how you are connected not just to the transportation you are riding but to all of those who are sharing the journey with you.

Once you feel that you are centered, choose a spot in front of you that is approximately three feet from your current position. Choose a spot that is close to the ground, perhaps just a foot or two above the floor of the bus or train. Slowly lower your eyes to this point on the ground

490

without lowering your neck, it is important to maintain proper posture throughout the exercise. As you feel your eyes begin to dip towards the floor, focus exclusively on all of the sensory information they are providing you. From there, slowly incorporate the sensations that are being provided by the rest of your senses.

In order to tune out all of the noise and movement that naturally comes with riding public transportation, focus on your breathing and concentrate on taking deep rhythmic breaths at a nice slow pace. Once you have found a rhythm that works for you, consider one of the options below as a means of focusing your attention and attaining a state of mindfulness that might not seem possible otherwise. Remember, practicing mindfulness meditation while using public transportation is even trickier to get the hang of than the other types of mindfulness meditation in these pages. Don't get discouraged if you can't clear your mind as easily as you may be able to elsewhere, as with any other skill practice makes perfect.

Chapter 38. Affirmations For Over Coming Anxiety

Anxiety, as you have learned thus far, is something that is largely pervasive, annoying, something people wish they had less of but is entirely common. Many people suffer from anxiety, and in recognizing that fact, you are better able to feel less ashamed. Do not be ashamed of your anxiety—so many people around you probably share some of your same anxiety symptoms and you would never realize it. Nevertheless, it is something that you should make an effort to correct. As you master these methods, learning to create affirmations and learning to fake it until you make it, you will be able to get a better hold on any symptoms that arise for you.

Creating Affirmations

Affirmations are short sentences that you tell yourself in order to serve as a reminder or as a replacement for a negative thought. They are easy to use and are most often used as a quick and easy repetition in order to overcome negative thinking. You can use them specifically for anxiety, but they can also be used for general mood regulation, encouraging good habits, and many other situations in your life that require more self-discipline.

Your affirmation can be anything, so long as you ensure that it follows the right structure—it must be present, positive, and personal. By ensuring these three things, you are able to make an affirmation that is largely functional simply because you will be able to control it.

When you ensure that your affirmation is positive, you are respecting the cycle between thoughts, feelings, and behaviors. You know that a positive thought will lead to positive feelings, which will lead to positive behaviors, which is what you are hoping to achieve with your positive affirmation. After all, any affirmation you are developing is meant to help you cope with anxiety, which is largely comprised of negative thinking in the first place. The reason it must be positive can be clearly understood with the following example: Consider two affirmations and decide which seems more motivational or helpful for your anxiety:

I will not let my anxiety control me

I control my anxiety by remembering my breathing techniques

Chances are, you would find the second statement more useful in controlling your anxiety. This is for a very good reason—you are creating an action for yourself instead of telling yourself what not to do. When you know what not to do, you still do not know what you should be doing, after all. You will be unsure whether what you should be doing is crying, letting anger take control, or even just abandoning ship altogether. You do not have a clear action. However, when you tell yourself that you will control anxiety through breathing techniques, you remind yourself that you have a method to ensure that things are okay and you have an action plan for when anxiety starts to rise.

Next, you must make sure that your affirmation is present-tense. The reason for this is that you want to ensure that your affirmation is currently true. By creating an affirmation that is present-tense and repeating it to yourself, you tell yourself that it is currently true at that moment, which can sometimes be enough to trigger the behavior you needed to see. You are able to essentially trick your brain into action by saying that you are engaging in whatever behavior your affirmation is asking for.

When you make your affirmation something future tense by saying something like, "I will control my anxiety," you do not tell yourself when it will happen. It could happen tomorrow, it could happen a year for now, or it could happen right that moment, but it is ambiguous. Remember, part of anxiety is a concern about uncertainty, and ambiguity absolutely breeds uncertainty.

Lastly, your affirmation must be personal. Remember what self-discipline taught you—only you can control yourself, and you can only control yourself. Keep in mind that those are two different things altogether, though they look like someone was distracted when writing—the only one who can make you do anything is yourself, and the only thing you have utter control over is yourself. Because of that, the only way you can ensure your affirmation is true is through making sure that it is personal. You want to be the subject that is doing whatever action is in your affirmation in order to make sure that you can absolutely guarantee that the affirmation will be true. For example, you could say, "Jill will control anxiety through breathing," but you cannot enforce that. You can, however, enforce, "I am encouraging Jill to control her anxiety through breathing." Now, your affirmation focuses on something you can control.

Some examples of anxiety-related affirmations can include:

- I am safe where I am right now
- I control my actions, even when I am anxious
- I have everything I need to control my anxiety

- I use my breathing to keep myself under my own control

Notice how each and every one of those examples starts with "I," involves some sort of statement, and is present tense. Those are perfect examples. You can create any sort of affirmation for yourself, so long as it matches that pattern.

When you are using affirmations, you want to use them with plenty of repetition. You will be repeating them to yourself regularly, and because of that, you want to develop some sort of routine for yourself. For example, pair your affirmation reciting with some other activity that you do regularly. You may decide to pair it with getting into your car as you buckle up. When you match up your repetition of affirmations with an activity that you do regularly or automatically already, you can then make that affirmation just as habitual.

If you choose to get into the car and buckling up as your example, every time you do, you will recite your affirmation to yourself at least 10 times as you do. It does not matter how many times you get in and out of your car—you will repeat those affirmations. If you happen to get in your car at least 10 times, then you are reciting those affirmations at least 100 times that day. Do not worry though—the more repetition you implement the better. Over time, the thoughts become habitual and will happen without you thinking about them. That is how you know it is working and that your mind is accepting them as true.

As you make them true for yourself, you will have to also correct yourself every time you come close to making your affirmation not true as well— for example, if you are going to lose control of yourself, you should recite your affirmation to you. Your affirmation is a sort of back-up plan, reminding you of what to do in that particular situation and by reminding yourself, you are able to better gain control over the situation at hand. If you are close to losing control of your anxiety and recite the affirmation, you remind yourself that you can, in fact, control it, and you trigger your breathing exercises. If you feel like you are going to lose your temper, you can recite your affirmation related to that and feel the desire to lash out fade away.

Fake it until You Make it

When you are struggling to get that anxiety under control, sometimes, the best solution is to actually fake that you are in better control of it. Some of the techniques you have already studied already introduced this topic—when you engaged in the breathing and relaxation techniques, you were forcing your brain to accept a state that it was not naturally in. You essentially fooled it into thinking that you were calmer than you actually were just because you changed your pace in breathing. Much of your body behaves like this, and you can actually change a lot of your own feelings just by acting the part. Even if you do not feel confident right at that moment, you will the more you practice it.

Anxiety is particularly tricky in the sense that not only does it trigger certain feelings from you, but it is also triggered by certain physical states. This makes it essentially self-fulfilling—it can encourage the feelings that add fuel to the fire, making it easily escalated, and therefore destructive if left unchecked. However, when you instead begin to respond to your anxiety in ways that are not anxious, the anxiety starts to melt away.

Stop and think about what you would not do during an emergency—you would probably not remain calm as you spoke or smile. You would not be relaxed or eating or breathing slowly. You would not have a relaxed body posture. You would not relax back in your chair. All of those would not match an actual emergency that would require action.

When you behave in any of those ways when you are anxious, even if you only choose one of those behaviors, you are able to tell your mind that there is no real threat. If there were a threat, you tell your mind, then you would not be talking calmly or resting. You would not be breathing deeply and calmly. If there were an actual threat to yourself at that moment, you would be panicking, running away, or otherwise attempting to escape something that is not actually there at that moment in time.

One way to trigger this is by keeping candy or gum on your person at all times. When you begin to feel anxious, you can stop, take out that candy or gum, and put it in your mouth. Think about it this way—if you were actually in danger, or you were actually in an emergency, would you have the time to stop, pull out a stick of gum, open it, put away the wrapper, put the packaging away, and put the gum in your mouth to chew? No, probably not— you would be focusing on survival or helping someone else to survive. You would not be able to salivate if you were under threat, but even though you are feeling anxious at that moment, you are able to salivate with the gum in your mouth. That contradiction triggers your brain to stop, reevaluate, and instead switch to calmness rather than focusing on the negative or the fear associated with whatever you are doing at that particular moment.

Because anxiety has a tendency to be about what will come next, you are able to trick yourself, telling yourself that what will come next is not a debilitating disaster, but rather some sort of sweet treat instead. Your body will quickly cease the fear and anxiety and shift instead to something more relaxed.

Conclusion

If you have gotten to this point it is because you are committed to learning about the ways in which affirmations and meditation can have a profoundly positive effect in your life.

As such, the next step is to put what you have learned into practice.

Practicing affirmations

Now you understand the power that affirmations have, you will find it easy to apply them in your life. With positive affirmations, there is so much that you can accomplish. The best thing about using affirmations is that they require minimal effort, and are completely free of charge. This is excellent, considering the power that they have to alter your circumstances.

There are two types of affirmations that you can make, and there are positive affirmations and negative affirmations. Through this book, you have learned that it is the positive affirmations which are truly life changing. You will have negative thoughts, as that is typical of human nature. However, you can resist the urge of giving your negative thoughts the power to become negative affirmations. Rather, recognize them for what they are and transform them into positivity by using a positive affirmation.

If you have been dealing with a touch financial situation, and are looking to double your earnings, use the power of positive affirmations. A change will surely happen, though you must be patient enough to wait for it, and conscious enough to recognize it. The beauty about affirmations is that they always happen as you expect them to happen. That is why if you want them to work miracles in your life, ensure that you rid yourself of questions and doubt. Trust that things are working in your favor, and look forward to a life that is better than you could have ever imagined.

Practicing meditation

Now that you have the tools, you can deal with anxiety and stress. All you have to do is to meditate.

Thousands of research reports continue to prove how meditation influences both the mental and physical wellbeing. Meditation can bridge the gap between you and many worldly wants as well: your sleep gets better, you are able to regulate your weight, your relationships become more satisfactory and you have the ability to reduce physical pains that occasionally come and go.

Although its practice is still being blindsided by many factors, the practice is bound to receive the recognition it deserves eventually. With the internet of things, the spread of the practice is almost reaching a rampant state with the topic of meditation resting on the lips of both professionals and paupers. Even in the event that most of these people are just talking about it without putting any practice, the fact that it has gained such a massive amount of popularity is nothing but astounding. This is a positive thing though, as the positives of meditation outweigh the negatives.

For those who are a bit skeptical about engaging in it because of various reasons, I hope this book serves as a beacon of light to dispel any misbeliefs and doubts one might carry about the practice. The main purpose of meditation is to reach within and access oneself. We all spend so much time on a daily basis trying to find people and things. It all falls in place easier if you discover the most important thing to find is yourself.

So, thank you once again for your kind attention. If you have found this book to be useful or helpful, in any way, please tell your friends and family, or anyone whom you believe to be interested in this topic, about this book. It will surely help them find the balance they seek in life. In addition, they are surely going to benefit in the long run.